KU-438-822

R

Manlin

A COMPANION TO THE
BAPTIST CHURCH HYMNAL
(*Revised*)

A COMPANION TO THE BAPTIST CHURCH HYMNAL

(Revised)

BY

J. O. BARRETT   B. GREY GRIFFITH

FRANK BUFFARD   J. O. HAGGER

AND

HUGH MARTIN (*Editor*)

THE PSALMS AND HYMNS TRUST

6 SOUTHAMPTON ROW, LONDON, W.C.1

First published 1953

MADE AND PRINTED IN GREAT BRITAIN BY
MORRISON AND GIBB LIMITED, LONDON AND EDINBURGH

CONTENTS

PRINCIPAL AUTHORITIES

The following are among the books consulted:

Dictionary of Hymnology. Julian.

Handbook to the Church Hymnary. Revised Edition. Edited by James Moffatt and Millar Patrick.

Hymns Ancient and Modern, Historical edition.

English Hymns. S. W. Duffield.

The New Methodist Hymn-book, Illustrated in History and Experience. John Telford.

Companion to the School Hymn-book of the Methodist Church. W. S. Kelynack.

The English Hymn. L. F. Benson.

Songs of Praise Discussed. Percy Dearmer.

The Hymnal 1940 Companion.

On Baptist authors:

A Handbook to the Baptist Church Hymnal. Edited by Carey Bonner and W. T. Whitley.

Some Baptist Hymnists. Carey Bonner.

FOREWORD

THE need has been felt for some time for a Companion to the *Baptist Church Hymnal* (*Revised*) which would provide information about the hymns and their writers. Much of the material here assembled has long been available to students who knew where to find it, but such works of reference are not generally accessible and naturally need supplementing and adapting for our special purpose. So there is a good deal here that has had to be searched for in many different quarters and the compilation of the book has been a lengthy business. Information about some of our authors is very scanty and we should welcome supplementary material or corrections. This volume itself supplements, and at some points corrects, an earlier book with much the same aim, *A Handbook to the Baptist Church Hymnal* by Carey Bonner and W. T. Whitley.

To keep the book at a manageable size and price we reluctantly decided not to include treatment of tunes and composers. Where a hymn is so wedded to a tune that some mention seemed inevitable, reference will be found in the note on the hymn. For the same reason of size and price we have had to impose severe limits upon our description of many of the hymns. This also accounts for the telegraphic rather than literary style of the notes.

The hymns are considered in the order in which they appear in the *Hymnal*, but there are indexes of first lines and of the names of authors and translators which should make it easy to find what is wanted. Biographical information about an author or translator is given under his first hymn in the book, but there is a cross reference after his name at each subsequent entry. Thus, 'Isaac Watts (2)' at the head of a hymn means that a note about him will be found under hymn number 2.

In addition to my debt to my colleagues on the editorial committee and to Mr. C. H. Parsons, secretary of the Psalms and Hymns Trust, I wish to acknowledge the help of Messrs. A. Hayden and R. F. Newton in reading the proofs and in making available the results of their researches into the biographies of many of the hymn-writers.

We hope that the information now made generally available in convenient form for the users of our *Hymnal* will not only prove of interest but will make for more intelligent and more worthy worship. Happily we can use hymns and make them the expression of our own worship and aspiration without knowing who wrote them or when or where. Often, however, such knowledge lights up the meaning of the hymn and helps us to sing it with added sympathy and insight. Behind our hymns there is often adventure, romance, tragedy, heroic Christian witness, long faithfulness in service in church or Sunday school, patient discipleship on a bed of pain. With the aid of our hymn-book we may enter in our measure into the experience of the saints, famous and humble, of the Church Universal. Here are voices speaking to us from many ages and from many lands, out of many Christian traditions, all bearing witness to our one Lord.

The hymn-book should be more used than it is for reading in our personal devotions. Many hymns are prayers, or might inspire them. Some in our collection that would perhaps be out of place in public worship would be brimful of helpfulness in the intimacies of private prayer. Ministers, too, might very profitably from time to time speak in sermons and addresses about the story and message of our hymns. We hope our work may be found serviceable for both these purposes.

May this Companion help us to emulate the Apostle and to sing with the spirit and with the understanding also.

HUGH MARTIN.

HYMNODY IN THE CHRISTIAN CHURCH

THE story of the Church's song is lengthy and involved, and it is possible here to give only its main outline.

The Early Centuries

The first hymn-book of the Christian Church was the Psalter. The Jewish converts brought their Scriptures with them, and from then until now the Psalms have been the basic element in Christian hymnody. They were soon supplemented by distinctively Christian songs. Some, like the Magnificat and the Benedictus, were taken from the New Testament. As early as A.D. 112 the younger Pliny asserts in his well-known letter to Trajan that 'The Christians sing, antiphonally, a hymn of praise to Christ as God'. The creeds were sung, and by the fourth century the original Te Deum was composed, the song which has nobly expressed the faith and gratitude of the Church for fifteen hundred years.

Strangely enough, the rise of heresy gave impetus to hymn writing. The Syrian Church produced hymns expressing the Christian faith in answer to the hymns of the Gnostics, and in both East and West hymns were written to counter the influence of Arian hymnody.

Ambrose (340–97), Bishop of Milan, made hymns popular in the West. He wrote them, and set them to simple melodies. They were sung unaccompanied, without harmony, for harmony was then unknown. St. Augustine listened to them and was deeply impressed, even though critical of their emotional effect. Their use spread rapidly, but slowly the quality of words and music degenerated, and they ceased to be an aid to devotion. Repressive measures were taken in the Eastern church, and when Pope Gregory the Great (540–604) came to power in the West he banned Ambrosian music and made the severe liturgical chant obligatory. The Gregorian chant was sung by the clergy and choir. Congregational singing was suppressed.

The Middle Ages

Yet hymns were still written. From Fortunatus, a contemporary of Gregory, comes the hymn which Canon Ellerton paraphrased as 'Welcome, happy morning', and each succeeding century has its notable song writer. 'The day is past and over' is a translation of a Greek hymn of the sixth or seventh century, which is still used in the Greek Church. In the eighth century John of Damascus was writing Christian songs. 'The day of Resurrection' is taken from one of his poems. To a suggestion in one of the hymns of Joseph the Hymnographer in the ninth century we owe 'O happy band of pilgrims'.

In the West many schools of music were established in the monasteries which grew up all over Europe in those dark, chaotic days. Hymns were written for saints' and festal days, and for the Daily Offices. By the tenth century metrical singing and harmonization were developing.

In the twelfth century the Abbey of Cluny was at the height of its wealth and fame. There St. Bernard, born early in that century of English parents, composed the satire on the vices and follies of his age from which some of our best-known hymns are extracted, e.g. 'Jerusalem the golden'. He was overshadowed by his namesake St. Bernard of Clairvaux (1091–1153), the eloquent and saintly monk who has contributed so richly to our hymnals. Our hymnody would be immeasurably poorer without 'Jesus, Thou joy of loving hearts' and 'Jesus, the very thought of Thee'. The wandering friars also made their contribution, notably that lover of God and all His works, St. Francis of Assisi (1182–1226). The joyous faith of that gentle and blameless soul is reflected in 'All creatures of our God and King'.

Yet once again the use of song and music became debased. Secular words and melodies were introduced even into the service of the Mass. It is revealing that the Council of Trent (1545–63), considered the possibility of excluding music from church services in the interests of reverence and decency.

The Reformation

In Roman theory all that is essential in worship is done by the clergy. Martin Luther (1483–1546) believed in the priesthood of all believers, and therefore in the right of every believer to offer his own prayer and praise. Others had believed this before him. The Bohemian Brethren had used a hymnal since 1504, the first hymn-book in the vernacular. Luther wrote hymns which were simple, direct, and evangelical. His main inspiration was the Psalter, as in his paraphrase of Psalm xlvi. 'a safe stronghold our God is still', the greatest of all his hymns. He drew his tunes from the Roman service books, from current vernacular hymns, and from popular folk-songs. He made singing an important part of worship. His hymns, with their clear expression of the Gospel, became as great a force in the Reformation as his translation of the Bible. In 1524 he published the first hymn-book of evangelical Germany.

The years which followed were full of national and sectarian strife. After the disastrous Peasants' Revolt came the Emperor's attempt to suppress Protestantism. For thirty years central Europe was ravaged by bitter war. Löwenstern's 'Lord of our life and God of our salvation' reflects the experiences endured in this period. Martin Rinkart's 'Now thank we all our God' voiced the heartfelt thanksgiving for the ending of these appalling decades of pestilence and famine and death.

In the seventeenth century a new note is heard in German hymnody. Hitherto hymns had been concerned with the object of the believer's faith, rather than with his desires and emotions. But in some of the hymns of the mystics and pietists a more subjective and personal note appears. 'Commit thou all thy griefs' by Paul Gerhardt (1607–76), and 'God calling yet! Shall I not hear?', by Tersteegen (1697–1769), are illustrations of this.

In Geneva, John Calvin (1509–64), was leading the song of the Church in another direction. His aim was to return to the practice of the primitive church. Apart from the Ten Commandments and the Nunc Dimittis only Psalms

were to be sung in worship. Manmade hymns were excluded.
The method of chanting the Psalter in prose was unknown,
and Calvin, with the gifted groups he gathered round him,
rewrote the Psalms in metrical form and set them to attractive
tunes, some of which, like the 'Old Hundredth', we still use.
These metrical Psalms, sung in unison and without instru-
ment, became immediately and widely popular. They gave
the Huguenots the inspiration to fight and endure, and
they spread to many countries, including our own.

The Psalters

The Psalmody of Luther and Calvin stimulated the
translation of the Psalms into English. Both England and
Scotland adopted the metrical form, and followed Geneva
in excluding hymns from public worship.

In England the first authorized metrical Psalter was published in 1652. It was popularly known as 'Sternhold and
Hopkins', after the two men who were the chief contributors
to its contents. They furthered the enthusiastic revival of
psalm-singing under Elizabeth. A new version by Tate and
Brady was published in 1696 and sanctioned for public worship.

By 1850 most churches had replaced or supplemented
the metrical versions by collections of hymns. The singing
of the metrical Psalms was always additional to the reading
of the Psalms appointed for the day. The present almost
universal practice of chanting the appointed Psalms began
early in the nineteenth century.

Attempts were made to provide a Psalter which could
be used in both England and Scotland, but they failed.
After various experiments Scotland adopted in 1650 a
metrical version which is still the authorized version for
the Presbyterian churches of Scotland. The Psalms were
the only part of worship in which the congregation joined
until the introduction of the paraphrases of Scripture in
the middle of the eighteenth century. The use of hymns did
not become general in Scotland until after 1873.

The songs a people sing have always exercised a potent
influence. For long years the metrical Psalms were the
Church's only song-book, and it would be interesting to

examine the effects of this on theology and character, particularly in Scotland. Its influence on our hymnals can be more readily assessed. The Psalms imparted to our earlier hymns some of their own dignity and objectiveness, as contrasted with the sentimentality and self-centredness of many later hymns. More directly, a surprising number of these Psalms found a place in our hymn-books, and the Psalters have given us some of our finest tunes.

Isaac Watts

There were many who loved the Psalter, yet who felt that something more was needed. The spirit of some Psalms was less than Christian. The facts of the Christian revelation and the riches of Christian experience found no expression in them. To sing only the Psalms meant that the name of Christ was not used in corporate praise.

Christian songs were being written by men of the calibre of George Herbert (1593–1632) and Thomas Ken (1637–1711), but with no thought of these being used by a congregation. Others were avowedly seeking to find a place for hymns in worship. Baptist Hymnody is the subject of the next chapter, but it should be mentioned here that hymns were being sung at Broadmead Baptist Church, Bristol, by 1671, and that Benjamin Keach as early as 1673 introduced the singing of a hymn at the Communion Service, and soon after issued a hymnal for congregational use, comprised of his own hymns and those of Joseph Stennett. The Independents were even sooner in the field, for William Barton's congregation were using in 1651 his short *Collection of Psalms and Hymns*. These men, together with hymn-writers like Baxter, Bunyan, and Addison, were slowly opening the door of worship to the entrance of Christian song.

It was a Congregational minister, Isaac Watts (1674–1748), who threw that door wide open. This slightly built and delicate man had a powerful and original mind. In 1719 he published a version of the Psalms. It was not a complete Psalter, for he omitted Psalms he thought unfit for Christian worship. His aim was to see 'David converted into a Christian', and, like Luther, he interpreted the

Psalms in the language of the Gospel. His method is plain when Psalm lxxii. is compared with his paraphrase of it in the first great missionary hymn 'Jesus shall reign'.

His writing of hymns followed logically on this. In them he gave expression to Christian truth and experience which were outside the range of the Psalter. Published in 1706, they met with an immediate welcome and firmly established hymn-singing as part of Christian worship.

The Wesleys

Others were inspired by his example, among them Philip Doddridge (1702–51), scholar, poet, and Congregational minister in Northampton.

But it was the work of John Wesley (1703–91), and of his younger brother Charles, which dominated the hymnody of the eighteenth century. When John sailed to Georgia as a missionary of the S.P.G. he was already interested in hymns. He had taken Watts' collection and George Herbert's *The Temple* with him to study. This interest was greatly strengthened by the hymns and hymn-singing of a party of Moravian emigrants on board. He was deeply impressed by the rich spiritual experience exemplified by their lives and voiced in their hymns. One result was that before he left America he issued in 1737 a collection of psalms and hymns for congregational use, and was arraigned by the authorities for introducing these unauthorized novelties.

But more important than this was the use the brothers made of hymns in their evangelistic work. John wrote few original hymns, but he was an inspired translator, especially of German hymns. Charles wrote more than 6,000. Most of them are less objective than Watts' hymns and more evangelical. These simple, direct hymns fastened the truths they preached in the minds of their converts, and the singing of them was a powerful evangelical agent to others.

The Wesleys were not the only distinguished hymnwriters of the period. A. M. Toplady (1740–78) was a bitter opponent of Wesley. He wrote 'Rock of Ages', esteemed by some the greatest hymn in the English language, as an assertion of the Calvinist faith which he believed

Wesley was undermining. William Cowper (1731–1800) and John Newton (1725–1807) published the *Olney Hymns* in 1779. Some are morbid and introspective, but the best reveal their ardent faith and have found a loved and honoured place in all our hymnals.

It was in this period that Welsh hymnody revived. Hymns were sung in the ancient British Church, and the records of Welsh singing go far back in her history. But religion was at a low ebb for long years before the Reformation, and for many years after. It was the Methodist revival which awakened song and produced hymn-writers who have given us memorable hymns and tunes. Foremost in their ranks is William Williams (1717–91), the poet and preacher of Pantycelyn. To him we owe 'Guide me, O Thou great Jehovah' and 'O'er the gloomy hills of darkness'.

The Nineteenth Century

The nineteenth century produced a wealth of hymns. Bishop Heber (1783–1826) wrote some of our best-loved ones, including 'Holy, Holy, Holy' and 'From Greenland's icy mountains'. This brilliant scholar and gentle saint sought to weld his hymns into the framework of the liturgy. He tried to obtain authorization for their use, but without success. He adopted the freer rhythms of contemporary poetry, as in 'Brightest and best of the sons of the morning'. His hymns lack the scriptural strength of earlier hymns, but breathe a sure and deep devotion.

In 1827 John Keble (1792–1866) published *The Christian Year*. These poems were scarcely hymns, but from them centos were extracted to form some of our finest Christian songs. They were the source of 'New every morning is the love' and of 'Sun of my soul'.

Keble was the leader of the Oxford movement and exercised a strong influence on John Henry Newman (1801–90), who wrote 'Lead, kindly Light' twelve years before he entered the Roman Communion and 'Praise to the Holiest' twenty years after. Frederick Faber (1814–63), who followed him into the Roman Church, carrying with him his love for the hymns of Cowper and Newton, has enriched our hymnals with 'Souls of men, why will ye scatter' and 'Hark, hark my soul'.

Maurice and Kingsley, the Christian socialists, were writing hymns, and many writers from the Evangelicals. James Montgomery, Horatius Bonar, and Bishop Bickersteth were among them, and those notable women Charlotte Elliott and Frances Ridley Havergal.

Others were discovering the riches of medieval hymnology. Many of the ancient breviaries included a hymnarium, with psalms, responses, and hymns used by priests and choirs in the Daily Offices. From these, and other sources, John Chandler, Edward Caswall, and J. M. Neale were recovering treasure for congregational use.

This work of translation had important results for Anglican hymnody. Hymns were an accepted part of public worship among Baptists and Independents by the end of the seventeenth century, while the Church of England recognized only the Psalms. This did not prevent collections of hymns being used. By 1820 hymnals were used in Anglican churches all over England, though often opposed and sometimes suppressed by authority. Most of the hymns were borrowed from the Dissenters, which may have been one reason for official disapproval. The discovery that hymns had a place in the ancient worship of the Church created a different attitude. In 1861 an influential committee, under the chairmanship of Sir H. W. Baker, published the first edition of *Hymns Ancient and Modern*. It contained 273 hymns, 132 of these being translations from the Latin. It was designed to be used alongside the Book of Common Prayer, having hymns appropriate to the services and saints' and festal days of the Church. Its publication met with abuse as well as enthusiasm, but it steadily superseded the great variety of hymns in use and gave hymns a recognized place in Anglican worship. The compilers had enlisted the aid of leading composers of church music, and of younger musicians like Dr. Dykes. Their music proved immediately popular, and their tunes were freely borrowed by Dissenters and by those Anglicans who continued to use earlier hymn-books.

America had added a number of hymns to our hymnals.

Among them are 'O sacred Head, once wounded' by J. W. Alexander, and 'Stand up, stand up for Jesus' by George Duffield. Bishop Phillips Brooks wrote 'O little town of Bethlehem' and W. P. Merrill 'Rise up, O men of God'. We also use hymns written by those who were in revolt against the harsh Calvinism of their day—H. W. Longfellow and his brother Samuel, O. W. Holmes, J. W. Chadwick, and F. L. Hosmer.

More distinctive are the Gospel hymns of the second half of the nineteenth century. Those of Ira D. Sankey and Fanny Crosby are the most familiar. Their lively rhythm and monotonous harmonization made them easy to sing. The Salvation Army has made such hymns familiar in almost every land. At their best they are genuinely moving; at their worst they cannot be described in polite language.

Present and Future

It is difficult to judge the hymns of our own century. They reflect the interests and standards of the time, as hymns have always done. The spread of education and the influence of broadcasting have led to a desire for a finer literary and musical quality, leading sometimes to the introduction of poems which are hard to recognize as hymns to the praise of God. The widespread desire for social justice and international peace is echoed in such hymns as Scott Holland's 'Judge eternal, throned in splendour'. Hymnals need frequent revision if they are to express faithfully and with reality the prayer and praise of the worshipper.

Here we must leave the story of the past. The future is full of shadows, but the days of great hymn-writing are not over. Only when the Church becomes indifferent and faithless does it cease to sing. Meanwhile, let us enjoy and use worthily the treasures which we possess. Our hymnals, cradled in Scripture and nurtured by the faith of the centuries, are a glorious gift of God to His people. No books reveal more clearly the essential unity of the Church. Their voices are gathered from every age and from every section of the Church and united in a chorus of praise where differences are forgotten and we have become 'one Body in Christ'.

F. BUFFARD.

HYMNS AMONG THE BAPTISTS

ISAAC WATTS has sometimes been called 'The Father of English hymnody'. In point of time, however, though not in skill, Benjamin Keach (1640–1704) has the place of honour. Isaac Watts published no hymns until three years after Keach's death. Keach was a tailor by trade, self-educated, and became minister of the General Baptist Church at Winslow, Buckinghamshire. In 1664 he issued a *Child's Instructor* which contained hymns. The whole edition was seized and destroyed, and Keach was fined, imprisoned, and put in the pillory for having expressed views contrary to those of the Prayer Book. He rewrote the book from memory, and it subsequently ran into several editions. Keach came to London and in 1668 was ordained as elder of the Southwark Baptist Church. While there, under the influence of new friends and of his second wife, he transferred his loyalty to the Particular Baptists and established a church at Horsley Down. Here in 1673 he introduced the singing of hymns of his own composition after the Lord's Supper, and in 1676 published a hymn-book, followed in 1691 by his *Spiritual Melody* containing three hundred original hymns. It must be admitted that Keach's gifts as a hymn-writer were negligible. Much he wrote can only be described as doggerel. One or two examples may be quoted from his *Spiritual Melody*.[1]

> Our wounds do stink and are corrupt,
> Hard swellings we do see;
> We want a little ointment, Lord,
> Let us more humble be.

> Repentance like a bucket is
> To pump the water out;
> For leaky is our ship, alas,
> Which makes us look about.

---

[1] Quoted in *The Life and Faith of the Baptists* (1946 edition), H. Wheeler Robinson, p. 48.

Nevertheless all honour is due to Keach for his work as a pioneer in Christian praise. It was he who was responsible for the introduction of congregational hymn-singing into the regular services of an English congregation.

In 1691 in his *Breach Repair'd* Keach replied to his critics, especially to Isaac Marlow's *Discourse Concerning Singing* (1690). Keach had previously argued for hymn-singing in *Tropes and Figures* (1682) and *Treatise on Baptism* (1689). Twenty-two members of Keach's church took such strong exception to congregational singing that they withdrew from the church, contending that such singing was artificial, and could not possibly reflect the spirit of the worshipper. Among the objections were: (1) You make that to be a constant ordinance which is an extraordinary spiritual gift. (2) You make that formal which is in right of performance spiritual, and ought to be left to the management of the Spirit instead of being confined to a limited form of words. (3) You use plurality of voices in that which ought to be performed by a single voice, there being no scripture warrant for using plurality of voices in singing more than in prayer. (4) There is no positive command in scripture that singing is to be a constant ordinance with the Church like prayer and preaching.[1] The dread of formality was doubtless very much in the mind of the objectors. So began a controversy which was to mark English Baptist life for a considerable period.

In 1673 Abraham Cheare's *Sundry Seasonable Lessons and Instructions to Youth* appeared. He and Keach were pioneers in the writing of hymns for children. In 1688 Bunyan in his *Solomon's Temple Spiritualized* spoke of singing by the congregation as belonging by God's appointment to the Church of the New Covenant, so long as the singing was confined to members of the Church. It seems surprising that Bunyan's church at Bedford did not sing at worship in his lifetime, and it was not until 1690 that the singing of hymns was introduced there. In London, Hercules Collins introduced hymn-singing at Wapping, arguing in

[1] *Home and Church* by Charles Stanford (concerning Old Maze Pond Church, London).

his *Orthodox Catechism* of 1680 that congregational singing was 'a public duty'. At the opening in 1687 of the restored Devonshire Square Baptist Meeting House the occasion was celebrated with hymn-singing.

There was a difference of approach to congregational hymn-singing on the part of General and Particular Baptists.[1] The latter decided at their Assembly in 1689 that no principle was at stake and that each congregation must be left to settle the question for itself. In 1679 Thomas Grantham, an influential leader among General Baptists, published *Christianismus Primitivus* in which he argued against 'musical singing with a multitude of voices'. He urged that psalms and hymns should be sung only by such as God 'has fitted thereto by the help of His Spirit', that congregational hymn-singing prevented instruction for 'when all speak none can hear', and that singing other men's words would open the way for forms of prayer. He also feared that congregational singing would lead to the use of instruments in public worship 'and then, farewell to all solemnity'.

In 1689 the General Baptist Assembly resolved 'to consider the question of promiscuous singing psalms, either the whole together, or they in conjunction with those who were not of their communion'. Those who favoured the practice were asked to show the Assembly 'what psalms they made use of for the matter, and what rules they did settle upon for the manner'. It was then revealed that it was not the metres of Sternhold and Hopkins but some composed by one Mr. Barton which were in use. The Assembly finally endorsed the opinion that the practice was foreign to evangelical worship, and that it was not safe for the churches to admit 'such carnall formalities'.

The publication in 1696 by Tate and Brady of a new version of the Psalms provided fresh tinder for the controversy. Joseph Stennett, senior, who has been described as the link in Baptist hymnody between the seventeenth and

---

[1] The General Baptists, the fruit of the movement begun by John Smyth and Thomas Helwys, were Arminian in their theology, while the Particular Baptists held the Calvinistic doctrine of election, according to which the Atonement was only for those whom God had chosen for salvation. The General Baptists held that it was universal, for all men.

eighteenth centuries pointed out that after the supper in the Upper Room the Lord and his disciples sang together. He himself published in 1697 a book of hymns for the Lord's Supper, and followed it with another for baptismal services, while Keach issued a new edition of his hymn-book 'as now practised in several congregations' in 1700.

The General Baptists continued to regard hymn-singing with some disfavour into the early part of the eighteenth century, and among the more conservative section until the end of the century. In 1733 a case was presented from Northamptonshire to the General Baptist Assembly complaining that some churches in that district had 'fallen into a way of singing the Psalms of David or other men's composures with tuneable notes and a mixed multitude'. It is to be noted, however, that on this occasion the Assembly decided to take no action.

Benjamin Beddome (1717–98) was from 1740 writing hymns for the use of his own congregation at Bourton-on-the-Water, and Daniel Turner (1710–98), the cultured and influential minister of the Abingdon Church for fifty years, contributed hymns to collections such as that made by John Rippon at the end of the eighteenth century. To this period also belong Dr. Samuel Stennett, John Fawcett, whose memory will always be linked with 'Blest be the tie that binds', and Dr. John Ryland, who at the age of twenty in 1773 wrote the first of his one hundred hymns. In the north, Alverey Jackson, who settled as pastor of the Baptist Church at Barnoldswick in 1717, immediately 'made an essay to restore the Gospel Ordinances of singing psalms, hymns, and spiritual songs'. A sermon by him on the duty of singing which it is said must have lasted two hours survives.[1] In 1719 the Association agreed that singing was a moral duty in the churches. Not far away in the Rossendale Valley a group known as the Deighn Layrocks (the larks of Deighn village) became Baptists and soon began to enrich the congregational worship of the churches around Goodshaw and Lumb. They composed their own hymn tunes

[1] R. J. V. Wylie, *The Baptist Churches of Accrington*, p. 118. B.Q. iv. 43.

and so overcame the objection against singing other men's compositions in Christian worship. It was not until 1829 that the Baptists of Accrington used hymns by Isaac Watts to supplement their own. It was in this district, too, that the orchestras which had been introduced to assist congregational hymn-singing were displaced by organs. Cloughfold led the way in 1852 and Lumb followed in 1858.

The records of Suffolk Baptist life provide us with an interesting picture of the musical side of Baptist worship in that part of the country at the end of the eighteenth century. A certain 'Octoginta' describes a visit paid by his father in 1794 to Wattisham Chapel. A tablet was hung on the pulpit with L.M. printed upon it. This was exchanged for S.M. or C.M., according to the metre required. It seemed that only one tune was available for each metre and at first none for peculiar metres. There was a contempt for the use of musical instruments in worship, especially for the bass viol. On one occasion an 'audacious youth' smuggled one into the chapel gallery. A deacon espied it, and hurrying upstairs called out in broadest Suffolk words which may be translated 'What is that thing doing here? It has no soul, it cannot praise God. Take that thing away.' [1]

It was for long a serious hindrance to good congregational singing that the verses of the hymns had to be read out two lines at a time. Samuel Medley of Liverpool (1738–99) improved on this by having his hymns printed on leaflets and distributed to the congregation, the custom spreading to other churches.

Many new congregations of General Baptists came into being in the Midlands and in Yorkshire in the middle of the century, partly no doubt as a result of the Methodist movement, and these like the Methodists practised congregational hymn-singing. It was not long after the formation in 1770 of the New Connexion of General Baptists that a collection of hymns was prepared for their use and issued in Halifax in 1772. The Midland section issued *Barton Hymns* in 1785. A third collection appeared in 1793, *Hymns and Spiritual Songs*, and a new and revised collection in 1800. In 1785–87

[1] A. J. Klaiber, *The Story of the Suffolk Baptists*, p. 97.

there was a lively controversy between Gilbert Boyce, a respected Lincolnshire minister who condemned hymn-singing and Dan Taylor,[1] then in London, who defended it. In 1793 John Deacon published a hymn-book for the use of General Baptist Churches, and a second enlarged edition was issued in 1804. In 1830 a revised form of the book was formally adopted as the *General Baptist Hymn Book*. This was displaced in 1851 by *The New Hymn Book*, compiled by the Reverends J. B. and J. Carey Pike. In 1879 another book, *Baptist Hymnal*, edited by the Rev. W. R. Stevenson, was published, containing nine hundred and twenty hymns, and incorporating a considerable number of the best contemporary hymns. The word General was dropped from the title, in part because the two wings of the Denomination had drawn much closer together, and because it was hoped, as proved to be the case, that some Particular Baptist congregations would use the book.

As the eighteenth century drew to its close Particular Baptists were using the collection of hymns issued in 1787 by John Rippon of Southwark, an outstanding name in Baptist hymnody. The book was an appendix to Isaac Watts' *Psalms and Hymns*. Within thirteen years ten editions appeared. Rippon collaborated with Thomas Walker in the production of a book of tunes in 1811 to accompany his hymn-book. This too was widely used. *The Bristol Hymn Book* of 1769 was also in use among them. John Haddon in 1828 issued for Particular Baptists *A New Selection*. That and the subsequent supplement *Praise Waiteth* of 1871 were in wide use. In 1858 *Psalms and Hymns* appeared, containing one thousand hymns, and in 1866 *Our Own Hymn Book* containing one thousand one hundred and twenty-nine psalms and hymns, edited by C. H. Spurgeon. It was used at the Metropolitan Tabernacle for which it had been prepared, and by many other congregations whose ministers had been trained by Spurgeon.

[1] Dan Taylor (1738–1816) was the minister of the first General Baptist Church in Yorkshire, at Hebden Bridge, and took the lead in founding in London in 1770 the New Connexion of General Baptists. The name was intended to mark its distinctiveness from the old General Baptists who had become practically Unitarian.

Among the more strongly Calvinistic Particular Baptist Churches the principal books were William Gadsby's *Selection of Hymns* (1814), David Denham's *Selection* (1837), and another book with the same title by John Stevens.

It seems surprising when one considers the artistic and musical genius of the Welsh people that it was not until 1774 that Benjamin Francis of Shortwood issued a collection of Welsh hymns. Joseph Harris of Swansea published another book in 1796 and Titus Lewis of Carmarthen a third in 1798. A book issued in 1821 by the Rev. Joseph Harris found general acceptance. Among other hymn-books were one edited by the Rev. Robert Jones of Llanllyfui, another issued in 1867 compiled by the Rev. Lewis Jones of Pwllheli and a *Handbook of Praise* prepared by a committee and issued in 1881.

In Scotland a collection of hymns issued in 1751 by Sir William Sinclair, 'minister of the Gospel of God and servant of Jesus Christ', may well have been the first or one of the first to be produced in Scotland for a Protestant congregation. Subsequent books were a collection by D. Niven in 1786 and *The Christian Hymnal* edited by the Rev. Oliver Flett of Paisley in 1871.

Baptists were responsible for other innovations regarding hymns. They were pioneers in the singing of hymns written by women. Anne Dutton (1698–1765), wife of a Baptist minister in Huntingdon, issued a selection of 'Sixty-one hymns on several subjects'. Anne Steele (1716–1778), daughter of the Baptist minister at Broughton, Hants, who wrote under the *nom de plume* of Theodosia also contributed, and more enduringly, to Baptist hymnody. She is represented in the 1933 *Revised Baptist Church Hymnal* by two hymns.

From the evidence available it appears that Baptists were pioneers in issuing a collection of hymns by various authors. John Ash of Pershore, a schoolmaster, collaborated with the Rev. Caleb Evans of the Bristol Academy in producing the *Bristol Hymn Book* in 1769, containing four hundred and twelve hymns by various authors. The venture met with immediate and lasting approval, for a tenth edition was issued in 1827. While the editors naturally drew largely on Baptist writers they introduced other hymns, including some by John Newton. In 1806 a new selection of seven hundred evangelical hymns appeared in which over two hundred authors were represented. The editor, John Dobell, a Customs House Officer, introduced a further innovation in the provision of notes concerning the authors.

With the issue of *The Baptist Church Hymnal* in 1900, a book which received the warm commendation of Dr. John Julian, editor of *A Dictionary of Hymnology*, we enter on the modern period. The editors introduced two hundred new hymns by one hundred and twenty different authors. Baptists were not uncritical of the new book, especially because of the absence from it of old well-loved tunes, some of which were brought back after protest against their exclusion.

The 1933 *Revised Baptist Church Hymnal* saw the disappearance of about one hundred and fifty of the hymns in the 1900 book on the ground that they were not in general use. Among the new hymns eleven were from the Early or Middle Ages and twenty-two from the period covered from Luther to Wesley. More than one hundred modern tunes were discarded and many old classics were reintroduced. Among the Baptist hymn-writers whose hymns appeared here for the first time in a Baptist hymnal were the Rev. F. Goldsmith French, *Lord of the reapers*, the Rev. W. Y. Fullerton, *I cannot tell why He*, *Whom angels worship*, the Rev. W. J. Mathams, subsequently a minister in the Church of Scotland, *God is with us*, *Christ of the Upward Way*, *Jesus, Friend of little children*, W. H. Parker, a nineteenth-century Nottingham Baptist, *Tell me the stories of Jesus*, Miss Alice Pullen, *Thou Perfect Hero-Knight*, written for the Children's House, Bow, where she was on the staff, and the Rev. L. J. Egerton Smith, formerly minister at Burnham-on-Crough, *For all the love*. The contribution by American composers of varied denominations also calls for mention. Twenty new hymn-writers in the U.S. were introduced, including nine women, and among their hymns which have become well known to English congregations are Samuel Johnson's *City of God, how broad and far* and M. J. Savage's *What purpose burns within our hearts*. Many congregations welcomed the inclusion of such 'Gospel' hymns as Mrs. Hawks' *I need Thee every hour* and Mrs. Stockton's *God loved the world of sinners lost*.

The Revised Hymnal has met with general approval among Baptist congregations, and is now very widely used.

Baptists have made a contribution, though not an important one, to the writing of hymn tunes. We have already noted the original tunes composed by the Baptists of the Rossendale Valley in the eighteenth century. They have had their successors, but for the most part Baptists have drawn on the larger treasury of hymn tunes in use in the Church of Christ, to the great enrichment of their services. *The Revised Baptist Church Hymnal*, for example, contains tunes by only about a dozen Baptist composers. The main contribution of Baptists to Christian hymnody has been, as this chapter has shown, in the introduction of congregational hymn-singing, in the writing of hymns, and in the preparation of collections of hymns. All in all, it has been a distinctive and notable contribution to that volume of praise which is ever ascending to the throne of God.

JOHN O. BARRETT.

NOTES ON THE HYMNS AND THEIR AUTHORS

THE hymns are treated in the order in which they appear in the *Hymnal*. The indexes of first lines and of the names of authors and translators will help in tracing information. Biographical information about an author or translator is given under his first hymn in the book, but there is a cross reference after his name at each subsequent entry. Thus 'Isaac Watts (2)' at the head of a hymn means that a note about him will be found under hymn number 2.

1 ALL PEOPLE THAT ON EARTH DO DWELL
WILLIAM KETHE (Floruit 1550–1600)

A paraphrase of Psalm c, appeared first in *Anglo-Genevan Psalter*, 1561, also in a Psalter published the same year by John Daye, and the Scottish Psalter, 1564. Authorship uncertain but ascribed in Scottish Psalter to William Kethe, by others to Sternhold and Hopkins. Kethe the most probable as he was in Geneva in 1559 and helped in the production of *The Anglo-Genevan Psalter*. The Scottish Psalter changed 'fear' into 'mirth' in ver. 1 and 'the Lord ye know' into 'Know ye the Lord' in 1650 Psalter. The misspelling of 'folck' as 'flock' has persisted. Isaac Watts corrected the spelling of 'folck' but his version lacks the spirit of gladness which this version possesses.

William Kethe was an exile from the Marian persecution of 1555–8 in Frankfurt and Geneva and was said to be of Scottish birth. He was envoy of Geneva to English-speaking congregations on the Continent. The exiles left Geneva in 1559 but Kethe may have remained to complete his work on the Bible and the Psalms. In 1563 and 1569 he was chaplain to the forces under the Earl of Warwick and held the living at Childe Okeford in Dorsetshire. He composed popular as well as religious ballads and was described as a 'ready rhymer'. He has twenty-five Psalm versions in the Anglo-Genevan Psalter of 1564–5.

John Daye, 1552–84, of Dunwich Walden, Essex, a music printer, was a zealous reformer and suffered imprisonment and at one time was an exile. He printed first edition of Queen Elizabeth's *Prayer Book*, Foxes' *Book of Martyrs*, the first English music book and Archbishop Parker's translation of the Psalms and other psalters.

2 BEFORE JEHOVAH'S AWFUL THRONE

ISAAC WATTS (1674–1748)

Isaac Watts' version of Psalm c, altered by John Wesley. First in Watts' *Psalms of David*, 1719, where the first verse ran:

> Sing to the Lord with joyful voice,
> Let every land His name adore;
> The British Isles shall send the noice
> Across the ocean to the shore.

Wesley altered this to:

> Nations attend before His throne
> With solemn fear, with sacred joy.

Watts' correction of Kethe's spelling should be noted in ver. 3, 'we are His people'.

Isaac Watts, perhaps the best known of English hymn-writers. Born in Southampton, son of a prominent Independent who had been imprisoned for his views. His father kept a boarding-house. Isaac refused an offer of a University education as this would have involved allegiance to the Church of England, and entered an Independent Academy. He was a good student and for six years acted as tutor to the family of Sir John Hartopp. He became pastor of the Independent Church in Mark Lane, London, in 1702, resigning in 1712 on health grounds. Onward for thirty-six years he lived at Abney Park, Stoke Newington, London, as guest of Sir Thomas Abney and later of his widow. The grounds have become a cemetery. He published many books both theological and lyrical and one on logic became a text-book at Oxford. Edinburgh conferred the D.D. on him in 1728.

Dr. Johnson included him in his *Lives of the Poets*. His was a gracious spirit and did much to sweeten the relations between Dissenters and Anglicans and nothing helped more than the hymns he composed which were and are used by all sections of the Church. He was the originator of some of the Scottish paraphrases and wrote over 600 hymns.

See also 23, 101, 112, 119, 136, 157, 162, 253, 274, 303, 304, 306, 395, 401, 445, 446, 469, 488, 729 and from *Psalms of David Imitated* 2, 7, 22, 44, 48, 50, 191, 517, 549, 577, 578.

3 OH, WORSHIP THE KING

ROBERT GRANT (1779–1838)

A happy rendering of Psalm civ, suggested by Kethe's version. The writer is so akin to the changing scenes of nature that the hymn could almost be classed as a hymn of nature worship. First appearance, *Christian Psalmody* 1833. There have been slight alterations, ver. 1 (line 2), ran 'Oh gratefully sing His unchangeable love'; ver. 3 (line 4) had 'girdle' not 'mantle' and ver. 6 began 'O Lord of all might how boundless Thy love'.

Sir Robert Grant was the son of Charles Grant, M.P. for Inverness, Director of East India Company and a well-known philanthropist. Educated Magdalene College, Cambridge, Fellow of same. Called to the Bar, 1807, King's Sergeant in the Court of the Duchy of Lancaster and one of the Commissioners in Bankruptcy. Member of Parliament for several constituencies; Privy Councillor, 1831; in 1833 carried through a bill for the emancipation of the Jews. Judge-Advocate-General in 1831. Governor of Bombay, 1834, when he was knighted. A medical college was erected to his memory after his death. His hymns were contributed to *Christian Observer* and to H. V. Elliott's *Psalms and Hymns*, 1835. His brother Lord Glenelg published twelve of his hymns in 1839.

4 YE SERVANTS OF GOD

CHARLES WESLEY (1707–88)

Published in 1744 in *Hymns for times of trouble and persecution*, the title of which is suggestive of the background both of Methodism and the nation. There were six verses and there have been slight alterations. It is No. 1 of 'Hymns to be sung in Tumult' and the notes of confidence and robust faith cannot be missed.

Charles Wesley was probably the most prolific hymn-writer of any age. Born Epworth 1707, the youngest son of Samuel and Susannah Wesley and brother of John. Educated Westminster School and Christ Church, Oxford. Graduated 1729 and became college tutor. In the same year became one of the Oxford 'Methodists'. Ordained in 1735 and went with John to Georgia as secretary to General Oglethorpe but stayed only a few months. He and John came under the influence of the Moravians and especially of Peter Bohler in 1738. He and his brother now worked together. In 1756 he gave up itinerary work and settled in Bristol and in 1771 moved to London. The brothers were not wholly in agreement as to John's policy of ordinations and separation and Charles asserted that he had lived and would die in communion with the Church of England. His great contribution was his hymnwriting; it is claimed that he wrote 6,500. Most of these have now been forgotten but a very large number are in constant use in all the Churches and among them some of the finest in our language.

See also 84, 117, 123, 141, 147, 149, 168, 182, 209, 231, 241, 259, 270, 277, 301, 311, 317, 373, 394, 422, 458, 464, 465, 467, 491, 495, 542, 583, 593, 608, 613, 720.

5 ANGELS HOLY, HIGH AND LOWLY

JOHN STUART BLACKIE (1809–95)

First appeared in Dr. Bonar's *Bible Hymn Book* (1845). This is a rendering of the 'Benedicite'. Blackie said the hymn was composed for a beautiful melody he had heard used for convivial purposes which he thought better fitted for sanctuary worship. The Benedicite is the LXX rendering of Daniel iii between verses 23 and 24 and is not in the Hebrew version. It passed into the canticles of the Church through the Greek and the Latin.

Born Glasgow, educated Marischal College, Aberdeen, and Edinburgh University. He lived a short while on the Continent and then was called to the Bar, 1834. He became Professor of Latin in Aberdeen, 1841, and Professor of Greek, Edinburgh, 1850. At one time he edited the *Sunday Magazine* and published in 1857 *Lays and Legends of Ancient Greece*.

6 SING TO THE LORD A JOYFUL SONG
JOHN SAMUEL BEWLEY MONSELL (1811–75)

Based on Psalm cxlv. First published in *Hymns of love and praise for the Church's year*, 1863, when the author was vicar of Egham.

Son of the Archdeacon of Londonderry. Educated Trinity College, Dublin; ordained 1834; chaplain to Bishop Mant and rector of Ramoan and then held two livings in England, Egham and St. Nicholas, Guildford. He was a fine preacher and of a happy disposition. His household 'was full of the beauty of holiness and the spirit of gaiety playing like sunshine over all the troubles of life'. He urged that hymns should be more fervent and joyous. Published eleven volumes of poetry and over 300 hymns, some seventy of which are still in use. He wrote a hymn to gather money for the rebuilding of his church and while the work was in progress was struck by a falling stone and died soon afterwards. A verse of the hymn seemed to have contained a premonition of his death.

> Dear body, thou and I must part;
> Thy busy head, thy throbbing heart
> Must cease to work and cease to play,
> For me at no far distant day.

See also 18, 98, 126, 151, 228, 471, 524, 599, 680.

7 GIVE TO OUR GOD IMMORTAL PRAISE
ISAAC WATTS (see 2)

From *Psalms of David*, a paraphrase of Psalm cxxxvi. The original had eight verses.

8 ALL THINGS PRAISE THEE, LORD MOST HIGH
GEORGE WILLIAM CONDER (1821–74)

From the appendix of the *Leeds Hymn Book*, 1874.

Educated Highbury College; in 1845 co-pastor High Wycombe Congregational Church; 1849 pastor, Belgrave Chapel, Leeds; 1864, Cheetham Hill, Manchester, and 1870, Queen's Road,

Forest Hill, London. He helped in the compilation of the *Leeds Hymn Book*, 1853, and published an appendix to that book in 1874.

9 OH, GIVE THANKS TO HIM WHO MADE
JOSIAH CONDER (1789–1855)

Born in Aldersgate, London. Son of an engraver and bookseller, at fifteen joined his father in his shop. At twenty-two he joined with Ann and Jane Taylor (see 746) in publishing *The Associate Minstrels*. This work was highly commended for Conder had real literary ability. The business did not prosper and Conder knew straitened means. For twenty years he owned and edited the *Eclectic Review* and edited the newspaper *The Patriot*. He wrote much and was greatly interested in nonconformity. He edited the first official hymn-book for the Congregational Union in which were sixty-two of his own hymns. He married the grand-daughter of Roubiliac, a sculptor and a descendant of the Huguenots. One of his grandsons was Colonel Claude R. Conder, archaeologist, well known for his survey of Palestine, and another, Charles Conder, the artist.

See also 54, 77, 273, 359, 487, 501, 570, 587, 595.

10 OH, PRAISE THE LORD OUR GOD
EDWARD HAYES PLUMPTRE (1821–91)

Written as a processional hymn and in the hope that it might serve for Sunday Schools and for social gatherings. Published in *Lazarus and other poems*, 1864.

Educated King's College, London, and University College, Oxford. Fellow of Brasenose, Oxford. Ordained 1846. Chaplain, King's, London; Dean of Queen's College, Oxford; Prebendary of St. Pauls; Professor of New Testament Exegesis, King's College, London. In 1881 Dean of Wells. Boyle lecturer in 1886, member of Old Testament Committee of revisers of the Bible. He was a reputable scholar and wrote several volumes of verse.

See also 677, 710.

11 NOW THANK WE ALL OUR GOD
MARTIN RINCKART (1586–1649)

A paraphrase of Ecclesiasticus l. 22–24, written in 1630. The first two verses were to serve as grace after meat in the author's household, the third was added as a doxology. Tradition connects the composition with the Peace of Westphalia. The date for that, however, is 1648. The hymn has become a great German hymn of thanksgiving and is sung on national occasions in that land.

The son of a cooper. In 1617 archidiaconus of Ellenburg where he spent the rest of his life. These covered the strenuous and austere years of the Thirty Years War. Ellenburg became a refugee centre and suffered both famine and pestilence. Rinckart was the only minister of religion and he spent himself and his resources in the service of others. He was a man of great influence and many stories are told of his contacts with the military commanders whom war brought to the town. His hymn should be read with the realization of that background of stark horror and sin. He was also a poet, dramatist, and musician.

Catherine Winkworth (1829–78), the translator, was daughter of Henry Winkworth of Alderley Edge, Manchester, and Catherine spent most of her life in that area. She was a fine translator of German songs and poems. Her *Lyra Germanica* was a devotional classic of the nineteenth century. She published other volumes of translations. Dr. Martineau praised her work, saying of it, 'not quite the life of Wesley's versions of the Moravian hymns but . . . more conscientious and obtaining a result as poetical as exactitude permits, short of native music'. Her later years were spent in Clifton, Bristol. She was always interested in the higher education of women and impressed others with her gifts of mind and soul.

See also 30, 87, 213, 300, 346, 520, 643, 709.

12 SING PRAISE TO GOD WHO REIGNS ABOVE
JOHANN JAKOB SCHUTZ (1640–90)

A lawyer in Frankfurt and a learned and a pious man. He was concerned with the doctrine of the Church and in later life separated from the Lutheran Church and became one of the early separatists in Germany. He issued two tractates in 1675, one of which contained five hymns he had written.

Frances Elizabeth Cox (1812–97), the translator, was born in Oxford. She had a felicitous turn of translation and published two volumes, *Sacred Hymns from the German*, 1841, and *Hymns from the German*, 1864. Baron Bunsen guided her in the choice of hymns she translated.

See also 128, 338.

13 STAND UP AND BLESS THE LORD
JAMES MONTGOMERY (1771–1854)

Written on March 15, 1824, for the Sunday School Anniversary of the Sheffield Red Hill Wesleyan School and published in *Christian Psalmist*, 1825.

Born at Irvine, Ayrshire, became a great hymn-writer, composing some 400 hymns. He had an adventurous career. His father was an Ulster Scot of peasant stock who became a Moravian minister in Irvine and later a missionary to the West Indies where he and his wife died. James went to the Moravian school at Fulneck and, failing to enter the ministry, became a baker. This was uncongenial, and James, who had been experimenting in verse, tried when he was eighteen to get his poems published. In 1794 he joined the staff of the *Sheffield Register*, a paper of liberal views. Gales, his senior, a printer, had to flee the country to avoid prosecution. James took on the editorship and changed the name of the paper to *Sheffield Iris* and continued as editor for thirty-one years. He was twice fined and imprisoned in York Castle for articles on the fall of the Bastille and on a political riot in Sheffield. He lectured on poetry and was a great advocate of Foreign Missions and the Bible Society. Public opinion towards him changed and in 1833 he was awarded a royal pension of £200 per annum, and after his death a statue was erected to him in Sheffield. There are more than a hundred of his hymns still in use. Canon Ellerton pays a high tribute to him saying he was our first great hymnologist who collected hymns and wrote hymns and made people understand something of what a hymn meant. It is to him we owe the great missionary hymn, 'Hark the song of Jubilee' (541).

He published many poems: *The West Indies*, 'in honour of the abolition of the slave trade', 1807; *The world before the Flood*, 1813; *Songs of Zion*, 1822; *Pelican Island*, 1828; *Poet's Portfolio*, 1835; *Original Hymns*, 1853.

See also 16, 32, 85, 114, 342, 387, 429, 493, 521, 541, 574, 589.

14 LET EVERY VOICE FOR PRAISE AWAKE
THOMAS DAVIS (1804–87)

A solicitor who later was ordained and became incumbent of Roundhay, Leeds. He wrote six volumes of verse. This hymn appeared in *Hymns New and Old*, 1864.

See also 252.

15 LET US WITH A GLADSOME MIND
JOHN MILTON (1608–74)

A paraphrase of Psalm cxxxvi. In the Psalter the refrain 'For His mercy endureth for ever' appears to have been the response of the singers in the Temple. Milton uses it as the second sentence of every verse. Our present version has been greatly shortened and altered. Milton's last verse ran:

> Let us therefore warble forth
> His mighty majesty and worth.

Two of the omitted verses ran:

> O let us His praises tell
> That doth the wrathful tyrants quell.
> That His mansion hath on high
> Above the reach of mortal eye.

Milton wrote the hymn when he was fifteen years of age.

It is impossible in a short note to express adequate appreciation of the genius of one who was second only to Shakespeare in his

C

mastery of the English tongue. Milton was a Londoner who lived through the stormy period of the civil war and the Restoration. He was educated at St. Paul's School and Christ's College, Cambridge. There were three periods of literary activity: his shorter poems, his controversial and political writings, and then the great poems in the grand style. He laboured for the freedom of the press and has given us perhaps our finest statement on that issue. He worked too for reform of Church and legislation, e.g. his efforts at reform of the divorce laws. He took the side of Cromwell against Charles and held office under the Commonwealth as secretary for foreign tongues. He was afflicted with blindness but continued his offices till the eve of the Restoration. He was an Independent who held Baptist views. He lived in retirement after the Restoration, escaping retrospective action by the new government. Then he completed *Paradise Lost and Regained*, 1667–71. He had domestic troubles and his blindness made him dependent upon others and he felt himself at times deserted. He was not only a great polemical writer but the poet of Puritanism. The worth of his later poems was recognized by his political opponents. Dryden said of him 'this man cuts us all out and the ancients too'. His influence on English hymns is slight, but his name stands high and glorious in the English tradition. He was buried in St. Giles, Cripplegate.

See also 171, 567.

16 SONGS OF PRAISE THE ANGELS SANG

JAMES MONTGOMERY (see 13)

Based on Luke ii. 13–14, entitled 'Glory to God in the highest'. Published in Cotterill's *Selection*, 1819.

17 THE GOD OF ABRAHAM PRAISE

THOMAS OLIVERS (1725–99)

In 1770, thirty years after his conversion, Olivers heard Meyer Lyon sing the Yigdal, the Hebrew confession of faith, in Duke Place Synagogue in London. He wrote the hymn telling a friend he had rendered it from the Hebrew giving it a Christian character. Lyon found a tune for it, 'Leoni'. It was published first as a tract and then in Wesley's *Pocket hymn-book for the use of Christians of all Denominations* in 1785. While Henry Martyn was waiting in 1805 to sail to India he found the hymn of great devotional help.

Olivers was a strange character and his story is a strange story. He was born in Tregynon, Montgomeryshire, and was early left an orphan with few to help him. He struggled through boyhood, uneducated and uncared for. He wandered about as an itinerant cobbler and when in Bristol heard Whitefield preach from the text, 'Is not this a brand plucked from the burning?' This was the moment of his conversion. He at once turned to hard work to pay off his debts and soon became an itinerant Methodist preacher. He acted thus for twenty-two years and then Wesley made him in 1775 supervisor of the Methodist Press. Wesley discharged him in 1789 because he said, 'his mistakes are insufferable and pieces were inserted without my knowledge'. He then lived in retirement in London. He was an ardent controversialist and the author of tunes as well as hymns. The tune, 'Helmsley', set to Hymn 168, is his composition.

18 O, WORSHIP THE LORD

J. S. B. MONSELL (see 6)

Published in *Parish Hymnal*, 1873. It was written for Epiphany.

19 ROUND THE LORD IN GLORY SEATED

RICHARD MANT (1776–1848)

Based on Isaiah's vision in the Temple (Isaiah vi. 1–3). Originally there were four eight-lined verses and the hymn opened with:

> Bright the visions that delighted
> Once the sight of Judah's seer;
> Sweet the countless tongues united
> To entrance the prophet's ear.

Educated Winchester and Trinity College, Oxford, Fellow of Oriel. Ordained 1802. Became curate to his father in Southampton. Vicar of Coggeshall, Essex, 1810; Bampton lecturer, 1811; rector of St. Botolph's, Bishopsgate, 1815; and in addition in 1818 rector of East Horley, Surrey. In 1820, Bishop of Killaloe and Kilfenoragh and was translated to the See of Down and Connor in 1828 which in 1833 was united with Dromore. He was a great champion of the Church of Ireland and wrote its history. He wrote several hymns which were published in *Scripture Narratives*, 1831, and *Ancient Hymns from the Roman Breviary, with original hymns*, 1837.
See also 312.

20 GLORY TO GOD ON HIGH

JAMES ALLEN (1734–1804)

Published in *Kendal Hymn Book*, 1757, which he edited. Because of its unorthodoxy Allen's version was considerably altered by Toplady and Rippon, since he, consonant with the views he held, in the original hymn identified the Son with the Father and the Father with the Son.

Intended for the Anglican ministry, he was attracted by the Rev. Benjamin Ingham who at first an Anglican had become a Methodist, and then joined the Countess of Huntingdon's connexion and eventually formed the Inghamites who were Independents with some peculiar views. James Allen had been for a year at St. John's

9

College, Cambridge, and then became an Inghamite itinerant preacher. Later he joined the Sandemanians who held heterodox views on the Person of our Lord. He founded his own community with a chapel on his estate at Gayle in Yorkshire.

21 SING HALLELUJAH FORTH

JOHN ELLERTON (1826–93)

Translated from the Latin hymn popular in the tenth and the eleventh centuries. The translation was published in *Hymns Ancient and Modern*, 1868.

Born London, educated King William's College, Isle of Man, and Trinity College, Cambridge. He was influenced by F. Denison Maurice as a youth and was able to pass through the Tractarian movement without identifying himself with either side. He had the piety of the Evangelicals and the objective adoration of the High Church party and over all the intellectual freedom of the Broad Church. Ordained in 1850 and after several curacies, vicar of Crewe Green and chaplain to Lord Crewe 1860. He was greatly interested in the cultural life of the artisan and gave much time to the work of their institutes. Another of his interests was music, and he organized the first choral association in the Midlands. He accepted the living of Hunstock, Shropshire, 1872, and Barnes, Surrey, 1876, where his health broke down. He translated hymns from the Latin and wrote many himself. He was joint compiler of the 1889 edition of *Hymns Ancient and Modern*. He wrote hymns for schools and Bible classes, produced a *Temperance Hymn Book* and the *London Mission Hymn Book* and helped in the *Hymnal Companion to the Book of Common Prayer*. In all he composed eighty-six hymns. He refused to take any copyright of his hymns believing that if any hymn helped in the praise of Christ the author should feel very grateful. During his last hours he was singing or repeating hymns. He had been nominated for a prebendal stall at St. Alban's Cathedral, but ill health and death made it impossible for him to be installed.

See also 125, 440, 441, 442, 554, 556, 560, 562, 563, 600, 692.

22 FROM ALL THAT DWELL BELOW THE SKIES

ISAAC WATTS (see 2)

A version of Psalm clxxvii, published in *Psalms of David*, 1719.

23 COME, LET US JOIN OUR CHEERFUL SONGS

ISAAC WATTS (see 2)

Published in *Hymns and Spiritual Songs*, 1707. The fourth verse is omitted. The caption was 'Christ Jesus, the Lamb of God worshipped by all creation, Rev. v. 11–13'.

24 ALL CREATURES OF OUR GOD AND KING
St. Francis of Assisi (1182-1226)

A most felicitous rendering of Francis' famous Hymn to the Sun. It is an improvization on Psalm cxlv with the current troubadour style adapted to quite another service. The hymn reveals the spirit of the author. Composed in 1225, a year before his death, when, nearly blind, he lay in the torrid heat of the summer. He was very ill, in miserable conditions, and yet then he composed this masterpiece.

St. Francis was one of the most attractive characters of medieval Christendom, known to his contemporaries and followers as 'the gay troubadour of God'. He was converted when he was twenty-five after living a dissipated life. His father was a wealthy merchant, but Francis, whose real name was Giovanni, renounced all claim to wealth and wedded, as he said, Lady Poverty. He founded the order of poor brothers which was known by his name and this grew rapidly, receiving at length papal sanction. Many stories are told of his self sacrifice and his love for all creatures. He sought to emulate the example of his Master and poured out his life in service for others. Perhaps the best known story is of his receiving the gift of the stigmata, the Master's wound marks, in his own body. He died at the early age of forty-five, and when death was approaching asked that he might be taken from his hut, stripped of all his clothes, and so go to his Lord with no material possession.

William Henry Draper (1855-1933), the translator, was educated at Keble College, Oxford. Ordained, 1880; held several charges and from 1919 was Master of the Temple. He translated Greek and Italian hymns and published *Hymns for Holy Week* and *The Victoria Book of Hymns*. He also edited *Seven Spiritual Songs by Thomas Campion* and *Hymns for Tunes* by Orlando Gibbons.

25 ANGEL VOICES EVER SINGING
Francis Pott (1832-1909)

Both the hymn and the tune by E. G. Monk were written at the request of Rev. W. K. Macrorie, who became Bishop of Maritzburg, for the opening of an organ at Wingate Church, Lancashire, in February 1861.

Educated Brasenose College, Oxford. Ordained, 1856; Rector of Northill, Beds, retiring 1891. He was a member of the original committee which produced *Hymns Ancient and Modern* and in 1866 published *Hymns fitted to the order of Common Prayer*. He also translated from the Latin, Hymn 129.

26 LET ALL THE WORLD
George Herbert (1593-1632)

There are two hymns in our collection composed by George Herbert, this and Hymn 284. Both come from the book *The*

Temple, the theme of which is the worship of a child of God in His Temple. The whole book breathes simple dignity and shows fine craftsmanship.

Herbert died of consumption at the early age of thirty-nine and was buried beneath the altar of his church at Bemerton near Salisbury. When on his death-bed he gave to his executor a MS. of *The Temple* asking that if it was thought that it might turn to the advantage of any dejected soul it was to be published. All Herbert's hymns which are in use are from this work. George was the younger brother of Lord Herbert who has passed into history both as a soldier and a philosopher. He was born 1593 in Montgomery Castle, educated Westminster School and Trinity College, Cambridge. Fellow of his college and in 1619 public orator. His early ambition was for a career at Court, but in 1630 he was ordained and became rector of Bemerton. His hymns were in great favour with the Puritans and John Wesley included forty-seven. He was also a musician and sang his hymns to the accompaniment of lute or viol. He was the friend of poets and held in high regard by Bacon. His biography was written by Izaak Walton.

See also 284.

27 LO! GOD IS HERE

GERHARDT TERSTEEGEN (1697–1769)

Born in the Netherlands. Perhaps the greatest poet of mysticism. An orphan at six, his early life was in straitened circumstances. He was destined for the Reformed ministry, but domestic circumstances made it necessary for him to earn a living and he joined his brother in keeping a shop in Mulheim. Through physical pain he learned the way of prayer and was converted. Henceforth he dedicated his life to God and practised austerity and meditation. The cottage in which he lived alone became known as 'the Pilgrim's Cottage', and there he kept himself by weaving silk ribbons. He had his 'dark night of the soul' and this lasted five years. On his emergence he wrote in his blood a new covenant with God. Mysticism kept him from the services of the Reformed Church, but he formed no sect of his own. He stressed the inner light, direct access to God without the ordinary means of grace. He lived laboriously, working at his weaving, spending hours in prayer and meditation, addressing meetings and conducting a large correspondence. People flocked to him with their problems, even bringing their sick for a healing touch. He was a constant sufferer himself but he continued his work till over sixty years of age. Among his writings is a collection of hymns, *Geistliches Blumen-Gärtlein.*

John Wesley translated twenty-seven and paid his tribute to the influence of Tersteegen on his own soul.

See also 218, 299.

28 O, PRAISE OUR GOD TO-DAY
ROBERT WALMSLEY (1831–1905)

Written for Sunday school anniversaries and especially for those held in Lancashire.

A jeweller in Sale, Manchester, very interested in Sunday school work and the Manchester Sunday School Union. He was a Congregationalist and most of his hymns were written for the Whitweek festivals which were a feature of Sunday schools in Manchester. He published forty-four hymns in *Sacred Songs for children of all ages*, 1900.

29 PRAISE THE LORD
ANON

The hymn was found pasted on a leaf in *Psalms, Hymns and Anthems of the Founding Hospital*, 1798, and headed Hymn from Psalm cxlviii, Haydn. The author is unknown. It has been attributed to Bishop Richard Mant and appeared in a Dublin Collection during his episcopate in Ireland. The famous Foundling Hospital in London was founded by Captain Coram in 1738.

Singing was an important part of the curriculum. In 1774 there was issued the hymn-book referred to above and in 1809 an appendix. Handel was greatly interested in the hospital; he helped to collect money for a chapel and presented an organ and annually gave a recital of 'Messiah' from which the hospital received £7,000.

30 PRAISE TO THE LORD, THE ALMIGHTY
JOACHIM NEANDER (1650–80)

A thanksgiving hymn based on Psalm ciii. verses 1–6 and Psalm cl.

Born Bremen and died when he was thirty. His student life was marked by riotous behaviour. He was converted under one Undereyk, minister of St. Martin's Church, to whom he afterwards acted as colleague. He had pietistic sympathies and became an ardent evangelist. He was also headmaster of a school and his evangelistic work provoked such opposition that he was forced to leave the town. He lived in a cave on the banks of the Rhine which is still known as Neander's cave. He became second preacher at St. Martin's in 1679, and again encountered opposition. He died a year later. He was a scholar and a poet and wrote some sixty hymns which were published in 1680 and also composed music for the hymns.

31 YE HOLY ANGELS BRIGHT
RICHARD BAXTER (1615–91)

The basis of this hymn is in Baxter's 'A Psalm of Praise' to the tune of Psalm cxlviii appended to *The Poor Man's Family Book*

13

dated August 26, 1672. There were sixteen verses; the first two were changed by R. R. Chope and the last two are Chope's own. It is therefore a composite effort. The *Poor Man's Family Book* was written with the request that rich men should give it to their tenants and poor neighbours, 'either this or some fitter work'. The hymn as we have it first appeared in Chope's *Hymnal*, 1858.

Born Rowton, Shropshire, Baxter was son of a Puritan who had suffered for his views. Educated Wroxeter School, but no university.

He ventured on a life at Court but was out of sympathy with Charles I and studied theology. For a few months a schoolmaster, and then ordained, serving at Bridgenorth and Kidderminster. He was a chaplain in the Parliamentary Army. His great work was done in Kidderminster where he acted as pastor for fifteen years. He wrote during that period sixty books, including *A Call to the Unconverted*, 1657, and in 1650 the equally well-known *Saint's Everlasting Rest*. He rebuked Cromwell for assuming supreme power and after the Restoration served as chaplain to Charles II. Again he disliked Court life and resigned and refused a bishopric when so doing. He became a nonconformist minister after the Act of Uniformity and served as a minister at Acton for which he was imprisoned for six months. He built a chapel in Bloomsbury but never occupied it. In 1685 he was tried by the notorious Judge Jeffreys who told him he had written books 'enough to fill a cart'. He went again to prison where he was befriended by Matthew Henry. He was released in 1687 and the last four years of his life were years of peace and quiet. Baxter was ever for moderation. Dean Stanley called him 'the greatest of Protestant Schoolmen'. He was a prolific writer but his prose was better than his verse.

See also 331.

Richard Robert Chope (1830–1928). Little is known of Chope beyond the dates of his birth and death. It was when he was a curate at Stapleton that he worked on Baxter's hymn.

32 HOLY, HOLY, HOLY LORD

JAMES MONTGOMERY (see 13)

Published 1853.

33 HOLY, HOLY, HOLY, LORD GOD ALMIGHTY

REGINALD HEBER (1783–1826)

Julian says this hymn is a splendid metrical paraphrase of Revelation iv. 8–11. Heber composed it when he was vicar of Hodnet, 1807–23. It was published after his death in *A Selection of Psalms and Hymns for the Parish Church at Banbury*. Lord Tennyson said it was one of his favourites and it was sung at his funeral in 1892. In the autograph copy the second verse has 'and ever art to be'. Heber said he endeavoured never to use fulsome or indecorous language.

Born Malpas, Cheshire. Died Trichinopoly, India. Educated Grammar School, Whitchurch, Salop, and Brasenose College, Oxford. He had a brilliant academic career, winning the Newdigate prize for a poem on Palestine. When Sir Walter Scott pointed out to him that no tools were used in the building of the Temple, Heber added the following lines in a few moments:

> No hammer fell, no ponderous axes rung;
> Like some tall palm the mystic fabric sprung.

He was Fellow of All Souls; travelled in the Middle East; rector of the family living at Hodnet till 1823; Prebendary of St. Asaph, 1812; Bampton Lecturer, 1815, his subject 'Personality and Office of the Comforter'; after twice refusing, became Bishop of Calcutta in 1823; this covered the whole of India and involved much travel. The change of climate and the heavy duties weakened Heber and he died of a stroke while on his journeyings. The next year was published *Hymns written and adapted for the Weekly Church service of the year*. He included other than his own hymns. There is a figure to his memory in the national Cathedral in Washington, U.S.A.

See also 90, 249, 402, 494, 523, 573.

34 O GOD OF LIFE, WHOSE POWER BENIGN
ARTHUR TOZER RUSSELL (1806–74)

His only hymn in our collection though he wrote over 140. Published 1851 in the author's *Psalms and Hymns partly selected and partly original for the use of the Church of England*.

Son of Thomas Clout, a Congregational minister who changed his name to Russell. The father made a reputation by editing the works of Puritan fathers. Educated St. Saviour's School, Southwark, Merchant Taylor's, Manchester College, York, and St. John's, Cambridge. Ordained 1829 and held several curacies and livings. He was an extreme High Churchman and became a moderate Calvinist through a study of Augustine. He published sermons; a memorial to Thomas Fuller; *Hymn Tunes original and selected*; and *Psalms and Hymns*, referred to above.

35 HOLY FATHER, CHEER OUR WAY
R. H. ROBINSON (1842–92)

For the congregation of St. Paul's, Upper Norwood, in 1869, with the text Zechariah xiv. 7, 'At evening time it shall be light'.

Educated King's College, London. Ordained 1866. Vicar of Octagon Chapel, Bath, 1869, and St. German's, Blackheath, 1884, a proprietary chapel. Published sermons on *Faith and Duty* and *The Creed of the Age*.

36 FATHER OF HEAVEN, WHOSE LOVE PROFOUND

EDWARD COOPER (1770–1833)

Contributed to a Staffordshire collection of *Psalms and Hymns*, 1805. Educated Queen's College, Oxford, Fellow of All Souls; Rector of Hamstall-Redware, 1788–1809; Yoxall, Staffs, 1809–33. He was a popular preacher and published seven volumes of sermons. Dr. Bickersteth, Bishop of Exeter, advised his younger clergy to use these sermons rather than their own compositions and even the last Archbishop of Tuam confessed that when pressed for time it was his habit to read one of Cooper's sermons.

37 GOD IS IN HIS TEMPLE

WILLIAM TIDD MATSON (1833–99)

Based on Psalm xi. 4 and published in 1853.

Born, West Hackney. Educated by Rev. J. M. Gould and St. John's College, Cambridge. He was converted when he was twenty years of age and at first associated himself with the Methodist New Connexion and then became a Congregationalist. He held pastorates at Havant, Gosport, Highbury, and Portsmouth. He published several volumes. Julian says he lacked lyrical power, yet his hymns are above the average.

See also 226, 256.

38 IMMORTAL, INVISIBLE

WALTER CHALMERS SMITH (1824–1908)

Written 1867. Based on 1 Timothy i. 17. There have been several alterations in the original script.

Educated Grammar School and University, Aberdeen, and at New College, Edinburgh. Ordained 1850 and held charges at Islington, Milnathort, Glasgow, and Edinburgh. Moderator of Free Church of Scotland, 1893, when he retired. He was a highly cultured man and a poet of note. Among other publications was *Hymns of Christ and the Christian Life*, 1876, where this hymn occurs.

See also 83, 323.

39 LORD OF ALL BEING

OLIVER WENDELL HOLMES (1809–94)

Characteristic of the author, revealing wide sympathy with nature and with mankind and also his sense of the Immanence of God. First printed in *The Atlantic Monthly*, December 1859, and at the end of Holmes' *Professor at the Breakfast Table* with the following explanation, 'Peace be to all such as may be vexed in spirit by any utterances these pages may have repeated. They will doubtless forget for the moment the differences in hues of truth we look at through our human prisms and join in singing (inwardly) this hymn to the Source of Light we all need to lead us, and the warmth which alone can make us brothers.'

Son of a Congregational minister, he qualified as a doctor from Yale and became Professor of Anatomy and Physiology at Dartmouth, 1838; Professor of Anatomy, Harvard, 1847–82. He was the chief founder of *The Atlantic Monthly* to which his famous contributions were made. He was an essayist, a poet, and a novelist, and in all three capacities showed gifts of wit and humour. His famous books are, *The Professor at the Breakfast Table*, *The Autocrat of the Breakfast Table*, *The Poet at the Breakfast Table*. He experienced a conflict between the harsh Calvinism of his forbears and his many coloured interests in humanity. As a consequence he became a Unitarian. Yet at heart he was ever an Evangelical and towards the end of his life fell back upon the great evangelical hymns. He said he believed more than some and less than others, and liked those who believed more better than he liked those who believed less.

See also 66, 604.

40 O LOVE OF GOD   Horatius Bonar (1808–89)

In *Hymns of Faith and Hope*, 1864.

Perhaps the greatest hymn-writer Scotland has produced. Educated Edinburgh High School and University. He began his ministry as an assistant at Leith and from 1838–66 was at Kelso, when he exercised a powerful ministry over the border country. His father was a solicitor and his family were represented in the ministry of the Church of Scotland for over two centuries. A great Evangelical, he was influenced by Edward Irving, sharing his strong views on the Second Advent. Editor of *Border Watch* and *Journal of Prophecy*. At the Disruption he stayed with the Free Church and became one of their stalwarts. He was very fond of children and many of his hymns were written for them. It was written concerning him: 'One said of him he was always visiting, another he was always preaching, another he was always writing, and another he was always praying'. In 1866 he became minister of Chalmers Memorial Free Church, Edinburgh; 1883, Moderator of Assembly. Aberdeen conferred D.D. in 1853. He wrote much poetry and seemed to have thrown off his hymns in a casual fashion and this has involved considerable editing. Over 100 of his hymns are still in use and there are eighteen in our collection. He published much, including *Songs for the Wilderness*, *The Bible Hymn Book*, *Hymns original and selected*, *Hymns of Faith and Hope*, *The Lord of Promise*.

See also 61, 234, 235, 283, 289, 292, 296, 315, 329, 376, 385, 498, 507, 508, 511, 576, 614.

41 FATHER AND FRIEND

SIR JOHN BOWRING (1792–1872)

Headed 'Omnipresence', *Matins and Vespers*, 2nd edition, 1874.

Born in Exeter of a family of landed gentry, trained for a commercial career. He was a remarkable man and had a remarkable career. A contemporary said of him that he could almost claim the name of universal genius. He was a characteristic Victorian, revealing the vigorous individualism of that era. He boasted that he knew 200 languages and could speak 100. However difficult it is to credit that claim yet he published *Specimens of Russian Poetry, Ancient Poetry and Romances of Spain, Specimens of Dutch Poets, Specimens of Polish Poets, Poetry of the Magyars, Poetry of Bohemia,* and he translated French and German works and published in Spanish a work on African slavery. He was a great free trader; he supported the decimal system and introduced the florin into our coinage. He became editor of the radical *Westminster Review.* In the House of Commons he represented in turn Clyde Burghs, Kilmarnock, and Bolton. In 1847 he was made consul in Canton and plenipotentiary to China, 1854, and afterwards Governor of Hong Kong and superintendent of trade with China. He was made F.R.S. and knighted in 1854. He was a strong supporter of the British Association for the Advancement of Science and was honoured at home and abroad and received many distinctions from his own and foreign countries. He published some thirty-six volumes. He was a Unitarian, and this should be remembered when we recall that he was author of the hymn 'In the Cross of Christ I glory'.

See also 47, 100, 118.

42 MY GOD, HOW WONDERFUL THOU ART

FREDERICK WILLIAM FABER (1814–63)

First appeared in his *Jesus and Mary*, 1849, entitled 'The Eternal Father'. Originally it had nine verses.

Born Calverley, Yorks, and died at the age of forty-eight at Brompton. Of Huguenot stock his early influences were Calvinistic. He wrote in his early days against the pretensions of Rome. Educated, Shrewsbury and Harrow, then Balliol and University College, Oxford; Fellow of University, 1837. At Oxford he came under the influence of J. H. Newman and also when on a continental journey had an interview with Pope Gregory which greatly influenced him. He was ordained in the Church of England in 1837, in 1842 was rector of Elton, Hants. In 1845 he entered the Roman Church and with eight others formed a community in Birmingham known as 'Brothers of the Will of God'. This community joined the oratory of St. Philip Neri under J. H. Newman and in 1849 established a branch in London which became the Brompton Oratory. There Faber spent the rest of his life. He was a great protagonist of the tenets of Roman Catholicism and in addition wrote 150 hymns corresponding to the number of the Psalms. His desire was to provide the Roman Church with a hymn-book such as was in use in Protestant churches. There are nine of Faber's hymns in our collection. Most of his hymns are unsuitable for Protestant use. Those in our collection reveal a truly devout spirit and sound an evangelical note.

See also 43, 111, 206, 210, 334, 386, 432, 564.

43 O GOD, THY POWER IS WONDERFUL

F. W. FABER (see 42)

44 OUR GOD, OUR HELP IN AGES PAST

ISAAC WATTS (see 2)

In the view of many the greatest hymn in the English language. It is based on Psalm xc and was published in *Psalms of David imitated in the language of the New Testament*, 1719. Three verses are omitted. John Wesley altered the opening phrases from 'Our God' to 'O God'. Watt's biographer says the hymn was composed in 1714, three years before the death of Queen Anne and at a time of great national anxiety. It is widely used on national occasions. Charlotte Brontë uses the hymn in her novel *Shirley*.

45 O THOU, IN ALL THY MIGHT SO FAR

FREDERICK LUCIAN HOSMER (1840–1929)

First appeared in the New York *Inquirer* in 1876. Its first use as a hymn seems to have been in Harvard's *University Hymn Book*, 1895.

Descended from one of the first settlers in Concord in 1635. Educated Harvard and Harvard Divinity School. Entered the Unitarian ministry and minister of First Congregational Church, Northboro, Mass, 1869–72 and Second Congregational Church, Quincy, Illinois, 1872–7. Then charges in Cleveland, St. Louis, and Berkeley, California, where he died in 1929. He prepared a service book for Sunday schools in 1877 *The Way of Life* and edited with W. W. G. Gannet and J. V. Blake *Unity Hymns and Carols*. In this 'theology and liturgy were frankly uprooted from a Christian basis and replanted in another soil'.

See also 260, 443, 515, 665.

46 O GOD, THE ROCK OF AGES

EDWARD HENRY BICKERSTETH (1825–1906)

In *Hymn Companion*, 1880, which he edited. In English Presbyterian *Psalms and Hymns*, 1867. It is extensively used.

Born Islington, educated at home and Trinity College, Cambridge. His father was the first secretary of the Church Missionary Society, and a leading Evangelical, who edited *Christian Psalmody*.

Ordained 1848, became in 1855, rector of Christ Church, Hampstead, where he remained for thirty years. In 1885, Dean of Gloucester and the same year Bishop of Exeter till 1900. He was a strong Evangelical and conducted retreats and conventions. He was also a scholar and wrote a commentary on the New Testament. He edited the Church of England's *Psalms and Hymns,* using largely his father's collection, and in 1870 published *The Hymnal Companion to the Book of Common Prayer.* This became the most widely used of evanglical hymn-books in the Church of England and in 1873 was in use in 1,500 churches.

See also 360, 437, 481, 500, 525.

47 GOD IS LOVE: HIS MERCY BRIGHTENS

Sir John Bowring (see 41)

Published 1825, the year he became editor of *Westminster Review.* It is a vigorous expression of robust faith and courage.

48 O, BLESS THE LORD, MY SOUL   Isaac Watts (see 2)

A free rendering of Psalm ciii. 1–7.

49 LORD GOD ALMIGHTY, IN THY HAND

George Thomas Coster (1835–1912)

Educated New College, London. Entered Congregational ministry and held several pastorates. He published, 1868, *Temperance and Religious Hymns;* in 1869, *Pastors and People;* and also other poetical and devotional literature.

See also 340, 535.

50 I'LL PRAISE MY MAKER WITH MY BREATH

Isaac Watts (see 2)

A very felicitous rendering of Psalm cxlvi. John Wesley when weak and near to death suddenly started singing these appropriate words.

51 YES, GOD IS GOOD   John Hampden Gurney (1802–62)

Son of Sir John Gurney, baron of the Court of Exchequer. Educated Trinity College, Cambridge, with a view to the law. He heard the call to the ministry and was ordained, 1827. Curate at Wycliffe's old parish at Lutterworth for twenty years, refusing offers of preferment. There he made his first collection of hymns in 1838. He went to Bryanston Square, London, in 1847 where he made a second collection in 1851. He was made Prebendary of St. Paul's in 1857 and was greatly interested in the work of the Religious Tract Society and the S.P.C.K.

See also 108, 278, 672.

Notes on the Hymns and Their Authors

52 THE SPACIOUS FIRMAMENT ON HIGH
JOSEPH ADDISON (1672–1719)

Appeared first in No. 465 of the *Spectator*, 1712. A paraphrase of Psalm xix. 1–6. Lord Selborne said of it, 'A very perfect and finished composition taking rank among the best hymns in the English language'.

Born Milston, Wilts, the son of the rector who was later Dean of Lichfield. Educated Charterhouse, where he met his great friend Richard Steele; then Queen's College and Magdalen College, Oxford. He was destined for the Church, but took up politics and literature. His patrons were the Whigs and he acted as their pamphleteer and they secured a pension for him in 1697 of £300 per annum. His poetical works suited the climate of the times. In 1704 he published *The Campaign* to celebrate Blenheim. He also produced a political tragedy, *Cato*. In 1716 he married Charlotte, Countess of Warwick, but domestic unhappiness drove him to conviviality. He died at the early age of forty-seven. Addison has always held a high place among men of letters and though his hymns lack the evangelical note, read against the background of his time they reveal a Christian attitude. John Wesley said, 'God raised up Mr. Addison and his associates to lash the prevailing vices and ridiculous and profane customs of the country and to show the excellencies of Christ and Christian institutions'. His greatest claim to fame was his association with Richard Steele in the production of the *Tatler*, *Spectator*, and *Guardian*. It was to the *Spectator* he contributed his hymns.
See also 58.

53 THERE IS A BOOK, WHO RUNS MAY READ
JOHN KEBLE (1792–1866)

The original had six more verses, and appeared in *The Christian Year*. It is based upon Romans i. 20.

Son of the vicar of Coln St. Aldwins, who was a high churchman and who acted as tutor to his son with whom there were strong and tender ties all through their lives. Educated Corpus Christi College, Oxford, which he entered at fourteen and graduated at eighteen, a double first and Fellow of Oriel at nineteen, a remarkable academic career. He remained as tutor in Oxford for nine years. In 1823 he left Oxford to act as curate to his father for the next thirteen years, practically without remuneration, in order to be with him in his declining years. He became vicar of Hursley near Winchester in 1833. In 1833, when he became Professor of Poetry at Oxford, the Oxford Movement began with an Assize sermon which Keble preached on National Apostasy. Newman judged that this sermon inaugurated the Tractarian Movement. Keble with Newman and Pusey formed the triumvirate of that movement and he wrote some of the most important *Tracts for our Times*. His influence was strong with the High Church party but he never left the Church of England as did others. He wrote a good deal, but his great work was *The Christian Year*. He had published this in 1827 with great diffidence and only under strong pressure from his friends. There was much opposition to it and one publisher actually refused to publish it at all and the Dublin Commission for the Discountenancing of Vice prohibited the sale, Archbishop Trench agreeing with the decision. This book had a wide circulation in this country and in America and from the profits which accrued Keble was able to rebuild the church at Hursley.

See also 183, 286, 506, 612, 622, 708.

54 BEYOND, BEYOND THAT BOUNDLESS SEA

J. CONDER (see 9)

In *Star of the East*, 1824, headed 'A thought on the Sea Shore', based on Acts xvii. 27. In our *Psalms and Hymns*, 1858. It has an extended use.

55 O GOD OF BETHEL   PHILIP DODDRIDGE (1702–51)

The justly famous paraphrase based on Genesis xxviii. 20–22, the story of Jacob's vow. The original MS. was dated January 16, 1736, but first published in *Scottish Translations and Paraphrases*, 1745. It was sung at the funeral of David Livingstone in Westminster Abbey. In 1781 a John Logan published the text as his own but began 'O God of Abraham' and added a verse. The hymn as it appears now is edited. The original ran:

> O God of Bethel by whose hand
> Thine Israel still is fed,
> Who through this weary pilgrimage
> Hast all our fathers led:
>
> To Thee our humble vows we raise,
> To Thee address our prayer,
> And in Thy kind and faithful breast
> Deposit all our care.
>
> If Thou through each perplexing path
> Wilt be our constant guide;
> If Thou wilt daily bread supply
> And raiment fit provide;
>
> If Thou wilt spread Thy shield around
> Till these our wanderings cease,
> And at our Father's loved abode
> Our souls arrive in peace:
>
> To Thee as to our Covenant God
> We'll our whole selves resign;
> And count that not our tenth alone
> But all we have is thine.

The present form was published in 1781.

Doddridge was of Puritan stock on both sides. His paternal grandfather was ejected from his living and his maternal grandfather was a Lutheran pastor who had fled Bohemia to escape persecution. His father was a London oilman and Philip was the youngest of twenty children. From his earliest days he was interested in religion and before he could read he learnt Old Testament history from pictures on Dutch tiles in his home. He was early an orphan and when fifteen went to Rev. Nathaniel Wood at St. Albans and at seventeen to Kibworth under John Jennings. He opened an academy in Market Harborough in 1729 on the advice of Isaac Watts and this moved the next year to Northampton where he became pastor of the Congregational Church and acted as president of the academy. Two hundred students passed through his hands and 120 entered the ministry. He suffered from consumption and sought recovery in Lisbon but died there at the age of forty-nine. He was a real scholar and a devout Christian. He wrote much and *The Progress of Religion in the Soul* became a devotional classic. He was greatly interested in the growing desire to establish foreign missionary societies but did not live to share the joy of 1792 when the Baptist Missionary Society was formed and pioneered the way for others. He wrote his hymns on sermons he had preached in order to help his flock remember. They were published after his death. He wrote some 364 and there are eleven in our collection. He was a great Nonconformist, a protagonist of dissenting academies and a divine. Aberdeen conferred the D.D. on him in 1736.

See also 75, 79, 170, 367, 377, 400, 478, 485, 581, 649.

56 FOR THE BEAUTY OF THE EARTH
FOLLIOTT SANDFRED PIERPOINT (1835–1917)

Published in *Lyra Eucharistica*, 1864, entitled, 'The Sacrifice of Praise'. It was written as a communion hymn and has been shortened and edited, the omitted verses emphasizing a view of the Eucharist we would not share.

Educated Grammar School, Bath, and Queen's College, Cambridge. He was a classical scholar and classics master at Somersetshire College. After retirement he lived in various places in the West Country. He published three collections of his poems.

57 LIFE OF AGES, RICHLY POURED
SAMUEL JOHNSON (1822–82)

Published in *Hymns of the Spirit* in 1864. Four verses are omitted. The hymn expresses the sense of the Immanence of God which characterized the thinking of the author.

Educated Harvard and Cambridge Divinity School. A radical in theology, refusing submission to any credal tests. He formed

the Free Church in Lynn, Mass., 1853, and remained till 1870.
He joined no denomination and was considered a Unitarian. He
was a reformer and an advocate of the anti-slavery movement. He
was also a scholar and published *Oriental Religions and their
relation to Universal Religion* and *The Worship of Jesus*, 1868.

See also 513.

58 WHEN ALL THY MERCIES, O MY GOD

J. ADDISON (see 52)

First appeared at the conclusion of an essay on gratitude in
No. 453 of *The Spectator*, August 9, 1712. There are verses missing.
Both this hymn and Hymn 52 were added by the University Printers
to Tate and Brady's version of the Psalms in 1818 and in this way
entered English hymnody.

59 ALL AS GOD WILLS

JOHN GREENLEAF WHITTIER (1807–92)

From 'My Psalm', 1859.

Born of Quaker parentage, he ranks among the foremost of
American poets. He began life as a farm boy and when a boy
heard a Scotch pedlar singing Burns's songs and bought a copy.
This bred in him the desire to write verse and his sister sent some
of his efforts to a paper edited by William Garrison. From this
beginning a friendship developed between the two which led
Whittier into journalism. His first book, *Legends of New England*,
was published in 1831. He became successively editor of *The
American Manufacturer*, *The New England Review*, and *The
Pennsylvania Freeman*, a strong anti-slavery paper. He was a
member of the Society of Friends and wore their distinctive
dress and used their mode of speech. His best poetry was written
after he was fifty years of age. He said of himself, 'I am not
really a hymn-writer for I know nothing of music, only a very
few of my poems were written for singing. A good hymn is the
best use to which poetry can be devoted but I do not claim
that I have been successful in writing one.' He also said, 'Two
hundred years of silence have taken the "sing" out of the
Quakers'. There are over fifty of his hymns in use and we
have eight in our collection. Phoebe Cary wrote of him in her
memorial verse:

> But not thy strains with courage rife,
> Nor holiest hymns, shall rank above
> The rhythmic beauty of thy life,
> Itself a canticle of love.

See also 91, 92, 93, 350, 357, 378, 444.

60 GOD MOVES IN A MYSTERIOUS WAY
WILLIAM COWPER (1731–1800)

First appeared in John Newton's *Twenty-six letters on religious subjects to which are added hymns*, 1774; then in the *Olney Hymns*, signed 'C'. Its original title, 'Light shineth out of the darkness'. There is a legend which has received a wide circulation that Cowper wrote the hymn after he had been providentially saved from suicide, but though Cowper once did attempt suicide, there is no basis for the legend. There is another story which is well authenticated, that during the hungry forties of the nineteenth century a Lancashire mill owner called his operatives together to tell them things were so bad that he could not see how to continue to operate the mill. Silence followed the announcement and foreboding fell on the assembled workpeople till a girl was heard singing the verse which begins: 'Ye fearful saints fresh courage take'. The whole company took up the singing and the fresh courage came. So this hymn is the answer of Cowper's faith to the calamities of his own life.

His father was chaplain to George II, his grandfather, Judge of Common Pleas; his elder brother became Lord Chancellor and the first Earl Cowper. His mother was descended from John Donne. He was a timid boy and suffered much at school from bullying that left its mark on his life. He took refuge then in a text, Psalm cxviii. 6, 'I will not fear what man doeth unto me'. Later he went to Westminster School and was friendly with Warren Hastings. He was called to the Bar in 1754 but did not practise. He suffered from recurring fits of melancholia. Eventually he went to live at Olney and collaborated with John Newton. Together they produced the *Olney Hymns*. When Newton left for London, Cowper found it possible to shed some of the extreme Calvinistic views which he had held. Lady Austen prevailed on him to write. He translated Homer, published *The Task*, and became ranked among the great English poets. His hymns were written out of his own experience and the shadows on his own life can be discerned in what he wrote. Their deep feeling has encouraged and comforted sufferers ever since.

See also 115, 196, 262, 288, 344, 601.

61 O EVERLASTING LIGHT
H. BONAR (see 40)

Headed 'Christ is all' in 2nd series *Hymns of Faith and Hope*, 1864.

62 THE LORD'S MY SHEPHERD
FRANCIS ROUS (1579–1659) and WILLIAM BARTON (1597–1678)

The relation of Hymns 62 and 64 to Rous and Barton and their relation to one another is an interesting story and belongs to the tempestuous story of Puritanism. Francis Rous was M.P. for Truro and Speaker in Barebone's Parliament. In 1646 the Westminster Assembly of Divines authorized that Rous' version of the metrical Psalms should be sung throughout the country, their object being uniformity of worship. The House of Lords preferred Barton's version and submitted this to the Assembly. The Commons ordered Rous' version, 'it and none other to be sung in all the churches and chapels within the Kingdom'. The Scots disapproved and appointed a revision committee which had to compare Rous' version with those of Boyd and Sir William Mure of Rowallan and Barton and the Scottish Psalter of 1564–5. Barton claimed that the metrical Psalter in use in Scotland was composed out of 'mine and Mr. Rous's'. These two hymns come from the metrical Psalter.

Barton was vicar of Mayfield, Staffs, and then St. Martin's, Leicester. He was the friend of Richard Baxter and was described as a 'conforming Puritan'. He did not like Sternhold and Hopkins' version of the Psalms and produced *The Book of Psalms in Metre*, 1644. It was this version the House of Lords preferred. He published in 1688 *Six Centuries of Select Hymns and Spiritual Songs collected out of the Bible*. Barton was a formative influence in English hymnody and the Independents especially adopted his hymns and thus they passed into the service of other churches.

See also 64, 73, 130, 569.

63 THE KING OF LOVE MY SHEPHERD IS

SIR HENRY WILLIAMS BAKER, BT. (1821–77)

This well-known and well-loved hymn was written for *Hymns Ancient and Modern*. The author repeated the third verse on his death-bed. Baker recast an earlier paraphrase by George Herbert which began:

> The God of Love my Shepherd is
> And He that doth me feed;
> While He is mine and I am His,
> What can I want or need?

Son of Vice-Admiral Sir Henry Loraine Baker. Educated Trinity College, Cambridge. Ordained 1844. Held the living of Monkland, Leominster, 1851, until his death. He was a High Churchman and believed in the celibacy of the clergy. His great service was rendered in connexion with *Hymns Ancient and Modern*. He was chairman of the Committee and exercised his authority as editor with such freedom as to earn much resentment, one critic suggesting that A and M represented 'Asked for and Mutilated'. He translated Latin hymns and edited original hymns. He published *Family prayers for the use of those who have to work hard* and for the same class, *A Daily Text Book*.

See also 78, 120, 197, 568, 666, 683.

64 I TO THE HILLS   F. Rous and W. Barton (see 62)

65 THERE'S NOT A BIRD WITH LONELY NEST
Baptist Wriothesley Noel (1799–1873)

From Noel's *A Selection of Psalms and Hymns*.

Son of Sir Gerard Noel, Bart., and Lady Noel, Baroness Barham. Educated Trinity College, Cambridge. Ordained into the Church of England, 1826, and incumbent of St. John's Episcopal Chapel, Bedford Row, and Chaplain to the Queen. He was a great evangelist. In 1848 accepted the truth of New Testament Baptism and became pastor of John Street Baptist Church for twenty years. He afterwards conducted evangelistic campaigns with great success. He was President of the Baptist Union in 1867. He edited two hymnals, the selection above and *Hymns about Jesus*.

See also 476.

66 O LOVE DIVINE, THAT STOOPED TO SHARE
O. W. Holmes (see 39)

Printed in *The Professor at the Breakfast Table*, 1859, though written 1849.

67 ETERNAL GOD, WHOSE CHANGELESS WILL
Joseph Estlin Carpenter (1844–1927)

Published in *Hymns of Worship*, 1927.

Unitarian minister and scholar. After charges in Clifton, 1866, and Leeds, 1869, became professor in Manchester College, London, 1875, transferred to Oxford, 1889. Became principal in 1906. He was particularly known as a specialist in the comparative study of religions. His scholarship and fine personal qualities were widely recognized, far beyond his own communion. He was the author of many books on the Bible and Eastern religions. He edited *Hymns for Use in Manchester College, Oxford*, 1894.

68 A SAFE STRONGHOLD OUR GOD IS STILL
Martin Luther (1483–1546)

By general consent the greatest hymn out of Germany. Appeared first in Klug's *Gesangbuch*, Wittenberg, 1529. Legend, unverified, says it was written before Luther's appearance at the Diet of Wurms and that he sang it as he entered the town. The third verse repeats what Luther had said two days before, 'Though there are as many devils in Wurms as there are tiles on the roofs nevertheless I will go'. There are several translations and this is by Thomas Carlyle (*Fraser's Magazine*, 1831). Julian says that before 1900 there were over eighty renderings in fifty-three languages. It is a paraphrase of Psalm xlvi and became the battle hymn of the Reformation. It was sung by the army of Gustavus Adolphus before the battle of Leipzig, and often since in times of national crisis. There are two or three inaccuracies in Carlyle's version. Mr. Gaskell's version of verse 2

> Of Sabaoth the Lord,
> Sole God to be adored,
> 'Tis He must win the battle,

is nearer to the original.

Verse four is more closely rendered in *The Christian Singers of Germany*:

> Still shall they leave that word its might,
> And yet no thanks shall merit,
> Still is He with us in the fight,
> By His good gifts and spirit.
> E'en should they take our life,
> Goods, honour, children, wife,
> Though all of these were gone,
> Yet nothing have they won.
> God's Kingdom ours abideth.

Carlyle said, 'There is something in it like the sound of Alpine avalanches or the first murmur of earthquakes: in the very vastness of which dissonance a higher unison is revealed to us'. The hymn was greatly used by the Huguenots.

Born Eisleben, the son of a miner, Luther struggled to obtain an education at Magdeburg, Eisenach, and Erfurt. He entered the Augustinian convent at Erfurt and was ordained priest, 1507. He visited Rome, 1511, and has left his own account of the shock he sustained at the corruptions in the Church there. The appearance of Tetzel selling indulgences at Wittenberg brought on the climax and there Luther nailed his famous protest to the cathedral door. He refused a summons to Rome and published a treatise *The Babylonian Captivity of the Church*. He burnt publicly a papal bull issued against him. He refused to retract at the Diet of Wurms in 1521 and for a year he was lodged for safe custody at Wartburg by the Elector of Saxony. There he translated the scriptures and wrote other works. He returned to Wittenberg in 1522. His later activities were not all of them on the same high level. He had controversies with Erasmus, Henry VIII, and the Swiss Divines, and his actions in the Peasant's War were open to criticism. He remains one of the great figures in Christian story. He loved singing and found hymns a great help to him in his work, often singing as he journeyed. He wrote thirty-seven and said once that 'after theology no art can be placed on a level with music'.

See also 741.

69 MY SONG SHALL BE OF MERCY
HENRY DOWNTON (1818–85)

Published in *Hymns and Verses original and translated 1873*.
His father was sub-librarian, Trinity College, Cambridge.
Ordained 1840. In 1857 English Chaplain at Geneva. In 1873
rector of Hopton, Suffolk. He translated Naville's *Lectures on
Atheism*, 1865, and several Swiss and French hymns.
See also 530.

70 MOUNTAINS BY THE DARKNESS HIDDEN
THOMAS TOKE LYNCH (1818–71)

Published in *The Rivulet*, 1855.
At first a teacher and then minister, Highgate Independent
Church. The cause was in a poor way and Lynch resigned and
gathered a congregation, first at Mortimer Street and then Grafton
Street, Fitzroy Square, 1849–52. He suffered ill health and had to
withdraw from active work. In 1860 he began again first in Gower
Street and then in an iron building in Mortimer Street till his
death at the age of fifty-three. He had an odd appearance and his
appeal was to a select group. He was of great courage and
spirituality and both are revealed in his hymns. He published
The Rivulet from which his hymns are taken. He chose the title,
he said, 'for Christian poetry is indeed a river of the water of life
and to this river my rivulet brings its contribution'. The book
gave rise to bitter controversy splitting Congregationalism and
affecting Baptists. Lynch had strong defenders in Thomas Binney
and Newman Hall, but Spurgeon opposed him on the ground
that his hymns had 'a negative theology' and 'a non-doctrine
scheme'. Lynch showed a fine spirit, lacking all bitterness throughout the controversy, though the strain brought on a breakdown
and hastened his death. He was also a composer, composing
twenty-five tunes for his hymns. He was heard singing on his
death-bed, 'Guide me, O Thou Great Jehovah', and his last words
were, 'now I am going to begin to live'.
See also 80, 104, 180, 264, 267, 354, 368, 388, 409, 539, 565, 629.

71 GOD SENDETH SUN, HE SENDETH SHOWER
SARAH FULLER (*née* FLOWER) ADAMS (1805–48)

Contributed to the collection of hymns by Rev. W. J. Fox, a
Unitarian minister, published under the title, *Hymns and Anthems,
the words mostly from Scripture and the Poets*, 1840–41. Daughter
of Benjamin Flower, editor of *Cambridge Intelligencer* and later of
the *Political Review*. Her home town was Harlow, Essex, and the
family was Baptist. Her father suffered imprisonment for an
article commenting on the political action of the Bishop of Llandaff.

A schoolmistress in South Molton, Devon, sympathized with him and this led to their marriage. They had two daughters, Eliza, the elder, a gifted musician, and Sarah, who was gifted in letters. Sarah joined the Unitarians and worshipped under the Rev. W. J. Fox at South Place, Finsbury. Fox published the collection referred to above, and to this Sarah contributed thirteen hymns and Eliza sixty-three of the 150 tunes. Sarah married William Bridges Adams, an engineer and a man of radical political views, who built up a prosperous business. In 1841 Sarah published *Vivia Perpetua*, a dramatic poem, and 1845 *The Flock at the Fountain*, a catechism for children. She was a remarkable woman. Leigh Hunt called her, 'rare mistress of thought and tears', and Browning paid tribute to her worth. Eliza died of consumption, 1846, and Sarah, who had nursed her sister, in 1848 at the age of forty-three. She was buried in the Baptist Churchyard at Harlow and two of her hymns were sung at her funeral, this and 'Nearer my God to Thee'.

See also 265, 607.

72 PRAISE TO THE HOLIEST

JOHN HENRY NEWMAN (1801–90)

An extract from 'The Dream of Gerontius', dated January 1865; in 1868 in the appendix to *Hymns Ancient and Modern*, and thus into evangelical hymn-books. J. B. Dykes composed the tune 'Gerontius' for the 1868 edition. It was the favourite hymn of W. E. Gladstone and was sung at his funeral. From the evangelical point of view the doctrine of ver. 4 is dubious; there can be no higher gift than Grace.

Born London, the son of a banker with Huguenot blood and brought up an Evangelical. His childhood was lonely and he lived much in a world of dreams. Educated Trinity College, Oxford. Fellow of Oriel and Vice-President of St. Alban's Hall. From 1828–43, vicar of St. Mary's, the University Church, from which he profoundly influenced the University. He had personal gifts of charm and character, but his early habit of day dreaming persisted and seems to have caused him to view with longing an idealized past which never existed. He became a reactionary and looked askance on liberal views. He became leader of the Oxford Movement and one of the Tractarians. He shared with many others at that time the conviction of the need of a religious revival but felt that it must conform to the type of an earlier age. He had idealized the Middle Ages and longed for a reappearance of such a system, not realizing that it could never have endured in the Victorian era in which he lived. So he was a champion of authoritarianism, at war with liberalism which he considered the root of the malaise of the age. He did not find the authority he desired in the Church of England and after three years of hesitation joined the Roman

Church in 1848, after resigning St. Mary's in 1843. His association with the Romanists was not all he expected. He was viewed at first with suspicion in Rome. Monsignor Talbot told the Vatican he was the most dangerous man in England and he was never offered the opportunities he sought. For forty years he was at the Oratory of St. Philip Neri, Edgbaston, but he never seemed to be really happy in the Church of his choice. His *Apologia pro vita sua*, a most moving autobiography, was, he said, 'written in tears'. He was made Cardinal in 1879. From 1854–8 he sought to establish a Dublin Catholic University, but with no conspicuous success. He published *The Idea of a University*, which despite its keenness of insight reveals the impracticability of his mind. He was a saint and a scholar but he gives the impression of being shackled by his nostalgia for an idealized past which issued in a life of frustration.

See also 415, 616.

73 O THOU MY SOUL, BLESS GOD THE LORD

ROUS and BARTON (see 62)

Psalm ciii. 1–5, from *The Metrical Psalter*.

74 ETERNAL LIGHT! THOMAS BINNEY (1798–1874)

Writing in 1866 Binney says that the hymn was written about forty years earlier and was set to music and published by Power of the Strand on behalf of some charitable object to which the profits went. It was composed one evening after sundown at Newport, Isle of Wight, where Binney was minister.

Born of Presbyterian stock he was apprenticed to a bookseller, where he worked twelve to fifteen hours a day. He entered the Congregational College at Wymondley, Herts, and was there three years. He had three charges, the last being King's Weigh House, London. He became one of the leading London preachers and was a great controversialist with the Anglicans. He led the way in developing liturgical services in Nonconformist churches and his own church became well known for such. He wrote much religious verse but never thought of himself as a poet. *The Spectator* called him 'the great Dissenting Bishop'. He was twice called to the chair of the Congregational Union.

75 GRACE, 'TIS A CHARMING SOUND

P. DODDRIDGE (see 55)

The hymn resembles one by the Moravian, Esther Grunbeck, who was born in Gotha, 1717. In the hymn-book of the United Brethren her hymn opens:

Grace, Grace, oh that's a joyful sound.

Doddridge may have modelled his hymn on this.

76 GREAT GOD OF WONDERS

SAMUEL DAVIES (1723–61)

First appeared in Thomas Gibbon's *Hymns adapted to Divine Worship*, 1769. Gibbon says he took the hymn from Davies' MSS. which had been entrusted to him.

Born Newcastle, Delaware. He received his education through a revival movement. A Mr. Morris had been converted and opened a meeting house to which a minister, Rev. William Robinson, came and carried on a fruitful work. On his departure the friends wished to present him with money. This he refused, but the money was hidden in his saddle-bags. Robinson then devoted the money to the education of the young lad, Davies. In 1745 Davies was licensed by the Presbytery and became an influential preacher, though he suffered much opposition from the dominant Anglican Church in the province. In 1753 he visited England, seeking contributions to the College of New Jersey and in 1759 he succeeded the famed Jonathan Edwards. He wrote a few hymns and published some sermons, but his early death at the age of thirty-six cut short what promised to be a great career.

77 THOU ART THE EVERLASTING WORD

J. CONDER (see 9)

Headed 'Praise to Christ'. In *Congregational Hymn Book*, 1836.

78 OF THE FATHER'S LOVE BEGOTTEN

AURELIUS CLEMENS PRUDENTIUS (348–413)

The original poem was in Latin and is from a longer hymn by the Spanish poet Prudentius. The theme is that the believer should be mindful of the Saviour every hour of the day. Here He is praised as the Everlasting Son, of the Father's Love begotten. The last verse is a doxology added by J. M. Neale and altered by Sir H. W. Baker for *Hymns Ancient and Modern*. Prudentius was one of the best known and most prolific of early Latin Christian poets. He was trained in law and held judicial posts in two cities and an office of some dignity in the Imperial Court. When fifty-seven he entered a monastery and began his religious poems. Archbishop Trench said he made the Latin language a vehicle for new truths.

JOHN MASON NEALE, 1818–66, educated Sherborne Grammar School, Trinity College, Cambridge, Fellow of Downing College, gained the Seatonian prize for a sacred poem eleven times. At first an Evangelical he became a High Churchman and as a consequence suffered in his career. He was offered in 1843, Crawley, but ill health made it impossible for him to accept and he went to Madeira. He became Warden of Sackville College, East Grinstead, 1846. This was a home for indigent old men and carried a salary of £27 per annum. There he remained for the rest of his life. Ill health made it impossible to accept Provostship of St. Ninian's Cathedral, Perth. He inaugurated the Sisterhood of St. Margaret at East Grinstead, to minister to the bodily and spiritual needs of the sick in their homes. This has become a great organization. He founded, too, an orphanage, a middle-class school for girls and a house for fallen women at Aldershot. In all this he endured much opposition and for fourteen years was inhibited by his bishop. He wrote much but his greatest contribution was his translations. He claimed no rights in his hymns; a hymn, he thought, should become the common property of Christendom the moment it was published. On his death-bed they sang to him the hymns of Bernard of Morlaix and at his funeral his own translation of a hymn by Joseph the hymnographer, 'Safe home, safe home in port'. He left instructions that on his coffin there should be written 'J-M-Neale miser et indigens sacerdos, requiescens sub Signo Thau' ('poor and unworthy priest resting under the sign of the Cross'). His biographer writes, 'the most edifying moment to my soul was when I saw him in his last illness laying in dust all his works and all his talents and casting himself as a little child only on the atoning work of Jesus Christ'.

See also 107, 212, 403, 426, 438, 447, 448, 449, 543, 553, 638.

79 HARK! THE GLAD SOUND P. DODDRIDGE (see 55)

MS. dated December 1735, bearing the caption 'Christ's message from Luke iv. 18–19'. Published in Doddridge's posthumous collection, 1755. The hymn is shortened and it is 39 of Scottish Paraphrases. Dr. L. F. Benson says of it, 'It is as though the poet had been present in the Galilean synagogue when Jesus read the prophet's words about Himself and the poet had taken down those words from His lips and made them into a song'.

80 A THOUSAND YEARS HAVE COME AND GONE
T. T. LYNCH (see 70)

From his *Rivulet*.

81 WHILE SHEPHERDS WATCHED THEIR FLOCKS
NAHUM TATE (1652–1715)

First appeared in the supplement to *New Version of the Psalms*, 1700, edited by Tate & Brady. Then one of the six hymns permitted to be sung in worship besides the canticles and the Psalms. In 1708 edition there is a caption, 'Song of the Angels at the nativity of our Blessed Saviour', Luke ii. 8–15. It has continued unaltered and has been translated into Latin and several modern languages and remains one of the most popular of Christmas carols. In the

Earl of Oxford's *Fifty years of Parliament* the list of Poet Laureates has this entry, 'Tate, a butt of Pope and Swift mainly remembered for his Christmas carol, "While shepherds watched their flocks by night"'. The hymn remains the only remembrance we have of the man.

Son of a clergyman, educated Trinity College, Dublin. He was appointed Poet Laureate in succession to Shadwell and in 1702 Historiographer Royal. He wrote mostly for the stage, adapting other men's work, his only real success being his version of King Lear. He collaborated with Dryden. He produced with Nicholas Brady (1659–1726) *The New Version*, which supplanted the older version of Sternhold and Hopkins. He fell into dissolute ways and died in a sanctuary for debtors in the vicinity of the Mint.

See also 348.

82 IT CAME UPON THE MIDNIGHT CLEAR
EDMUND HAMILTON SEARS (1810–76)

Written 1849 and published in *Christian Register*, December 1850. It should be remembered that the author was an American writing against a background of uncertainty. In twelve years the Civil War devastated the United States and all the signs of trouble were patent in the Western world. There was revolution in Germany; England was grappling with the problems of the hungry 'forties and the Chartist movement; and the gold rush to California had started. Then Sears, an American, could sing of 'the age of gold when peace shall over all the earth its ancient splendours fling'.

Educated Schenectady and Harvard Divinity School. He was nominally a Unitarian and ministered to Unitarian churches. He was reputed to hold Swedenborgian views and he believed in the absolute divinity of Christ. He claimed descent from one of the Pilgrim Fathers. He recalls how he was greatly moved by hearing his father read Watts' version of Psalm xix. He early composed and wrote verses when he was ten, writing in chalk on his hat. His friends refused to believe he had done that and challenged him to write another which he at once did. He published *Regeneration*, 1854, *Pictures of Olden Times*, 1857, and edited the *Monthly Religious Magazine*.

83 EARTH WAS WAITING   W. C. SMITH (see 38)
From *Hymns of Christ and the Christian Life*.

84 HARK! THE HERALD ANGELS SING
C. WESLEY (see 4)

First in *Hymns and Sacred Poems*, 1739. It originally began:

Hark how all the welkin rings
Glory to the King of Kings.

John Wesley altered this to the present usage and so it appeared in Whitefield's *Collection*, 1753. There have been other alterations, e.g. originally there was no refrain, there were ten four-lined verses and the last couplet of ver. 1 ran:

> Universal Nature say,
> Christ the Lord is born to-day,

and in ver. 3 'heavenly' instead of 'heaven born'. The tune most commonly used is from Mendelssohn and was adapted by Dr. W. H. Cummings, organist of Waltham Abbey, published 1856.

85 ANGELS FROM THE REALMS OF GLORY
J. MONTGOMERY (see 13)

It appeared first on Xmas Eve, 1811, in *The Sheffield Iris*. Montgomery altered it and published it in *The Christian Psalmist* when it became immediately popular.

86 O COME, ALL YE FAITHFUL

The carol is wedded to the tune *Adeste Fideles* and the origin of both is obscure. Until recently the earliest MS. copy known was in the Wade MSS. at Stonyhurst, dated about 1750–60. On the strength of this it was suggested by Dom John Stephen that it had been written by John Francis Wade, a student at the R.C. College of Douai, in about 1740–43. In September 1946, however, the Rev. Maurice Frost, in a letter to the *Musical Times*, stated that he had found the Latin words of *Adeste Fideles*, set to the familiar tune, in a MS. from the Harmsworth Library. The catalogue dated this MS. *c.* 1687, because it contained a prayer for '*regem nostrum Jacobum*'.

The translation was made by Canon Oakeley for the Tractarian Church in Margaret Street, 1841. 'Now' has been substituted for 'Late' in the second last line.

Frederick Oakeley (1802–80) became incumbent of what is now All Saints, Margaret Street. He was extremely ritualistic and defended his actions vigorously. On being suspended by his Bishop he resigned from the Church of England and in 1845 was received into the Roman Church. He worked among the poor of Westminster and in 1852 was made a Canon of the R.C. Westminster Cathedral.

87 ALL MY HEART THIS NIGHT REJOICES
PAUL GERHARDT (1607–76)

The note of personal religion is noticeable in this joyous carol. There were fifteen verses of which six are taken. First appeared in Crüger's *Praxis Pietatis Melica*, Berlin, 1853. The translation is by Miss Winkworth, with slight alterations, in *Lyra Germanica*.

Born in Saxony, son of a burgomaster. His life span included the Thirty Years War. Because of this he did not enter the Lutheran ministry till he was forty-five and then was pastor of a small village church at Mittenwalde. He wrote and published hymns which became very popular and in 1657 was third deacon at St. Nicholas Church, Berlin. He was an influential and fearless preacher. The Great Elector, Frederich William I issued an edict restricting freedom of speech in order to stop disputations between the Reformed and the Lutheran Churches. Gerhardt refused to comply and was deposed from office and interdicted. He remained steadfast and was without employment for a year and knew privations and domestic trouble. In 1668 he was archdeacon of Lübben, but he was not happy in that charge. His hymns appeared in Crüger's collection as mentioned above. He was the typical German hymnwriter in the transitional period between confessionalism and pietism.

See also 116, 328.

(For Miss Winkworth, see 11.)

88 CHRISTIANS, AWAKE!   JOHN BYROM (1692–1763)

Originally written as a Xmas present for his daughter Dolly in 1749. There were forty-eight lines. In Byrom's note-book there is: 'Xmas 1750, the singing men and boys with Mr. Wainwright came here and sang Christians, awake!' It is said that the tune, 'Yorkshire or Stockport' was sung for the first time that day in Stockport Parish Church. Appeared in posthumous *Miscellaneous Poems*, 1773.

Born Kersal Cell, Manchester, of a merchant family. Educated Merchant Taylor's School, Trinity College, Cambridge. Fellow in 1714. In 1716 went to Montpelier, France, to study medicine, but after a year gave it up. He invented a system of shorthand and returned to England in 1718. He was given by Parliament the sole right to teach his system, which he did for twenty-one years. John and Charles Wesley were his pupils and Wesley's famous journal was largely written in this shorthand. He succeeded to the family fortune then. He was of a mystical turn of mind, had Jacobite sympathies, but came under evangelical influences. He heard Count von Zinzendorf preach, was much in the company of the Wesleys and called William Law his master. His fervent faith reveals itself in his hymns.

89 AS WITH GLADNESS MEN OF OLD
WILLIAM CHATTERTON DIX (1837–98)

First published in *Hymns of Love and Joy*, 1861. When it was published in *Hymns Ancient and Modern* he approved slight alterations.

Born Bristol, the son of a surgeon who had literary tastes and who wrote *The Life of Chatterton*, hence his son's name. Educated

Bristol Grammar School and then to business, becoming manager of an insurance company in Glasgow. He had his father's literary tastes and developed a felicitous style in hymn-writing. This hymn and others are found in most modern hymn-books. He published *Hymns of Love and Joy*, 1861; *Altar Songs*, 1867; *A Vision of All Saints*, 1871; *Seekers of the City*, 1878. He also put into metrical form some translations from the *Offices of the Eastern Orthodox Church* and of Abyssinian hymns.

See also 203, 668.

90 BRIGHTEST AND BEST   R. HEBER (see 33)

In *The Christian Observer*, 1811. Lord Macaulay's father, Zachary, was editor. Further issued in 1827 in *Hymns written and adapted to the weekly Church service*. The idea of the first verse has been criticized on the ground that it is suggestive of the worship of a star, but to endorse that would be to treat poetry as prose. Isaiah describes Lucifer as 'son of the morning' (xiv. 12) and Job xxxviii. 7 represents the morning stars praising God. It has become a very popular carol because of its tune, 'Epiphany Hymn', and its suggestive symbolism.

91 IMMORTAL LOVE   J. G. WHITTIER (see 59)

92 O LORD AND MASTER OF US ALL
J. G. WHITTIER (see 59)

93 WE FAINTLY HEAR   J. G. WHITTIER (see 59)

These three hymns by Whittier are from the poem 'Our Master' and first appeared in *Tent on the Beach and other poems*, 1867.

94 OH, MEAN MAY SEEM THIS HOUSE OF CLAY
THOMAS HORNBLOWER GILL (1819–1906)

Expresses in tender tones the Christian doctrine of the incarnation. This is the more significant since Gill began life as a Unitarian and on that ground was unable to proceed to Oxford where subscription to the Thirty-nine Articles was then a necessity.

He claimed that one of his ancestors was assistant to Richard Baxter at Kidderminster. Denied Oxford, he studied alone, his principal subjects being history and theology. He delighted in Watts' hymns; the comparison between their robust faith and the watered version of them in Unitarian worship began the estrangement from his early faith. His later years were spent at Blackheath. He joined the evangelical section of the Anglican Church and became a strong supporter of Puritan Protestantism. Dr. Dale drew largely on him when compiling his hymn-book for Carr's

Lane. He published *The Fortunes of Faith*, 1841; *The Anniversaries*, 1858; *Golden Chain of Praise Hymns*, 1869.

See also 246, 302, 362, 374, 456, 516, 651, 652, 662, 712.

95 IN ALL THINGS LIKE THY BRETHREN

JOSEPH ANSTICE (1808–36)

In *Hymns by the Rev. Joseph Anstice, M.A.*, London, 1836, the selection containing fifty-four hymns published privately by his widow. Originally it began:

> Lord, Thou in all things like wert made
> To us—yet free from sin.

The hymns were dictated to his wife during the last few weeks of his life.

Westminster School as a King's Scholar; Christchurch, Oxford. He won the Newdigate Prize in 1828 and two years later took a double first so had all the promise of a brilliant career. He was at Oxford with W. E. Gladstone who said of him, 'I bless and praise God for his presence here'. At twenty-three he was appointed Professor of Classical Literature in the newly established King's College, London, but at twenty-five had to retire through ill health and died when he was twenty-eight. He spent the few remaining years of his life at Torquay and continued tutoring to the end. He published, *The Influence of the Roman Conquest upon Literature and Arts in Rome*; *Selections from the Choice Poetry of the Greek Dramatic Writers translated into English Verse*.

See also 361.

96 LOVE CAME DOWN AT CHRISTMAS

CHRISTINA GEORGINA ROSSETTI (1830–94)

An exquisite lyric revealing the nature of a gifted and charming lady. It was published in her *Verses*, 1893.

A member of a famous artistic family and of a circle of literati and painters who have a niche in the hall of fame. Her father, Gabriele Rossetti, an Italian refugee, was Professor of Italian at King's College, London. She was born in Charlotte Street, Bloomsbury, the centre of an artistic colony. Her brother was Dante Gabriel Rossetti, and she sat as the model for his painting of the Virgin. She sat also for Holman Hunt, Millais and Madox Brown. She helped her mother to conduct a school. She was of a serious religious nature, deepened by sorrow and ill health. She broke an engagement because her fiancé had become a Roman Catholic. Her life was a quiet one and her biographer says, 'her days were spent as quietly as the noiseless and secluded days of a nun within the cloister walls'. She gave much time to poor children attached to the church in Regent's Park where she worshipped.

The *Encyclopaedia Britannica* says of her, 'All that we really need to know about her save that she was a great saint is that she was a great poet'. She published much in devotional books and poems: *Goblin Market*, 1862; *The Prince's Progress*, 1866; *Poems*, 1875; *A Pageant*, 1881; and *Verses*, 1893.

See also 160, 742.

97 THE FIRST NOWELL THE ANGEL DID SAY

Nowell is from the French Noël, identified with the Provençal Nadal, i.e. Latin Natalis, birthday: so the song of a birthday. Such carols were popular in France in the fifteenth century. They were repressed in Puritan times as too frivolous, but returned to use slowly after the Restoration. This traditional English carol is printed in William Sandys' *Christmas Carols, ancient and modern*, 1833. Sandys mentions three poor shepherds and comments that in medieval tradition there were four. In the Chester mystery play there are three and their names are given, Harvey, Tudd, and Trowle. The carol is wedded to the tune which seems to have been a popular West Country air.

98 BIRDS HAVE THEIR QUIET NEST

J. S. B. MONSELL (see 6)

From *Hymns and Miscellaneous Poems*, 1837, headed 'Humility of Christ'.

99 MASTER, WHERE ABIDEST THOU?

ELISABETH (*née* RUNDLE) CHARLES (1828–96)

Suggested by the disciples' question, John i. 38.

Born Tavistock, and from an early age gave sign of literary promise. She wrote much fiction, the best known being probably *The Schonberg-Cotta family*. She wrote also *The Voice of Christian Life in Song*, 1864. She was an ardent Anglican but showed a warm and tolerant attitude to all Christian people.

See also 230, 287, 497, 679.

100 HOW SWEETLY FLOWED THE GOSPEL'S SOUND

J. BOWRING (see 41)

First appeared in the 4th edition of *Matins and Vespers*, 1851.

101 MY DEAR REDEEMER AND MY LORD

ISAAC WATTS (see 2)

In *Hymns and Spiritual Songs*, 1707–9, headed 'Christ the Example'.

102 RIDE ON! RIDE ON, IN MAJESTY!

HENRY HART MILMAN (1791–1868)

Based on the narrative of the Triumphal Entry. The tone is of solemn procession. J. B. Dykes composed 'St. Drostane' for this hymn published in Heber's *Hymns written and adapted for the weekly church services*, 1827. It was for Palm Sunday. Probably written 1823. When Heber received the MS. he wrote the author, 'A few more such hymns and I shall neither need nor wait for the aid of Scott and Southey'. Originally the third line of ver. 1 went: 'Thy humble beast pursues his road'. Son of Sir Francis Milman, Bart., physician to George III. Educated Greenwich, Eton, Brasenose, Oxford. He had a brilliant academic career; won the Newdigate Prize for 'Belvedere Apollo' which Dean Stanley said was the best of the Oxford prize poems. Fellow of his college; Bampton lecturer, 1835; Professor of Poetry, Oxford, 1821–31. Ordained 1816. Vicar, St. Mary's, Reading, 1818; Canon of Westminster and rector of St. Margaret's, Westminster, 1835; Dean of St. Paul's, 1849. He wrote dramas and translated from Sanskrit and Latin and studied Indian thought and religious philosophy. He is best known as a historian and he applied the technique of historical approach to his *History of the Jews*, 1830. It aroused a storm of criticism and the sale of the book was stopped. He wrote other religious historical works. He was a great friend of Bishop Heber and the thirteen hymns he composed were at Heber's request.

See also 603.

103 WHEN THE SAVIOUR DWELT BELOW

JOHN RYLAND (1753–1825)

An honoured name in Baptist circles. His father was Baptist minister at Warwick where John was born. His father was his tutor, who opened a school in Northampton where at length John assisted. He was baptized when fourteen. In 1781 he became co-pastor with his father and in 1786, when his father left for London, sole pastor. He was on the committee of five which inaugurated the B.M.S. at Kettering on October 2, 1792. In 1794 he became pastor of the historic Broadmead Church, Bristol, and combined this post with the principalship of the college there. He continued these dual posts to his death. He succeeded Andrew Fuller as secretary of the B.M.S. in 1815. Robert Hall, his successor in Bristol, preached his funeral sermon which is printed in Robert Hall's works. He wrote books explanatory of the Baptist position and in the fashion of Doddridge wrote hymns on the subjects of his sermons. Some ninety-nine were published. He was a great scholar but his poetry was not of a high order.

See also 526.

104 OH, WHERE IS HE THAT TROD THE SEA?

T. T. LYNCH (see 70)

From his *Rivulet*. The hymn gathers the 'mighty works of God' and presents them in verse as an invitation to all in similar need.

105 THE GALILEAN FISHERS TOIL

CHRISTOPHER WORDSWORTH (1807–85)

Based on the experience of Peter and the others who saw the Master waiting for them on the shore (John xxi). Wordsworth maintained that the first duty of a hymn was to teach sound doctrine and thus to save souls, and this didactic purpose shows itself in all his hymns and sometimes lessens their poetic value.

Born Lambeth, the son of the rector, who after became Master of Trinity College, Cambridge: he was nephew of the great poet, William Wordsworth. Educated Winchester and Trinity, Cambridge, he graduated as senior classic and senior optime in the Maths. Tripos. He was a great athlete and in one of his anecdotes he tells how, in the Winchester–Harrow match, he 'caught out Manning'. Fellow of his college and classical lecturer and in 1836 Public Orator. At thirty he became headmaster of Harrow and inaugurated a great moral reform at the school; 1844, Canon of Westminster; 1848, Hulsean Lecturer at Cambridge; 1850–69 held the living in Stanford in the Vale of Berks; 1868, Bishop of Lincoln. He wrote much, including a commentary on the whole Bible. In 1862, *The Holy Year: hymns for every season of the year*, Canon Ellerton said of him, 'He was a most humble, loving, self-denying man and the man is reflected in his verse'.

See also 124, 294, 297, 552, 631.

106 O MASTER, IT IS GOOD TO BE

ARTHUR PENRHYN STANLEY (1815–81)

A versification of the Transfiguration with Peter's request. Originally six verses. Published *Macmillan's Magazine*, 1870.

Born Alderley, the son of the rector, who in 1837 became Bishop of Norwich, the nephew of the first Lord Stanley of Alderley. Educated Rugby under the great Dr. Arnold; Balliol, Oxford, where he won the Newdigate Prize for verse, the Ireland scholarship in Greek, first class classical honours, and the prizes for Latin, English, and theological essays; Fellow of University College and tutor for twelve years. 1850–2, secretary of Oxford University Commission. 1851, Canon at Canterbury; 1855, Professor of Ecclesiastical History at Oxford; and Canon of Christ Church; 1863, Dean of Westminster. Married the sister of the Earl of Elgin, who was a close friend of Queen Victoria. In this way Stanley was in close contact with the court and was highly thought of by the

Queen. He participated in the Old Catholic Congress in Cologne, 1872, and, because of his broad theological views, encountered much opposition. He published several religious historical works and also a life of 'Arnold of Rugby'. It is said that Tom Hughes made him the model for Arthur in *Tom Brown's Schooldays*. He had a gentle and attractive character and won the affection of those even who disagreed with him. He was anxious to develop congregational singing in the cathedral in Canterbury and most of his hymns were composed there.

See also 134.

107 ALL GLORY, LAUD AND HONOUR

THEODULPH OF ORLEANS (c. 821)

The original Latin was a long processional hymn for Palm Sunday. The legend is that Theodulph was imprisoned at Metz or Angers on a charge of conspiracy by Louis I. Theodulph himself, or choristers at his request, sang the hymn as the King with his court was going to the cathedral. His release followed immediately. It became a hymn sung with palms in hands by processions through towns, e.g. Hereford, Tours, and Rouen, where it was sung at the gates of the city. J. M. Neale, making his translation, added a note that till the seventeenth century there was another verse sung which we should not sing to-day:

> Be Thou, O Lord, the Rider
> And we the little ass
> That to God's Holy City
> Together we may pass.

Theodulph lived *circa* 821; he was born in Italy and became abbot of the monastery in Florence. Charlemagne brought him to France, 821, and he became Bishop of Orleans. He died in prison or soon after his release and probably from poison.

For J. M. Neale, see 78.

108 WE SAW THEE NOT

J. H. GURNEY (see 51)

Published in the collection which Gurney prepared for his church, St. Mary's, Marylebone. It is a free rendering of an earlier hymn by Mrs. Anne Richter. Gurney said of it, 'Successive alterations have left nothing of the original but the first four words and the repeated words'. Mrs. Richter was the daughter of Rev. Robert Rigby of Beverley. She married the Rev. W. M. Richter, chaplain of the County Gaol at Kirton Lindsey, Lincolnshire. She is said to have been descended from John Bradshaw who was the first to sign the death warrant of Charles I. She was a friend of Mrs. Hemans and composed verse for various magazines.

109 FIERCE RAGED THE TEMPEST

GODFREY THRING (1823–1903)

Based on the stilling of the storm (Mark iv. 39). Composed 1861, and first in R. R. Chope's *Congregational Hymn and Tune Book*, 1862. Son of the rector of Alford, Somerset, and brother of Lord Thring and Edward Thring, headmaster of Uppingham. Educated Shrewsbury and Balliol, Oxford. He succeeded his father as rector of Alford, 1858. Prebendary in Wells Cathedral. He resigned his living, 1893. He published several collections of hymns and specially *The Church of England Hymn Book*, 1882. His desire was to transcend what he called party hymn books, being anxious that all the great hymns should be at the disposal of the Church.

See also 142, 144, 536, 555, 632, 676.

110 MY SONG IS LOVE UNKNOWN

SAMUEL CROSSMAN (1624–83)

In *Young Man's Meditation*, 1664. Then in *Anglican Hymn Book*, 1868.

Born Bradfield, Suffolk, he became Prebendary of Bristol and wrote nine hymns.

111 O, COME AND MOURN WITH ME AWHILE

F. W. FABER (see 42)

Originally of twelve verses published in Faber's *Jesus and Mary*, 1849. The hymn has been considerably altered, e.g. ver. 1 (line 2) ran: 'See Mary calls us to her side' and then 'O come and let us with her mourn' in line 3. The original linked Mary and Jesus in a fashion that would be unsuitable and unacceptable in our churches.

112 WHEN I SURVEY THE WONDROUS CROSS

ISAAC WATTS (see 2)

The original title was 'Crucifixion to the world by the Cross of Christ' (Galatians vi. 14). Ver. 1 (line 2) ran: 'Where the young Prince of Glory died'. This has been restored in American editions. One verse has been omitted between 3 and 4:

> His dying crimson, like a robe,
> Spreads o'er His body on the Tree;
> Then am I dead to all the globe,
> And all the globe is dead to me.

Matthew Arnold called this the finest hymn in the English language. He was heard repeating the third verse shortly before his sudden death on April 15, 1888. Robert Bridges has written, 'This hymn stands out at the head of the few English hymns which can be held to compare with the best old Latin hymns of the same measure'.

113 WE SING THE PRAISE OF HIM WHO DIED
THOMAS KELLY (1769–1855)

Published in his *Hymns*, 1815, with the caption, 'God forbid that I should glory save in the cross'. The last two lines ran:

> 'Tis all that sinners want below.
> 'Tis all that angels know above.

They were altered by Kelly himself.

Son of an Irish judge. Educated Trinity College, Dublin, intended for the Bar but was converted and devoted his life to religious work. He was ordained and developed strong evangelic preaching. The Archbishop of Dublin inhibited him and Rowland Hill from preaching in his diocese because of his 'methodistical' activities. He seceded from the episcopal church. He was a man of considerable means and built churches which were run on congregational lines, though he did not join the Congregational body. He gave liberally, especially through the time of the famine in Ireland and was venerated by all and sundry. He published *Hymns on various passages of scripture*, 1804, containing 765 hymns. Some 140 of these are still in use and there are five in our collection.

See also 132, 138, 413, 637.

114 GO TO DARK GETHSEMANE J. MONTGOMERY (see 13)

He published two versions, one in *Selection of Psalms and Hymns*, 1820, the other in his *Christian Psalmist*, 1825. One verse was omitted:

> Early hasten to the tomb
> Where they laid His breathless clay;
> All is solitude and gloom,
> Who hath taken Him away?
> Christ is risen: He meets our eyes;
> Saviour, teach us so to rise.

115 THERE IS A FOUNTAIN W. COWPER (see 60)

Probably written 1771; published Cowper's *Collection of Psalms and Hymns*, 1772, and later in the *Olney Hymns*. It is a great evangelical hymn and used in all churches. The first verse with its vivid and to many minds crude imagery has been much criticized. Attempts have been made to alter it but without success. James Montgomery offered:

> From Calvary's Cross a fountain flows
> Of water and of blood,
> More healing than Bethesda's pool
> Or famed Siloam's flood.

But that version does not fit the rest of the hymn. Mrs. Oliphant, in her *Golden Treasury* of Cowper's poems, says it cannot be

44

believed that it is often used by any congregation of worshipping people in these days, yet Dr. T. R. Glover at his last Baptist Union Council meeting as president asked that this hymn should be sung, and Dr. Saintsbury says 'no finical or philistine dislike of the phraseology ought to blind any lover of poetry to the wonderful tranced adoration of its movement' (*History of English Prosody*, vol. 2, page 533).

116 O SACRED HEAD! NOW WOUNDED

BERNARD OF CLAIRVAUX (1091–1153)

Part of a rhythmical prayer 'to the various members of Christ's body suffering and hanging on the Cross'; so runs the Latin caption. It is in seven parts, to the feet, to the knees, to the hands, to the sides, to the breast, to the heart and to the head. It has been attributed to Bernard of Clairvaux but most probably was composed by Arnulf von Loewen, 1200–50. It was translated into German by Paul Gerhardt, 1656. Schaff writes, 'this classical hymn has shown an imperishable vitality in passing from the Latin into the German and from the German into the English and proclaiming in these tongues and in the name of the three confessions, Catholic, Lutheran, and Reformed, with equal effect the dying love of the Saviour and our boundless indebtedness to him'. The closing verse has been associated with the death-beds of many eminent Germans. It was sung in Tamil by the native assistants of C. F. Schwartz who died in Tanjore, 1798. Ritschl complained of the undue stress on the physical suffering of our Lord and yet as he lay dying asked that the first verse be repeated to him. Our version is based on Dr. J. W. Alexander's rendering in *The Breaking Crucible*. It appears in several forms.

Bernard was the son of a knight who was killed in the first crusade. He entered, when young, the monastery of Citeaux and his reputation led to his being chosen to head the band which formed the Abbey of Clairvaux. He was a great preacher and perhaps the most influential man of his day. Many of his sermons are still preserved.

See also 139, 154, 165.

James Waddell Alexander (1804–59), born in Virginia of Scottish stock. Educated New Jersey College and Princeton Theological Seminary. He held two pastorates and then the chair of Belles Lettres and Rhetoric in New Jersey College for twelve years. He served in the ministry in New York and then became Professor of Ecclesiastical History and Church Government at Princeton. In 1851 he became pastor of the Fifth Avenue Presbyterian Church, New York. He was greatly interested in hymnology and contemplated a collection of none but unaltered hymns. His own contributions were translations.

For P. Gerhardt, see 87.

117 ALL YE THAT PASS BY   C. WESLEY (see 4)

The first hymn in Wesley's *Hymns and Spiritual Songs, intended for the use of real Christians of all Denominations*, 1753. It is suitable for personal affirmation of faith. Its theology is the objective view of the atonement.

118 IN THE CROSS OF CHRIST I GLORY
                                        J. BOWRING (see 41)

The school of thought is almost completely different from that of the preceding hymn; the sacrifice of our Lord upon the cross is an example of love and courage which sweetens and lightens life. It appeared in Bowring's *Hymns*, 1825, and is based on Galatians vi. 14. The first line was placed upon the author's tombstone. It should be remembered that Bowring was a Unitarian.

119 NOT ALL THE BLOOD OF BEASTS
                                        ISAAC WATTS (see 2)

There is a story told by a London City Missionary of a Jewess finding this hymn on the paper in which some groceries were wrapped. The reading of the hymn sent her to the Bible and to faith in Jesus as Messiah. She suffered ostracism by her family. The theme is suggested by the Epistle to the Hebrews.

120 O, PERFECT LIFE OF LOVE!   H. W. BAKER (see 63)

Written 1875, published in revised edition of *Hymns Ancient and Modern*. It is deeply emotional and its artistic self restraint makes this a most useful hymn for use as a personal confession of faith.

121 AND DIDST THOU LOVE THE RACE
                                        JEAN INGELOW (1820–97)

Selected from a longer hymn in Miss Ingelow's *Poems*, 1863. It is a hymn of the Incarnation.

Born Boston, Lincs, daughter of a banker. She spent the first forty years of her life in the Fen country and then lived in London. She wrote poetry, successful novels, and charming fairy stories.

122 JESUS CHRIST IS RISEN TO-DAY

The hymn is anonymous. The original Latin carol is from a fourteenth-century MS. largely from Bohemia. The first English translation appeared *Lyra Davidica*, 1708. These were in the

46

main translations from Latin and German sources. This was a beginning of a breakaway from strict psalmody. The first version ran:

> Jesus Christ is risen to-day, Halle-Halle-lujah.
> Our triumphant holy day!
> Who so lately on the Cross
> *Suffered to redeem our loss*;
>
> Haste ye females from your fright,
> Take to Galilee your flight.
> To His sad disciples say
> *Jesus Christ is risen to-day*.
>
> In our Paschal joy and feast
> Let our Lord of Life be blest
> Let the Holy Trine be praised
> And thankful hearts to Heaven be raised.

Then in Arnold's *Complete Psalmodist*, 1779. The last verse was added by Chas. Wesley, the second verse altered, the second and third verses seem unrelated but this has persisted. In Heber's posthumous *Hymns*, 1827, it is wrongly attributed to Heber and the form is slightly different:

> ver. 1. Jesus Christ is risen to-day!
> Our triumphant holiday!
> Who so lately on the Cross
> Suffered to redeem our loss;
>
> ver. 3. For the pains which He endured
> Our salvation have secured.
> Now he reigns above the sky,
> Where the angels ever cry,

123 CHRIST THE LORD IS RISEN TO-DAY

C. WESLEY (see 4)

The original in *Hymns and Sacred Poems*, 1739, entitled 'Hymn for Easter day'. There were eleven four-lined verses. The present text was in Madan's *Psalms and Hymns*, 1760, and the alteration is due to him.

124 HALLELUJAH! HALLELUJAH!

C. WORDSWORTH (see 105)

First published *The Holy Year*, 1862, where there were five verses. It finely expresses the sense of triumph of the believer.

125 'WELCOME, HAPPY MORNING!'

VENANTIUS FORTUNATUS (530–604)

An exultant hymn linking the beauty and vigour of returning spring with the resurrection of our Lord. Our version is a free paraphrase by Canon Ellerton from a long Latin poem by Fortunatus. It was composed before 582 and addressed to Felix, Bishop of Nantes. A. S. Walpole in *Early Latin Hymns* comments, 'there is true poetical force and deep religious feeling and an appreciation of the beauty of spring when the earth puts on her gayest attire to meet her Risen Lord'. Tradition has it that Fortunatus sought to celebrate the success of Queen Radegunda in securing among other things a fragment of the true cross. She deposited this at the convent at Poitiers which she founded and where Fortunatus was Bishop; then Fortunatus wrote this hymn. A native of Italy, though he spent most of his life in Gaul, he lived during the Lombard invasion of Italy and during that period of change was the last of the classical poets. He studied rhetoric and poetry at Milan and Ravenna. He was much honoured in his day and finally settled at the Abbey of the Holy Cross at Poitiers and in 599 became Bishop. He wrote poems about the cross inspired by the possession of the relic. He wrote also lives of the saints, including Martin of Tours.

For Ellerton see 21.

126 CHRIST IS RISEN! HALLELUJAH!

J. S. B. MONSELL (see 6)

In *Hymns of Love and Praise*, 1863, headed 'Easter'.

127 O THOU WHO DIDST, WITH LOVE UNTOLD

Mrs. EMMA (*née* LESLIE) TOKE (1812–78)

Based on the story of Thomas and his reception by Jesus after his scepticism, John xx. 28.

The daughter of the Bishop of Kilmore and the wife of the vicar of Ashford. She wrote eleven hymns for the S.P.C.K. This one was for St. Thomas' Day.

128 JESUS LIVES!

CHRISTIAN FURCHTEGOTT GELLERT (1715–69)

First appeared in *Geistliche Oden und Lieder*, 1757. It had six verses of six lines each; the last line of each verse had in German— 'This shall be my confidence'. The translation is by Miss F. E. Cox who reduced the hymn to five verses of four lines. In her first version she followed Gellert's pattern but amended that for Rorison's *Hymns and Anthems*, 1851. Her first version was in her *Hymns from the German*, 1841. The Hallelujahs were added to the 1851 edition.

Son of a Lutheran minister, his first desire was for the ministry, and for a while he acted as assistant to his father. He was timid and read his sermons and this was disapproved by his congregation, and he became lecturer of literature and then professor of philosophy in Leipzig. He exercised a great influence and his lecture rooms were crowded. Among his students he had Goethe and Lessing. He wrote much and composed comedies and poems. In 1757 he published *Spiritual Odes and Songs* which was very popular. He was deeply religious and his generosity led to his impoverishment. His biographer says 'perhaps no grave has ever been watered by so many and such sincere tears'. His remains were buried in St. John's Church, Leipzig, in a vault alongside the tomb of J. S. Bach. The church was destroyed by bombing during the 1939–45 war.

For Miss Cox, see 12.

129 THE STRIFE IS O'ER

A medieval hymn of unknown authorship. It appeared first in the Jesuit *Symphonia Sirenum*, Cologne, 1695. It was translated by F. Pott in 1859 and included in his *Hymns fitted for the order of Common Prayer*, 1861, and revised for *Hymns Ancient and Modern*. Pott was a member of the committee which produced that book (see 25).

130 YE GATES, LIFT UP YOUR HEADS
F. ROUS and W. BARTON (see 62)

The version of Psalm xxiv. in the *Scottish Psalter*. This Psalter fitted the form of service in the Reformed Church in Scotland and was modelled on Calvin's order in Geneva. The Scottish reformers adopted the Anglo-Genevan Psalter of 1561. The General Assembly loaned £200 to a printer Lekprevick to print the Psalter, and the complete book was issued as part of the *Book of Common Order*, 1564. It included eighty-seven versions from Anglo-Genevan Psalter and forty-two from the English Psalter of 1562 and twenty-two by Robert Pont and John Craig, Scottish writers. There were tunes attached to the psalms and in 1615 common tunes added which were unattached. In 1643 an attempt was made to secure a common order in worship for Scotland and England and this meant a further edition. Francis Rous' version was accepted and this was revised by Rous and a committee of the Assembly. This was approved in 1650 and remains the version still in use.

131 THE GOLDEN GATES ARE LIFTED UP
Mrs. CECIL FRANCES (*née* HUMPHREYS) ALEXANDER (1818–95)

From *Hymns Descriptive and Devotional*, 1858.

Born Wicklow, daughter of Major Humphreys. Miss Humphreys was a very attractive woman and her hand was sought in marriage by two outstanding men in the Irish Church, Professor Archer Butler and the Rev. Wm. Alexander whom she married. Alexander had led rather a stormy life in Oxford and when he married was a curate. He became Bishop of Derry and Raphoe and in 1896 Archbishop of Armagh and Primate of all Ireland. He was himself a poet. Mrs. Alexander had been writing poetry before her marriage and in 1848 published *Hymns for Little Children*. This went into 100 editions and is still used. The profits she devoted to a school for deaf mutes in Londonderry. She published many other books of poems and the best of them were collected by her husband after her death. Both Tennyson and Stopford Brooke paid high tribute to her.

See also 205, 634, 733, 737, 752, 761, 781.

132 LOOK, YE SAINTS   T. KELLY (see 113)

First appeared in his 3rd edition, *Hymns on Various Passages of Scripture*, 1809. There are two slight changes.

133 GOLDEN HARPS ARE SOUNDING
FRANCES RIDLEY HAVERGAL (1836–79)

Written December 1871. Her sister in her memorial of F. R. H. writes: 'When visiting at Perry Bar she walked into the boys' schoolroom and being tired leaned against the playground wall while Mr. Snepp went in. Returning in ten minutes he found her scribbling on an old envelope and at his request she handed it to him. It was this hymn just pencilled.' It is based on Ephesians iv. 8.

The youngest child of the Rev. W. H. Havergal, who himself wrote some 100 hymns and about fifty tunes, Frances wrote verse from an early age, some even when she was seven, which were printed in *Good Words*. She suffered ill health, was converted at fourteen and from that time realized the nearness of the Saviour. Her favourite name for Him was Master, for that she said involved complete submission. Her poetry was simple and expressive of consecration and love. She worked very hard in Christian service and died at the age of forty-three.

See also 172, 217, 233, 364, 375, 381, 382, 389, 391, 483.

134 CHRIST IS GONE   A. P. STANLEY (see 106)

First appeared as 'He is gone beyond the skies', was entitled 'Ascension'. Published in *Macmillan's Magazine*, June 1862. It has been altered in various collections. This version was in our *Psalms and Hymns*, 1880. It is extensively used and there are various versions. Originally seven verses of eight lines.

135 WHERE HIGH THE HEAVENLY TEMPLE STANDS
MICHAEL BRUCE (1746–67)

A paraphrase of Hebrews iv. 14–16. It differs considerably from the hymn printed in Logan's *Poems*, 1781. In the present form it is attributed to Michael Bruce whom Southey called, 'that youth of real genius' and who died when he was twenty-one. Logan had been his friend and after his death edited his poems, not always with real taste. Indeed Logan published as his own what Bruce had gathered in his last weeks. The son of a weaver, he did what many another Scots lad has done for education, worked by day and studied by night. He had five sessions at the Divinity Hall when his health completely broke and he went home to die.

See also 194.

136 WITH JOY WE MEDITATE THE GRACE
ISAAC WATTS (see 2)

In *Hymns and Spiritual Songs*, 1707–9, headed 'Our High Priest'. J. Wesley included it, omitting ver. 3 in his *Psalms and Hymns*, 1736–7. Whitefield used it in his collection, 1759. It was edited by Toplady for his collection, 1776.

137 O THOU, THE CONTRITE SINNERS FRIEND
CHARLOTTE ELLIOTT (1789–1871)

Written 1837, appeared 1843 in the collection made by her brother, H. V. Elliott. By error it was attributed to Wesley.

Born Clapham, a grand-daughter of Henry Venn. Her first ventures were in humorous verse, but an illness in 1821 left her a permanent invalid. She came into contact with Cesar Malan, an evangelist of Geneva. At first she resented his question as to whether she was a Christian, but after asked him how she could find Christ. 'Come to Him just as you are', he said, and she did. She devoted herself to religious work though in constant pain. Her hymns were published in *Psalms and Hymns* edited by her brother and also in *Hours of Sorrow Cheered and Comforted*, 1836; *Hymns for the Week*, 1839; *The Invalid's Hymn Book*, 1834–41; *Thoughts in Verse*, 1869.

See also 232, 269, 318, 326, 399, 486, 550.

138 THE HEAD THAT ONCE WAS CROWNED WITH THORNS
T. KELLY (see 113)

From the 5th edition of his *Hymns*, 1820, based upon Hebrews ii. 10.

139 O JESUS, KING MOST WONDERFUL
BERNARD OF CLAIRVAUX (see 116)

165 JESUS, THE VERY THOUGHT OF THEE
154 JESUS, THOU JOY OF LOVING HEARTS

These three hymns are from a long Latin poem of forty-two verses, probably of the eleventh century. Several authors have been suggested, but the most probable is Bernard since they seem most characteristic of him. The poem was certainly known in the eleventh century. There is no other evidence of authorship and as Dr. G. G. Coulton has said, 'Bernard disapproved of poetry'. The extracts which have become hymns give a finer representation than the whole poem which lacks a feeling of progress. David Livingstone used to repeat some of the verses in Latin as he journeyed through Africa. He wrote, 'That hymn of St. Bernard on the name of Christ although in dog Latin pleases me so; it rings in my ears as I wander across the wide, wide, wilderness'. Here is medieval piety at its best and the music of such devotion transcends the centuries.

139 and 165 were translated by Edward Caswall (1814–78), appearing in *Lyra Catholica*, 1849, before he became a Roman Catholic. He was born at Yately, Hants, son of the vicar. Educated Marlborough and Brasenose, Oxford. Ordained in the Church of England, for a few years a curate, and then joined the Tractarian Movement and went over to Rome in 1847. Three years after the death of his wife he became a Roman priest and in 1850 joined the oratory of St. Philip Neri at Edgbaston under Newman. His special ministry was visitation of the poor and sick. He translated old Latin hymns and published them in *Lyra Catholica*. He was very friendly with Newman.

Ray Palmer, 1808–87, translator of 154, born in New Jersey, son of a judge. At first a draper's assistant, then Philip's Academy, Andover, and Yale. Became a Congregational minister and corresponding secretary of the American Congregational Union. A wise teacher, devout and buoyant.

Other hymns of Palmer, 185, 261, 313.

Other hymns of Caswall, 165, 166, 275, 633, 644, 743.

140 ALL HAIL THE POWER OF JESUS' NAME!
EDWARD PERRONET (1726–92)

Few hymns are more widely known among English-speaking people. The best known tune is 'Miles Lane', which was printed in the *Gospel Magazine*, 1779, with no author or composer's name. Originally there were eight verses. Perronet included it in *Occasional Verses*, but did not reveal his authorship except in some acrostic verses which reveal his name. It has been altered and two verses omitted.

> ver. 5.   Let every tribe and every tongue
> That bound creation's call,
> Now shout, in universal song
> The crowned Lord of all.

The changes are in Dr. Rippon's *Selection of Hymns*, 1787. The omitted verses are:

> Let high born seraphs tune the lyre,
> And as they tune it fall
> Before His face, Who tunes the choir,
> And crown Him Lord of all.
> Crown Him ye morning stars of light,
> Who fixed this floating ball;
> Now hail the strength of Israel's might
> And crown Him Lord of all.

Son of the vicar of Shoreham, the family being French Huguenot refugees. His father was a friend of the Wesleys, and the son became one of their itinerant preachers. He broke with the Church of England, and became outright in his opposition, publishing a religious satire, *The Mitre*, in 1749. The Wesleys were not ready to go as far as Perronet and he joined the Countess of Huntingdon's Connexion. Even the Countess became annoyed with the violence of Peronnet's anti-Anglicanism. He then became the pastor of a small Independent Church in Canterbury. He wrote many hymns, but this is the only one remembered and used.

141 REJOICE! THE LORD IS KING   C. WESLEY (see 4)

From *Hymns for our Lord's Resurrection*, 1746, based on Philippians iv. 4. This is one of the three hymns for which Handel composed a tune. There is a verse omitted:

> He sits at God's right hand
> Till all His foes submit
> And bow to His command
> And fall beneath His feet,

and then the refrain.

142 CROWN HIM WITH MANY CROWNS
MATTHEW BRIDGES (1800–94) and GODFREY THRING (see 109)

Only the first verse was by Bridges. His hymn was in *Hymns of the Heart*, 1851. The present form was rearranged by G. Thring in the *Church of England Hymn Book*, 1880. Thring attached a note, 'The greater part of this hymn was originally written at the request of the Rev. H. W. Hatton to supply the place of some of the verses in M. Bridges' well-known hymn of which he and others did not approve. It was afterwards thought better to rewrite the whole so that the two hymns might be kept entirely distinct.' They are not, however, distinct.

Matthew Bridges was brought up in the Church of England. He published in 1825 *Jerusalem regained, a poem*; in 1828, *The Roman Empire under Constantine the Great*, in which he sought to examine the real origin of certain papal superstitions whose antiquity had been so often urged against the Protestants. He became influenced by the Tractarian movement and entered the Roman Church in 1848. He went to Canada and died at Quebec aged ninety-four.

See also 470. For Thring, see 109.

143 HAIL! THOU ONCE DESPISÈD JESUS

JOHN BAKEWELL (1721–1819)

In Madan's *Collection*, 1760. Bakewell gave the entire hymn to Toplady who altered it to his own views and published 1776. There is no doubt about Bakewell's authorship.

Born Brailsford, Derby. He was influenced for religion by reading Boston's *Fourfold State*. After conversion he preached in his district against opposition. He moved to London and met the Wesleys and Toplady and Madan. He conducted a school in Greenwich and also a Methodist class in his house. He remained a local preacher and died at the age of ninety-eight.

144 SAVIOUR, BLESSÈD SAVIOUR   G. THRING (see 109)

Written in 1862 under the caption 'Pressing on', and published *Hymns Congregational and others*, 1862. One verse omitted and the last verse slightly altered.

145 IN THE NAME OF JESUS

CAROLINE MARIA NOEL (1817–77)

Originally seven verses. A processional hymn for Ascension Day and in her book called *The Name of Jesus*, 1878. Philippians ii. 9–10.

Daughter of Canon G. T. Noel and niece of Baptist Noel (see 68). She wrote her first hymn when seventeen, but wrote none from the age of twenty to forty. She suffered much pain and this sent her back to hymn-writing and she wrote for other sufferers. Her hymns were collected in two works, the one referred to and the other *The Name of Jesus and other verses for the sick and lonely*.

146 HOW SWEET THE NAME OF JESUS SOUNDS

JOHN NEWTON (1725–1807)

This well-loved hymn should be read with the story of the author in mind. Towards the end of his remarkable life, when his faculties were fading, Newton said, 'My memory is nearly gone, but I remember two things, that I am a great sinner and Jesus is a great Saviour'. It is in the *Olney Hymns* where there is one more verse:

> By Thee my prayers acceptance gain,
> Although with sin defiled:
> Satan accuses me in vain,
> And I am owned a child.

In ver. 4 Newton wrote 'husband', and objection was made to that term for the Saviour, but Newton had based the hymn on Canticles I. and in the allegory of the Song of Solomon the term is fitting. There have been other alternatives suggested but the present emendation seems the least violent.

Newton's story is well known and can be summarized. His father was a shipmaster, his mother a godly woman who died when he was seven. He went to sea with his father, but was impressed into the Navy and became a midshipman. He was flogged for desertion and degraded and took service in a slave ship. He led, on his own confession, a dissipated life, but two things, reading Thomas à Kempis and deliverance from a great peril, led to his conversion. With his father's help for six years he commanded a slave ship. This, to us, surprising fact must be considered in regard to the background of his age and there is no question as to his devotion to Christ. He then became tide surveyor at Liverpool and offered himself for ordination. The Archbishop of York refused but the Bishop of Lincoln ordained him and he went as a curate to Olney where with Cowper he produced the *Olney Hymns*. He wrote 280 and Cowper sixty-eight. He then became incumbent at St. Mary, Woolnoth, London, where he did a great work till his death. He was a great Evangelical and used his own story with great effect. He composed his own epitaph:

> John Newton, clerk, once an infidel and libertine, a servant of slaves in Africa, was by the rich mercy of our Lord and Saviour Jesus Christ, preserved, restored, pardoned, and appointed to preach the Faith he had long laboured to destroy.

See also 156, 257, 325, 330, 423, 453, 582, 592, 606.

147 O FOR A THOUSAND TONGUES TO SING

C. WESLEY (see 4)

Written 1739 on the first anniversary of his conversion which took place on May 21, 1738. There are eighteen verses from which seven are taken. The 'thousand tongues' was suggested by the Moravian missionary, Peter Bohler, who was the means of his conversion. The essential factor in the conversion is expressed in the last two lines:

> Look and be saved through faith alone,
> Be justified by grace.

In the 1780 Wesleyan hymn-book this is No. 1.

148 I'VE FOUND THE PEARL   JOHN MASON (1646–94)

Son of a dissenting minister, educated in Northampton and Clare Hall, Cambridge. He had a curacy first and then was vicar of Stantonbury, Bucks, 1668, and of Water Stratford, 1674. He published, 1683, *Spiritual Songs or Songs of Praise to Almighty God*. In 1690 he preached a sermon, 'The Midnight Cry', in which he foretold the imminent second coming. It must be remembered that this doctrine figured more largely in Puritan times than in ours. The sermon evoked exaggerated enthusiasm and his followers made an encampment near a village where they lived on communistic lines. Mason gave up administering the sacraments and gave himself to preaching. His sermons and poems were collected and were praised by Isaac Watts.

149 THOU HIDDEN SOURCE   C. WESLEY (see 4)

In *Hymns and Sacred Poems*, 1749, headed 'Trust and Confidence'.

150 I AM NOT SKILLED   DORA GREENWELL (1821–82)

From *Songs of Salvation*, 1873.

The daughter of a landed gentleman, family misfortune made it necessary for her to live with her brothers, both clergymen, when she was twenty-seven. She made her home later with her mother in Torquay, Clifton, and London. She had a keen mind and a warm heart and her special interest was the care of mentally defective children. She wrote much and her devotional books have been greatly appreciated, Whittier comparing them with à Kempis, Fenelon, and Woolman. She pondered much the atonement and used as a device on her books a heart set against a black cross, which she borrowed from Luther, and both she placed in the midst of a white rose and added the motto *Et teneo et teneor*, 'I both hold and am held'.

151 REST OF THE WEARY   J. S. B. MONSELL (see 6)

From *Hymns of Love and Praise*, originally 'I' in ver. 3 (line 1) read 'I'll'.

152 O JESUS, FRIEND UNFAILING
SAMUEL CHRISTIAN GOTTFRIED KUSTER (1762–1838)

A hymn of quiet confidence in all circumstances.

Pastor of Friedrich Werder Church, Berlin. He was co-editor of a hymn-book to which he contributed two hymns, one of which Miss Burlingham translated.

Hannah Kilham Burlingham, 1842–1901, lived in Evesham. She was a good linguist. This hymn was translated in 1865.

153 O JESUS, EVER PRESENT
LAWRENCE TUTTIETT (1825–97)

In *Germs of thought on the Sunday Services*, 1864. It was said that Tuttiett, after visitation of the sick or a burial, tried to express in verse something of what he had been saying. This can be sensed in this hymn.

The son of a naval surgeon. Educated Christ's Hospital and King's College, London, to study medicine. His desire changed and he was ordained 1848 and became vicar of Marston, Warwick. In 1870 he was incumbent of the Episcopal Church, St. Andrews, and in 1880 honorary canon, St. Ninian's Cathedral, Perth. His last years were spent in Pitlochry. He published prayer annuals and collections of verse and *Hymns for Churchmen*, 1854; *Hymns for the children of the Church*, 1862; and *Germs of Thought*, 1864.

See also 167, 242, 650, 718.

154 JESUS, THOU JOY OF LOVING HEARTS
BERNARD OF CLAIRVAUX (see 116)

Commented on in connexion with Hymn 139.

155 O THOU MY SOUL   KRISHNA PAL (1764–1822)

This hymn has a special place in a Baptist hymnal. Its author was the first convert from Hinduism baptized in Bengal; the date, December 28, 1800, the place Serampore. Krishna Pal wrote several hymns in Bengali; this is the only one in our collection. It was translated by J. Marshman, one of the Serampore triumvirate. The fears and thoughts of Hinduism can be discerned in the background as that from which Christ had set the writer free.

Krishna Pal was a carpenter and Dr. John Thomas made contact with him when he was thirty-five. An accident brought the doctor and the patient into closer and more intimate contact and Krishna Pal decided for Christ. He endured much persecution from his own people but endured and was baptized by Carey in the River Ganga, Carey himself afterwards being charged with desecrating the river. Ward, the third of the trio, wrote a graphic account of the historic event and of the sacrament of Holy Communion which followed, and Thomas was delirious with joy. 'Sing, soul, sing, Sing aloud unutterable is my gladness.' He had waited fifteen years for the first fruit. Persecution persisted for Krishna Pal, but he built a preaching shed where he talked to his neighbours and wrote his hymns to Bengali tunes. The constant persecution tended to make his spirit fiery and caused much heart burning to the missionaries. He became a pioneer missionary to several places in India and in August, 1822, he died suddenly of cholera.

JOSHUA MARSHMAN, 1768–1837. The story of Marshman is the story of the beginnings of the B.M.S. He, with Carey and Ward, made their preaching centre, their school and college, their printing press at Serampore, a dynamic base of evangelism in India. To see his memorial one must look on the Christian Church in India to-day.

156 ONE THERE IS, ABOVE ALL OTHERS

J. NEWTON (see 146)

In the *Olney Hymns*, 1779, there were six verses based on Proverbs xviii. 24, 'There is a friend that sticketh closer than a brother'. The omitted verse is:

> Men, when raised to lofty stations
> Often know their friends no more;
> Slight and scorn their poor relations
> Though they valued them before;
> But our Saviour always owns
> Those whom He redeemed with groans.

157 JOIN ALL THE GLORIOUS NAMES

ISAAC WATTS (see 2)

From *Hymns and Spiritual Songs*, 1709, where there were twelve verses. Watts called it, 'The same as the 148th psalm'.

158 I'VE FOUND A FRIEND

JAMES GRINDLAY SMALL (1817–88)

First appeared in *The Revival Hymn Book*, 1863.
Educated Edinburgh High School and University, Dr. Chalmers being one of his professors. He went with the Free Church at the Disruption and held a charge at Bervie, near Montrose. He became Clerk to the Presbytery. He was greatly interested in psalmody and won a prize for a poem at the University. He published several volumes of verse.

159 'MAN OF SORROWS!' PHILIPP BLISS (1838–76)

First in *International Lessons Monthly*, 1875. Originally began, 'Man of sorrows, what a name'.
Originally a Methodist he became S.S. Superintendent of First Congregational Church, Chicago. He was a fine singer with a facility for verse and tuneful airs. He became musical companion to Major D. W. Whittle, an evangelist, and for their meetings prepared *Gospel Songs*. This was a departure in evangelizing and became popular, leading to the formation of other collections. The royalties on this book, amounting to £6,000, were devoted

58

to the work. Moody and Sankey found this collection on their return from an evangelistic campaign in this country and they combined their small *Sacred Songs and Solos*, known as 'Sankey's', with Bliss's collection. This was first issued as *Gospel Hymns and Sacred Songs* by P. P. Bliss and Ira D. Sankey. Bliss died in tragic circumstances trying to save his wife from a blazing train in which they were travelling.

160 NONE OTHER LAMB   C. G. ROSSETTI (see 96)

This moving hymn is from *The Face of the Deep*, 1892, Revelation v. 6, 'I beheld, and lo, in the midst of the throne stood a lamb as it had been slain'.

161 THOU ART THE WAY
GEORGE WASHINGTON DOANE (1799–1859)

From his *Songs of the Way*, 1824: on John xiv. 6. Bickersteth introduced it to *Hymns Ancient and Modern*, 1861. It was the only hymn by an American author in that collection.

Educated Union College, Schenectady, New York; ordained 1821. Professor of Belles Lettres in Trinity College, Hartford, Connecticut, 1824; rector of Trinity Church, Boston, 1828; Bishop of New Jersey, 1832. He was in close sympathy with the Tractarian Movement in England, a promoter of missionary movements and the establishment of Church Schools. He edited the first American reprint of Keble's *Christian Year*; published *Songs of the Way*, 1824. His *Collected Works* were issued in four volumes after his death.

162 NOW TO THE LORD A NOBLE SONG!
ISAAC WATTS (see 2)

In *Hymns and Spiritual Songs*, 1707–9, with the title 'Christ all in all'.

163 AWAKE, MY SOUL   SAMUEL MEDLEY (1738–99)

Son of a schoolmaster who was a friend of Sir Isaac Newton. He joined the Navy and was a midshipman in 1755. He was often in action and once was badly wounded. He was converted under his grandfather's preaching. He was baptized and joined the Eagle Street Baptist Church (now Kingsgate Chapel) in 1750, Dr. Gifford being the pastor. He opened a school in Seven Dials and began preaching. In 1767 he became the pastor of the Beechen Grove Baptist Church in Watford, 1767–72, and then went to Liverpool and to a very successful ministry, the church in Byrom Street being built to hold the increased congregations in 1790.

164 MIGHTY GOD, WHILE ANGELS BLESS THEE
ROBERT ROBINSON (1735–90)

Written for a Benjamin Williams, who became deacon of the Baptist Church at Reading. Williams was a small boy at the time and Robinson wrote it with the boy on his knee. He read it to him and then gave it into his hand.

Educated Swaffham Grammar School. His mother wanted him to be a clergyman of the Church of England, but lack of funds prevented this and he was apprenticed to a barber. He came under the influence of Whitefield in 1752 and himself dates his conversion 1755. He began preaching as a Calvinistic Methodist, but became a Baptist in 1759. Soon after he was pastor of Stone Yard Baptist Church, Cambridge. To supplement his income he farmed and did business as a coal and corn factor. He was a remarkable linguist and translated from the French. He wrote a history of Baptists and Baptism. He was passionately devoted to freedom and had much fellowship with the famous Dr. Priestley of Birmingham whose house was burnt by a mob during the early days of the French Revolution. His outspokenness and liberality of mind caused the Unitarians to claim him, but he remained a staunch Baptist to the end. He lived in a time of ferment and linked his religion to the changing scene.

See also 425.

165 JESUS, THE VERY THOUGHT OF THEE
BERNARD OF CLAIRVAUX (see 116)

See comment on Hymn 139.

166 WHEN MORNING GILDS THE SKIES
E. CASWALL (see 139)

The original German hymn of about 150 years old was first discovered in *Katholisches Gesangbuch*, 1828. Caswall offered this translation in his *Masque of Mary*, 1858. Robert Bridges 'tried to give a better version of it' in his *Yattendon Hymnal*, 1899. It was one of Canon Liddon's favourite hymns and was sung at his funeral.

167 O, QUICKLY COME, DREAD JUDGE OF ALL
L. TUTTIETT (see 153)

In *Hymns for Churchmen*, 1854.

168 LO! HE COMES, WITH CLOUDS DESCENDING
JOHN CENNICK (1718–55)

Considerably altered by C. Wesley, who wrote the first and second and fourth verses. The third verse was in Cennick's hymn in his *Collection of Sacred Hymns*, 1752, and was rearranged by Martin Madan, *Collection of Psalms and Hymns*, 1760. His poem had six verses, the third and fifth are omitted. The tune was composed by T. Olivers (see 17) and named 'Helmsley'. Olivers said he heard a boy whistling it in the street but no research has unearthed the tune among London songs.

John Cennick was of Quaker parentage though brought up in the Church of England. He was of Bohemian stock. He became attached to the Wesleys and John appointed him teacher of a school for colliers' children at Kingswood. He was the first Methodist lay preacher. He took the side of Whitefield against the Wesleys and finally joined the Moravians and was used by them in Germany and Northern Ireland.

See also 414, 615, 642.

169 HARK! 'TIS THE WATCHMAN'S CRY

Found in *The Revival* magazine, 1859. Anonymous.

170 YE SERVANTS OF THE LORD   P. DODDRIDGE (see 55)

His custom of using hymns to help his sermons is clear here. The hymn is entitled 'The active Christian'. Ver. 5 (line 3), Doddridge wrote 'favourite' instead of 'faithful'. Dean Alford says 'the substitute adjective was more a matter of duty than choice'. It appeared in the posthumous edition of his works.

171 THE LORD WILL COME AND NOT BE SLOW

J. MILTON (see 15)

In *Poems upon several occasions*, 1673. There is a group of paraphrases headed 'Nine of the Psalms done into metre where all but what is in a different character are the very words of the text translated from the original'. Headed, April 1648, J. M. There are some verses omitted.

172 THOU ART COMING   F. R. HAVERGAL (see 133)

In *Under the Surface*, 1876, F. R. H. wrote, 'It was on Advent Sunday, December 2, 1873, I first saw clearly the blessedness of true consecration'. This was the first hymn she wrote after that experience.

173 OUR BLEST REDEEMER   HARRIET AUBER (1773–1862)

One of the two hymns in her *Spirit of the Psalms*, 1829, for Whitsuntide. It has been translated into several languages, including Latin. There is an oft repeated story that Miss Auber scratched the hymn on her bedroom window in Hoddesdon. Several people claimed to have seen it, but the glass has disappeared and the story may be a pleasant myth! Descended from Pierre Auber, a refugee in 1685 from the revocation of the Edict of Nantes, she spent her life in the villages of Broxbourne and Hoddesdon in the vicinity of what is now the conference centre of High Leigh. She desired to make elegant Sternhold and Hopkins versions of the Psalms. C. H. Spurgeon used some of her versions in his *Tabernacle Collection*. She wrote much poetry but nothing else approaching the beauty of this far-famed hymn. Her memory was cherished for many years in the villages where she lived.

174 COME, GRACIOUS SPIRIT

SIMON BROWNE (1680–1732)

Modelled on Isaac Watts. First in Browne's *Hymns and Spiritual Songs*, 1720. It has been altered and adapted often. It was written in the first person singular and was altered to the plural later. The last verse is due to W. Mercer's *Church Psalter and Hymn Book*, 1864.

Became an Independent minister, first in Portsmouth and in 1716, of the important church in the Old Jewry. Published in addition to his collection of hymns a book of sermons. His spiritual life was a shadowed one. He engaged in the controversies of his time and had a great respect for Isaac Watts. He had an unfortunate encounter with a highwayman and inadvertently killed his man, and this affected him. He lost his wife and son and he had the delusion that God had destroyed his 'thinking substance'. Toplady said of him, 'Instead of having no soul he wrote, reasoned, and prayed as if he had two'. He spent his declining years at Shepton Mallet, translating classical authors, writing books for children, and working at a dictionary.

175 SPIRIT OF TRUTH, INDWELLING LIGHT

JOHN ERNEST BODE (1816–74)

From his *Hymns from the Gospel*, 1860.

Educated Eton, Charterhouse, and Christ Church, Oxford. He was the first holder of the Hertford scholarship. Tutor of Christ Church for six years; rector of Westwell, Oxon, 1847, and Castle Camps, Cambridge, 1860; Bampton lecturer, 1855. He published some volumes of poems.

See also 473.

176 O BREATH OF GOD   ALFRED HENRY VINE (1845–1917)

Appeared in *Methodist Recorder*, 1901.

Son of the Rev. John Vine, Wesleyan minister. Educated King Edwards School, Birmingham, and King's College, London; entered Wesleyan ministry, 1867. Published three volumes of poetry.

See also 406.

177 ⎰COME, HOLY GHOST, OUR SOULS INSPIRE
and ⎱   JOHN COSIN (1594–1672)
178 ⎰CREATOR SPIRIT BY WHOSE AID
                    JOHN DRYDEN (1631–1700)

Both these hymns are translations of a Latin hymn, *Veni Creator Spiritus*. The original cannot be traced back beyond the ninth century; its author is unknown. There is inconclusive evidence that it was written by Archbishop of Mainz, Rabanus Maurus, 776–856. The hymn had a great vogue in the Middle Ages. There is a story told by Joinville of the sailing of the French crusaders: The captain of the ship carrying King Louis called to his seamen who stood at the prow, 'Are you ready?' They answered, 'Aye, Aye, let the clerks come forward'. When they came, he called to them, 'Sing for God's sake'. With one voice they chanted *Veni Creator Spiritus*. Then he called to the seamen, 'Unfurl the sails for God's sake'. When the Latin hymn was sung it was accompanied with the special ringing of bells and the use of incense and lights, and it has been used for ordinations in the Catholic Church since the eleventh century. There have been several translations and none considered really satisfactory—an evidence of the deep impression the hymn has made. The first English translation was 1549 in the *Book of Common Prayer*. Then in Cosin's *Collection of private devotions in the practice of the Ancient Church*, 1627. Canon Ellerton says that Cosin translated this hymn for private use every morning at nine, the hour when God the Holy Spirit came down upon the church. Cosin was one of the revisers of the Prayer Book, 1661–2, and thus his version was inserted in the ordination service.

In Dryden's version fifteen lines are omitted. John Wesley adapted this for his *Psalms and Hymns*, 1738. There have been several alterations of phrases and words.

JOHN COSIN, educated Caius College, Cambridge. After being chaplain to the Bishop of Durham he was prebendary of Durham, Archdeacon of the East Riding. In 1640 Chancellor of University of Cambridge, Dean of Peterborough. His collection was criticized by the Puritans and one, whom he had severely treated, influenced the Long Parliament to suspend him. He retired to France, but at the Restoration became Bishop of Durham. There he spent large sums on the cathedral and the library and took part in the final revision of the *Book of Common Prayer*.

JOHN DRYDEN. Born of Puritan parents he became one of the chief literary figures of the Restoration; Poet Laureate, 1670. Most of his work was the production of plays, some too coarse even for that not over squeamish age. Educated Westminster and Trinity College, Cambridge. He joined the Roman Catholic Church when James II became King. He remained Roman Catholic at the Protestant Revolution of 1688 and was deprived of his laureateship and other emoluments and turned to the stage. He translated many Latin poems and some hymns. He is buried in Westminster Abbey.

179 COME TO OUR POOR NATURE'S NIGHT
GEORGE RAWSON (1807–89)

Contributed to *Leeds Hymnbook*, 1853. Practised as a solicitor in Leeds. He was a Congregationalist and helped in their *Leeds Hymnbook*. He also helped in the compilation of our *Psalms and Hymns*. He contributed twenty-seven hymns to our collection, altering some and writing new ones. He wished to be known only as 'A Leeds Layman'. His own hymns were published, *Hymns, Verses, and Chants*, 1876; *Songs of Spiritual Thought*, 1885. He was deeply spiritual and a very humble man.

See also 200, 266, 332, 436, 490, 496, 626, 627, 783.

180 GRACIOUS SPIRIT, DWELL WITH ME
T. T. LYNCH (see 70)

From *The Rivulet*, verses 4 and 5 omitted. There are all the marks of Lynch's deep spiritual feeling and poetic gift.

181 SPIRIT DIVINE, ATTEND OUR PRAYERS
ANDREW REED (1787–1862)

From *The Evangelical Magazine*, June 1829. The London Board of Congregational Ministers issued on February 10, 1829, a call to 'solemn prayer and humiliation in the eastern district of the metropolis'. On Good Friday of that year special services of prayer were held and this hymn was written for that occasion. Notice how each verse is built on a different metaphor: light, fire, dew, dove, wind. Reed himself said, 'We never rise to the highest nor are our moralities safe till we can say, "of Him and through Him and to Him are all things" '.

Son of a watchmaker. Educated Hackney College for the Congregational ministry. Minister of New Road Chapel, St. George's-in-the-East. When this was overcrowded he built Wycliffe Chapel where he was, 1831–61. He published a supplement to Watt's collection, 1842, and later *The Hymn Book*. He composed in all twenty-one hymns.

He was a great organizer and philanthropist and was influential in founding the London Orphanage Asylum, Lower Clapton, and the Asylum for Fatherless Children, near Croydon, the Asylum for Idiots, near Reigate, the Infant Orphan Asylum, Wanstead, the Royal Hospital for Incurables, and the Eastern Asylum for Idiots. For all these he gathered £129,320, a formidable sum now and more so then. He was also a great supporter of missionary work. To his son who asked him to write his biography he wrote, 'I was born yesterday, I shall die to-morrow, and I must not spend to-day telling what I have done but in doing what I may for Him who has done all for me. I sprang from the people, I have lived for the people, the most for the most unhappy. The people when they know it will not suffer me to die out of loving remembrance.'

182 COME, HOLY GHOST, OUR HEARTS INSPIRE
C. WESLEY (see 4)

From *Hymns and Sacred Poems*, 1740, entitled 'Before reading Holy Scripture'. There are two alterations, 'Thine' for 'Thy' in ver. 1 (line 2) and 'celestial' for 'prolific' in ver. 3 (line 1), the second alteration made by John Wesley in 1780.

183 WHEN GOD OF OLD
J. KEBLE (see 53)

A shortened version of the original in *The Christian Year*, 1827, as a Whitsuntide poem based on Acts ii. 2–4.

184 HOLY SPIRIT, TRUTH DIVINE
SAMUEL LONGFELLOW (1819–92)

Contributed to Unitarian *Hymns of the Spirit*, 1864, entitled 'Prayer for Inspiration' and is indicative of the Unitarian conception of Inspiration.

The younger brother of the poet. Educated Harvard for Unitarian ministry; held charges, Fall River, Mass; Brooklyn and Germanstown, Penn. He resigned in 1866; published the life of his brother. He collaborated with Samuel Johnson in compiling *A Book of Hymns*, 1846. He was a radical in theology and excluded from a second edition in which Johnson joined any hymns with a distinctive Christological theme.

See also 370, 466, 557.

185 COME, HOLY GHOST, IN LOVE
Attributed to KING ROBERT II OF FRANCE

Part of the great medieval hymn *Veni Sancte Spiritus* known as 'The Golden Sequence'. It was retained in the liturgy after the reforms of the sixteenth century. It has been acclaimed as a masterpiece of Latin sacred poetry. Its author is unknown. Several have been credited with it such as Hermanus Contractus, King Robert II of France, Stephen Langton, Innocent 3rd. It was not found in any MSS. before 1200 and has always been associated with Whitsuntide. For Ray Palmer, see 154.

186 BREATHE ON ME, BREATH OF GOD

EDWIN HATCH (1835–89)

Published privately in a pamphlet *Between doubt and prayer*, 1878. It is significant of deep devotion and consecration. Originally ver. 3 (line 2) read: 'Blend all my soul with Thine'.

Son of Nonconformists, educated King Edward School, Birmingham, Pembroke College, Oxford. His circle in Oxford included Burne Jones, William Morris, and Swinburne. He wrote literary articles while a student, was ordained, and for a while worked in an East End Parish. He served for three years, Professor of Classics, Trinity College, Toronto. In 1867, Vice-Principal St. Mary's Hall, Oxford; Bampton Lecturer, 1880, and also Grinfield Lecturer. Rector of Purleigh, 1884, and University Reader in Ecclesiastical History. Hibbert Lecturer, 1888.

His scholarship had a great hold on his generation. His particular field was historical research and Harnack translated his Bampton lectures. After his death Harnack said, 'In his learning that of England's great old theologians, Ussher and Pearson lived to me again. He was a glorious man whose loss I shall never cease to mourn.' He was only fifty-four when he died.

187 COME, HOLY SPIRIT, COME JOSEPH HART (1712–68)

A shortened version of the hymn published in *Hymns composed on various subjects*, 1759.

He gives us an outline of his life in the preface to his *Hymns*. Born of pious parents, received a good education and at one time taught languages. In his early manhood he knew alternating periods of concern and dissolute living. Occasionally he attended Whitefield's Tabernacle but was converted in Moravian Chapel, Fetter Lane, London. The text of the sermon he gives 'Revelations iii. 10'. He preached to large congregations in Independent Chapel, Jewin Street, 1760–68. He held strong Calvinistic views and was a severe critic of John Wesley. He composed hymns which he published as above. He was buried in Bunhill Fields, some 20,000 people gathering to hear the funeral sermon.

188 COME THOU, OH COME

A Latin hymn suggested by a passage in Anselm's *Orationes*. Gerard Moultre, translator (1829–85), educated Rugby and Exeter College, Oxford. He became vicar of Southleigh, 1869, and Warden of St. James' College. He wrote religious poetry and made many translations from Greek, Latin, and German.

189 COME DOWN, O LOVE DIVINE
BIANCO DA SIENA (?–1434)

From a collection of hymns by Bianco *Laudi Spirituali*. It was little known and this was copied by Telesforo Bine in 1851 from a MS. owned by Francesco de Rossi. This translation appeared in Littledale's *People's Hymnal*, 1867. W. H. Frere says the Italian *Laudi Spirituali* grew up with the Franciscan Movement. He died in Venice in 1434. The date of his birth is unknown and indeed little is known of him or his life. He joined a religious order founded by John Columbinus of Sienna in 1367 and spent the rest of his life in Venice. He has been described as an ardent young convert of the Jesuits at Sienna, 1367.

Richard Frederick Littledale, 1833–90, born Dublin, educated Trinity College, Dublin. He held two curacies at St. Matthew's, Thorpe Hamlet, Norfolk, and St. Mary the Virgin, Soho. He suffered bad health and his main service was literary. He was a high churchman, a controversialist, and a strong opponent of Rome. He did much by his writing to stay the drift to Rome during the Tractarian Movement. He was a student of liturgies and a notable translator of hymns from Greek, Latin, Syriac, German, Italian, Danish, and Swedish. He was joint editor of *The Priest's Prayer Book*, 1864, *The People's Hymnal*, 1867, and other writings.

190 AWAKE, O LORD
HENRY TWELLS (1823–1900)

A hymn of prayer for help and guidance in time of change by the author of 'At even ere the sun was set'. Educated King Edward's School, Birmingham, where his schoolfellows included Archbishop Benson, Bishop Lightfoot, and Bishop Westcott. Then St. Peter's College, Cambridge; master of St. Andrew's House School, Wells; headmaster, Godolphin School, Hammersmith. Rector of Baldock, Herts, 1870; Waltham on the Wolds, 1871; Hon. Canon of Peterborough, 1884. He retired in 1890 to Bournemouth where he built and helped to endow the Church of St. Augustine and served as priest in charge till his death. He worked on the committee for *Hymns Ancient and Modern*.

See also 199, 247, 558.

191 THE HEAVENS DECLARE THY GLORY, LORD
ISAAC WATTS (see 2)

Psalm xix, a felicitous rendering with a fine Christian application.

192 O WORD OF GOD INCARNATE
WILLIAM WALSHAM HOW (1823–97)

In supplement to *Psalms and Hymns*, 1867, which he compiled with T. B. Morrell. Based on Psalm cxix. 105. 'Thy word is a lantern unto my feet.'

Son of a solicitor. Educated Shrewsbury, Wadham College, Oxford. Ordained 1846. He was a singularly unambitious man though he reached high office in the church. He enriched hymnody with many treasures. Became rector of St. Andrew's, Undershaft, and suffragan Bishop of East London with the title of Bishop of Bedford, 1879; first Bishop of Wakefield, 1888. Declined the see of Manchester, without mentioning it to his wife, and also the see of Durham. He was a great human and an excellent pastor. London knew him as 'the poor man's bishop', 'the people's bishop', 'the omnibus bishop'. He had engraved on his pastoral staff *'Pasce verbo, pasce vita'*, a saying of St. Bernard, 'Feed with the word, feed with the life'. In addition to working with Morrell he was joint editor of S.P.C.K.'s *Church Hymns*, a collection less sacramental and more warm and evangelical than *Hymns Ancient and Modern*. Published in 1886 a collected edition of *Poems and Hymns*.

See also 204, 223, 371, 451, 537, 673, 674, 675, 713, 753, 772.

193 FATHER OF MERCIES IN THY WORD

ANNE STEELE (1717–78)

One of the greatest of Baptist hymn-writers. Born Broughton, Hants, the daughter of a timber merchant who was also the pastor of the Baptist Church. Her fiancé lost his life through drowning a few hours before the time fixed for the wedding. This had naturally a profound effect upon her. She published two volumes of poetry in 1760, *Poems on Subjects chiefly devotional* by 'Theodosia'. Her complete works were published with a memoir in 1863. This contained 144 hymns, thirty-four psalms, and various poems. Sixty-two of her hymns were in the Bristol Baptist collection 1769.

See also 208.

194 O, HAPPY IS THE MAN WHO HEARS

M. BRUCE (see 135)

A paraphrase of Proverbs iii. 13, 17.

195 LAMP OF OUR FEET   BERNARD BARTON (1784–1849)

From a poem of eleven verses on the Bible, 1827, published in *The Reliquary*, 1836. Originally line 1, ver. 5 read, 'And we, if we aright would learn', and line 3 'Must to its simple teaching turn'.

Born of Quaker parents he remained a Quaker and was known as the Quaker poet. Educated Quaker school at Ipswich, apprenticed at fourteen to a shopkeeper, then in business with his brother at Woodbridge, Suffolk, as a coal and corn merchant. He married and went to Liverpool, but his wife dying he returned to Wood-bridge and became a clerk in Alexander's Bank. He continued thus for forty years, devoting his evenings to literary work and correspondence. He was a friend of Charles Lamb, Lord Byron, Sir John Bowring, and Sir Walter Scott. Through the influence of Sir Robert Peel he was awarded a state pension of £100 per annum. His only daughter became the wife of Edward Fitzgerald of *Rubaiyat* fame. He published eight volumes of verse and after his death his daughter published *Poems and Letters*.

See also 280.

196 THE SPIRIT BREATHES UPON THE WORD

W. COWPER (see 60)

The hymn remains unaltered as it appeared in *Olney Hymns*, 1779.

197 LORD, THY WORD ABIDETH   H. W. BAKER (see 63)

In *Hymns Ancient and Modern*, 1861, with the caption, 'Thy word is a lantern unto my feet', Psalm cxix. 105.

198 BREAK THOU THE BREAD OF LIFE

MARY ARTEMISIA LATHBURY (1841–1913)

Composed 1880 for Chautauqua Literary and Scientific Circle. It was sung at Dr. Campbell Morgan's Bible School in West-minster Chapel every session.

Born Manchester, N.Y., daughter of a local preacher of Methodist Episcopal Church. Two of her brothers were ministers of that church. She was an artist by profession but contributed verse to religious periodicals for children and young people. She was very interested in the Chautauqua Movement and was known as its laureate. She founded the 'Look up Legion' in Methodist Sunday Schools.

See also 639.

199 THE VOICE OF GOD'S CREATION

H. TWELLS (see 190)

In 1889 edition of *Hymns Ancient and Modern*, 'The Word of God a light'.

200 WE LIMIT NOT THE TRUTH OF GOD

G. RAWSON (see 179)

The refrain at the end of every verse is the great sentence in the last sermon John Robinson preached to his flock at Leyden when they were determined to seek freedom in a new settlement across the Atlantic. The text was Ezra viii. 21–22. Robinson said, 'I am certain the Lord hath more truth and light yet to break forth out of His Holy Word'. So the Pilgrim Fathers set forth.

201 BOOK OF GRACE AND BOOK OF GLORY
THOMAS MACKELLAR (1812–99)

Written in 1843. Born New York. When fourteen entered Harper Bros. printing establishment. In 1833 went to Philadelphia as proof reader and became subsequently a partner of the firm known as MacKellar, Smith, and Jordan, type founders.

Published *Book of Grace*, 1843; *Sunday School Union Collection*, 1860; *Hymns*, 1885. He was an elder of the Presbyterian Church.

202 BOOK OF BOOKS
PERCY DEARMER (1867–1936)

Written to express modern appreciation of the Bible. Published *Songs of Praise*, 1925.

Educated Westminster School and Christchurch, Oxford. Vicar of St. Mary the Virgin, Primrose Hill, 1901–15. Secretary of London Christian Social Union, 1891–1912 and chairman of the League of Arts. Served as chaplain during the 1914–18 war. Professor of Ecclesiastical Art, King's College, London, 1919–36. Canon of Westminster, 1931. Published *The Parson's Handbook*, 1899; *Everyman's History of the Prayer Book*, 1934. He helped in the production of *English Hymnal*, 1906; *Songs of Praise*, 1925. *Oxford Book of Carols*, 1928, and co-operated with R. Vaughan Williams and Martin Shaw.

203 COME UNTO ME, YE WEARY
W. C. DIX (see 89)

In *The People's Hymnal*, 1867. Various changes have been made in the text from time to time, e.g. ver. 2 in the original went: 'Come unto me, dear children'. The hymn has become very popular.

204 O JESUS, THOU ART STANDING
W. W. HOW (see 192)

Written and published, 1867, in the supplement to *Psalms and Hymns* by Morrell and How. Based on Revelation iii. 20, 'Behold I stand at the door and knock'. One discerns How's deep sense of he call of the sacrifice of our Lord to every man.

205 JESUS CALLS US
MRS. C. F. ALEXANDER (see 131)

For St. Andrew's Day in S.P.C.K.'s *Hymns for Public Worship*, 1852. There have been alterations and some by the authoress, but the present version follows in the main the 1852 version.

206 SOULS OF MEN! F. W. FABER (see 42)

Originally there were thirteen verses with the heading, 'Come to Jesus' (Faber's *Hymns*, 1862).
Originally: verses 1 and 2, then

> It is God, His love looks mighty
> But is mightier than it seems!
> 'Tis our Father; and His fondness
> Goes far out beyond our dreams.

Then verses 3 and 4, and

> There is welcome for the sinner,
> And more graces for the good,
> There is mercy with the Saviour,
> There is healing in His blood.

> There is grace enough for thousands
> Of new worlds as great as this,
> There is room for fresh creations
> In that upper home of bliss.

Then after ver. 6:

> 'Tis not all we owe to Jesus,
> It is something more than all;
> Greater good because of evil,
> Larger mercy through the fall.

207 COME TO THE SAVIOUR NOW
JOHN MURCH WIGNER (1844–1911)

From *Supplementary Psalms and Hymns*, 1880, edited by his father J. T. Wigner, Baptist minister and member of the committee compiling our own *Psalms and Hymns*. Educated London University. In the home Civil Service.

208 THE SAVIOUR CALLS ANNE STEELE (see 193)

In *Poems on Subjects chiefly devotional*, 1760, headed invitation.

209 THY CEASELESS, UNEXHAUSTED LOVE
C. WESLEY (see 4)

In *Short Hymns*, 1762.

210 O, COME TO THE MERCIFUL SAVIOUR
F. W. FABER (see 42)

From *Oratory Hymns*, 1854, headed 'Divine Invitation'. It is in many collections and is extensively used.

211 BEHOLD A STRANGER AT THE DOOR!
JOSEPH GRIGG (1722–68)

There were five more verses in the original. The original ver. 5 read:

> Admit Him for you can't expel.
> Where'er He comes He comes to dwell.

Little is known of this author. He began life in humble circumstances. He was assistant minister to Rev. Thomas Bares, Presbyterian Church, Silver Street, London, 1743–7. He retired in 1747, married a wealthy widow and lived at St. Albans. He continued preaching and writing.

See also 475.

212 ART THOU WEARY   STEPHEN THE SABAITE (725–94)

In Neale's *Hymns of the Eastern Church*, 1862. In the 1st edition it was offered as a translation from the Greek of a hymn by St. Stephen the Sabaite, but in the 1866 edition Neale wrote that it contains so little from the Greek that it ought not to have been included in this collection. The original of ver. 7 (line 3) read, 'Angels, martyrs, prophets, virgins'.

Stephen was the nephew of John of Damascus and belonged like him to the monastery of Mar Saba. The monastery is still inhabited. It is situated on a lofty cliff with the ravine of the Kedron below and between Jerusalem and the Dead Sea. Many of its cells and chapels are cut out of the solid rock. There has been much persecution from the Persians and the Arabs and the place has the appearance of a fortress. Colonel Conder, in his *Palestine*, pp. 36–7, after a vivid description of the scenery, concludes, 'Here really out of the world the solitary hermits sate in the rocky cells which were their tombs; here in the awful prison of the Mar Saba monastery men are still buried, as it were, alive, without future, without hope, without employment, with no comradeship save that of equally embittered lives'.

For J. M. Neale, see 78.

213 LIFT UP YOUR HEADS   GEORG WEISSEL (1590–1635)

Based on Psalm xxiv. In German it was published 1642.

Born Domnau, Prussia, studied at various universities, and in 1614 rector of the school at Friedland. In Konigsberg, 1623, after theological studies became the pastor. He ranks as one of the most important early hymn-writers of Prussia.

For Catherine Winkworth, see 11.

214 TELL ME THE OLD, OLD STORY
ARABELLA CATHERINE HANKEY (1834–1911)

Published as a leaflet, 1867, 'The Story Wanted'. She wrote it, 'When I was weak and weary after an illness and especially realizing that simple thoughts in simple words are all we can bear in sickness'. She resented any other form than the original, i.e. she wanted each verse complete with no refrain. It is one of the best known gospel hymns.

Daughter of Thomas Hankey, a well-known banker and member of the Clapham Sect which had for its leader William Wilberforce. When a schoolgirl she taught in a Croydon Sunday School. At eighteen she started a Bible Class for shop assistants. She kept contact with her members all her life and some were present at her funeral fifty years later. She also started a Bible Class for girls of her own social circle. After a visit to South Africa to bring home an invalid brother she became intensely interested in missionary work. She published *Bible Class Teachings*, *A Booklet on Confirmation*, *A Collection of Hymns*, *The Old*, *Old Story*. She was also a welcome visitor to hospitals.

215 THERE IS NO LOVE
WILLIAM EDENSOR LITTLEWOOD (1831–86)

Vicar of St. James', Bath, 1872–81. Published *A Garland from the Parables*, 1857, from which this is taken.

216 I NEED THEE EVERY HOUR
ANNIE SHERWOOD HAWKS (1835–1918)

Published Lowry's, *Royal Diadem*, 1873. First appeared in a collection of gospel songs prepared for the National Baptist Sunday School Association meeting at Cincinnati, November 1872. The refrain was added by Dr. Lowry. The caption was 'Without me ye can do nothing' (John xv. 5). Mrs. Hawks said in her later years that she wrote the hymn when she was conscious of the nearness of the Master in the midst of daily cares and heard the words 'I need Thee every hour', and she took pencil and wrote.

When she married she lived in Brooklyn and joined the Baptist Church there under Dr. Robert Lowry who discovered her gift of hymn-writing and encouraged her in it.

217 I AM TRUSTING THEE   F. R. HAVERGAL (see 133)

Written September 1874. Published *Loyal Responses*, 1878, the caption 'Trusting Jesus'. This was her favourite hymn and was found in her pocket Bible after her death.

218 GOD CALLING YET!   G. TERSTEEGEN (see 27)

Sarah Findlater, 1823–1907, born Edinburgh, daughter of James Borthwick, manager North British Insurance Co., sister of Jane Borthwick. She married Rev. Eric Findlater, minister Free Church, Lochearnhead. With her sister published *Hymns from the Land of Luther*. There were 122 translations, fifty-three her own. Her daughters, Jane and Mary, are well-known novelists. She was a great linguist, very hospitable on a slender income, and together with her husband offering to the world a pattern of a simple, devout, happy, and hospitable Christian home.

See also 681.

219 THERE WERE NINETY AND NINE
ELIZABETH CECILIA DOUGLAS CLEPHANE (1830–69)

This well-known hymn was published first in *Children's Hour*, 1868. There are many stories of its origin. The Rev. James Dodds Dunbar, in *Memories of the Past*, says that Miss Clephane was a regular contributor to *Children's Hour*, and once being reminded that she had not sent her matter for the next number agreed to try her hand at a poetical contribution. She retired to a corner of the room and began to write. She soon produced this hymn. It quickly appeared in other periodicals. One, *The Christian Age*, May 1874, fell into Mr. Sankey's hands. At the close of a great evangelistic meeting in Edinburgh conducted by Mr. Moody the theme had been 'The Lost Sheep'. Sankey placed the paper cutting before him on the organ and improvised the music as he went along. The hymn and the tune have moved great multitudes throughout the English-speaking world. Miss Clephane had died some five years before this and till then her hymn had attracted little notice. Her sisters heard Sankey singing it in Melrose and recognized it as their sister's hymn.

Daughter of Andrew Douglas Clephane, Sheriff Principal of Fife and Kinross. After her father's death she lived first at Ormiston, East Lothian, and then at Bridgend, Melrose. She suffered impaired health, but was of a generous and happy disposition, being known in Melrose as 'The Sunbeam'. Eight of her hymns are published in the *Family Treasury*. She died when thirty-nine years old.

See also 237.

220 WHAT MEANS THIS EAGER, ANXIOUS THRONG
ETTA CAMPBELL (nineteenth century)

Written in 1863 after being at a revival where Miss Campbell heard an address on Luke xviii. 37. It was first published in *Song Victories*, much used in Moody and Sankey meetings. Sankey said this hymn was one of the greatest favourites in Britain. Miss Etta Campbell was a teacher at Morristown, New Jersey.

221 GOD LOVED THE WORLD
MARTHA MATILDA (*née* BRUSTAR) STOCKTON (1821–85)

Wife of a Baptist minister in New Jersey. Wrote this in 1871. Published in *Laudes Domini*, 1884.

222 JESUS, I WILL TRUST THEE
> MARY JANE (*née* DECK) WALKER (1816–78)

In her husband's *Psalms and Hymns for public and social worship*, 1864. She married, 1848, Rev. Ed. Walker, who was the first rector of Cheltenham. He was an ardent evangelical and edited *Psalms and Hymns* as above, in which he included hymns in use by the Plymouth Brethren. There were nine by his wife.

223 O MY SAVIOUR   W. W. HOW (see 192)
In *Psalms and Hymns*, 1886.

224 JESUS SINNERS WILL RECEIVE
> ERDMANN NEUMEISTER (1671–1756)

Mrs. Bevan's translation is in *Songs of Eternal Life*, 1858. The original appeared first in *Evangelischer Nachklang*, 1718. Educated Leipzig, where he became a tutor. Ordained 1697. Tutor at Weissenfels to the Duke's daughter, 1704, and later Court preacher. Later at Sorau where he was Court preacher and superintendent. Pastor of St. James's Church, Hamburg, 1715. He was a high Lutheran and strongly anti-pietistic, opposed to Moravianism on the ground of their subjectivism. He was erudite and a critic of poetry. Writing hymns was a life-long interest; he wrote 650.

Mrs. Emma Frances Bevan, 1827–1900, born Oxford, daughter of Rev. P. N. Shuttleworth, Warden of New College, and after Bishop of Chichester. She married R. C. L. Bevan, a banker, and later joined the Plymouth Brethren. She studied German mystics and published a catena of quotations from them. Published *Songs of Eternal Life*, 1858; *Songs of Praise for Christian Pilgrims*, 1859.

225 ROCK OF AGES
> AUGUSTUS MONTAGUE TOPLADY (1740–78)

One of the great hymns of the English language. Professor Saintsbury writes of it, 'Every word and syllable in this really great poem has its place and meaning'. First in *Gospel Magazine*, 1776, at the end of an article by Toplady, who was the editor, entitled, 'A remarkable calculation introduced here for the sake of the spiritual improvements subjoined. Questions and answers relating to the National Debt.' The article was a curious one, a calculation being made on the basis of how many sins each man commits in the day, half-day, hour, minute and second, and concludes, 'A living and dying prayer for the holiest believer in the World'. Then follows the hymn except line 2, ver. 4, which read, 'When my eye-strings break in death'. There is the familiar story that Toplady wrote the hymn when sheltering from a thunderstorm in a cleft in the rock in Burrington Combe in the Mendips some twelve years before the hymn was published, and indeed the very cleft is shown to tourists on the road to Cheddar. There does not seem much basis for the story and it was not heard till 1850! Toplady was always interested in the idea of our Lord as a Rock. Preaching on Isaiah lii. 11, he says, 'Chiefly may they sing who inhabit Christ the spiritual Rock of Ages'. The phrase, though of long usage, owes its place in English hearts to Toplady's use of it.

Son of a major who was killed at the siege of Carthagena. Educated Westminster and Trinity College, Dublin. He was converted in Ireland listening to a man preach who could not write his own name. He was at first attracted to the Wesleys, then ordained 1762, vicar of Broadhembury, Devon. He had lung trouble and thought London would suit him better. He obtained permission to preach in the chapel of the French Calvinists in Leicester Fields, London. He was editor, *Gospel Magazine*, for a while. A popular preacher attracting great congregations. He disputed with the Wesleys, taking the side of Calvinism against their Arminianism. He died when thirty-eight.

See also 310.

226 LORD, I WAS BLIND   W. T. MATSON (see 37)

Written 1857, headed 'Christ the Life of men'. Published in *A Summer Evening's Reverie and other poems*.

227 LORD! I REPENT SIR NATHANIEL BARNABY (1829–1915)

Born Chatham of a Kentish family, entered the naval dockyard and rose to the high position of Director of Naval Construction. He possessed great mechanical knowledge and was created a K.C.B. He was as a boy a member of the Baptist Sunday School in Chatham. When he married he moved to Lee and joined the High Road Baptist Church. For fifty years he was Superintendent of the Sunday School. His hymns were largely written for anniversary services. Some have appeared in *The School Hymnal* and six in *The Sunday School Hymnary*, including this one.

See also 698.

228 SINFUL, SIGHING TO BE BLEST

J. S. B. MONSELL (see 6)

In *Spiritual Songs*, 1857.

229 THINE FOR EVER!

MARY FAWLER (*née* HOOPER) MAUDE (1819–1913)

Written for her Sunday School class at St. Thomas Church, Newport, I.O.W., 1847. This and other hymns prefaced a little book, *Twelve letters on confirmation by a Sunday School teacher*. They were undiscovered for ten years and were then published without the authoress's knowledge in *Hymns Ancient and Modern*.

In her teens wrote three books which were published by S.P.C.K. She married Rev. Joseph Maude, vicar of St. Thomas, Newport, and after of Chirk, and an honorary canon of St. Asaph. There she conducted classes for colliers, and when widowed, classes for young men at Overton. She reached a great age and, when dying, young men of her class sang outside her door this hymn and then another, 'Will your anchor hold?' She sent out a message, 'Tell them it does not fail. It holds.' Two lines of this hymn are on her memorial tablet in Overton Church.

230 COME AND REJOICE WITH ME!
ELISABETH CHARLES (see 99)

231 O THOU WHO HAST REDEEMED OF OLD!
C. WESLEY (see 4)

From *Hymns and Sacred Poems*, 1749.

232 JUST AS I AM CHARLOTTE ELLIOTT (see 137)

Published in 1836 in *Invalid's Hymn-book*. It then appeared in *Hours of Sorrow cheered and comforted*, with the last verse added. It has been extensively translated, is in practically every hymn-book and is widely used in missionary work. The writer's niece says that Miss Elliott's brother, Rev. H. V. Elliott, was holding a bazaar for the building fund of St. Mary's Hall, Brighton. Charlotte was an invalid. She lay awake at night, 'tossed about with many a doubt' because of her inability to help. To conquer her feelings she took pen and wrote the hymn as a confession of an invalid's faith. It was headed 'John vi. 37: "Him that cometh unto Me I will in no wise cast out"'. The husband of the poet Wordsworth's daughter, Dora, wrote to Charlotte on July 28, 1847, saying the hymn had been sent to his wife who was on her death-bed and she said, 'This is the very thing for me'. The letter continues, 'Mrs. Wordsworth (her mother) tells me that your hymn forms part of her daily solitary prayers. I do not think Mr. Wordsworth could bear to have it repeated in his presence but he is not the less sensible of the solace it gave his one and matchless daughter.'

233 IN FULL AND GLAD SURRENDER
F. R. HAVERGAL (see 133)

From the Havergal MSS. headed 'Confirmation'. Her sister says, 'The epitome of her life and the focus of its sunshine'.

234 I HEARD THE VOICE OF JESUS SAY
H. BONAR (see 40)

Written in Kelso when Dr. Bonar was minister there, published in *Hymns Original and Selected*, 1846. According to the original

MS. the first draft was written in pencil with corrections and quaint marginal sketches. It is based on John i. 16, 'Of his fulness have we received and grace for grace'.

235 I WAS A WANDERING SHEEP   H. BONAR (see 40)
From *Songs of the Wilderness*, 1843.

1 Peter ii. 25. Originally of five verses of eight lines. It is extensively used.

236 COME, LET US TO THE LORD OUR GOD
JOHN MORISON (1750–98)

In the Scottish Paraphrases, 1781, based on Hosea vi. 1–4.

Educated University of Aberdeen. Held first a teaching post in Caithness. Went to Edinburgh where he studied Greek. He was influenced by Dr. Macfarlane of Canongate. He submitted twenty-four pieces for the committee preparing the Paraphrases. Seven were accepted. Morrison then settled in the parish of Canisbay, Caithness. Ordained 1780. He wrote poetry for the *Edinburgh Weekly Magazine*, and certain historical studies of Caithness.

237 BENEATH THE CROSS OF JESUS
E. C. CLEPHANE (see 219)

In *Family Treasury*, 1872. Printed anonymously. The authorship was acknowledged later.

238 O SAVIOUR, I HAVE NOUGHT TO PLEAD
JANE (*née* FOX) CREWDSON (1809–63)

Written shortly before her death, published posthumously in *A Little While and other poems*, 1864.

Born Cornwall. Married a Manchester manufacturer, Thomas D. Crewdson, 1836. She was always of delicate health and became a confirmed invalid. Her sufferings made her increasingly sensitive to spiritual realities. Her poems and hymns were published in *Aunt Jane's verses for children*, 1851; *Lays of the Reformation*, 1860; *A Little While*, 1864.

See also 598, 602, 671.

239 LORD, THY MERCY NOW ENTREATING
MARY ANN SIDEBOTHAM (1833–1913)

Contributed to *Children's Hymn Book*, 1881, bearing the initials A. N.

An accomplished musician and a life-long friend of Henry Smart. She was organist at her brother's church, St. Thomas on the Bourne, Surrey, and musical editor of *Children's Hymn Book*, S.P.C.K., edited by Mrs. Carey Brock. She was anxious to avoid

publicity and her contributions usually bore only the initials.
She composed songs and arranged a collection of words and music
for children, *The Birds' Nest*.

240 FATHER, HEAR THE PRAYER
Mrs. Love Maria (*née* Whitcomb) Willis (1824–1908)

Published anonymously in J. G. Adam's *Psalms of Life*, 1857.
It also appeared in Unitarian *Hymns of the Spirit*, 1864, and elsewhere. Mrs. Willis lived in New Hampshire and New York.

241 JESUS, MY STRENGTH, MY HOPE
C. Wesley (see 4)

In *Hymns and Sacred Poems*, 1740, headed 'A Poor Sinner'.
Some verses are omitted and the order has been changed.

242 GRANT US THY LIGHT   L. Tuttiett (see 153)

Headed 'Divine Guidance' in *Germs of Thought*, 1864. In the
1885 edition it begins, 'O Grant us light, etc.'

243 WE HAVE NOT KNOWN THEE
Thomas Benson Pollock (1836–96)

In the supplement to *Hymns Ancient and Modern*.
Educated Trinity College, Dublin. He began as a medical student,
but was ordained 1861. He held several curacies and in 1865 was
curate to his brother, Rev. J. S. Pollock of St. Albans, Bordesley,
Birmingham. It was a poor district and a great congregation was
gathered and they built one of the finest churches in the city.
The living was poor, but they gathered £100,000 for church and
school work. Both were interested in the Tractarian Movement
and their church became a stronghold of Anglo-Catholicism in
Birmingham. They met with much opposition. T. B. succeeded
his brother after thirty years of curacy, but he died ten months
later. He was a member of *Hymns Ancient and Modern* Committee,
contributed some hymns to St. Alban's Parish magazine, *The
Gospeller*.

244 AS HELPLESS AS A CHILD
James Drummond Burns (1823–64)

In *The Evening Hymn*, 1856. It is extensively used in this country
and the U.S.A.
Educated Heriot's Hospital, Edinburgh, High School, and
University, where he studied under Dr. Chalmers, and at the
Disruption went with the Free Church. He settled at Dunblane,
1845. He broke down in his first sermon, but was eventually ordained
in that year. He fell into ill health and in 1847 took charge of Free

Church Congregation, Funchal, Madeira, and in 1855 of a new congregation at Hampstead. He was a popular preacher. He died when only forty-one. He published *The Vision of Prophecy and other poems*, 1854; *The Heavenly Jerusalem or glimpses within the gates*. He wrote a short article on hymns in the eighth edition of *Encyclopedia Britannica*.

See also 268, 648, 765.

245 JESUS MEEK AND GENTLE

GEORGE RUNDLE PRYNNE (1818–1903)

In *Hymnal suited for Church Services*, 1858. It is used as a hymn for children, but the author did not so intend and later suggested that ver. 4 (line 3) should be amended to, 'Through earth's passing darkness' when it was sung by children.

Educated St. Catherine's College, Cambridge. Ordained 1841. Incumbent at Par, Cornwall, and two years later accepted a new parish, St. Peter's, Plymouth. He was an Anglo-Catholic and introduced confession and a daily eucharist in the face of much suspicion and opposition in such a Methodist stronghold. He had a lovable and saintly disposition and won the affection of his parishioners. He published *A Eucharistic Manual*, 1857; the hymnal we have mentioned; *The Soldier's dying vision*. He was a member of the revision committee of *Hymns Ancient and Modern*.

246 DEAR LORD AND MASTER MINE

T. H. GILL (see 94)

Published *Golden Chain*, 1869, caption 'Resignation'.

247 NOT FOR OUR SINS ALONE   H. TWELLS (see 190)

In 1889 supplement to *Hymns Ancient and Modern*, 'Plea for Divine Mercy'.

248 SHOW ME MYSELF, O HOLY LORD

Contributed anonymously to *The Plymouth Hymnal*, 1893, edited by Lyman Abbott. It was the descendant of *Plymouth Collection* which H. Ward Beecher gathered for the Plymouth Church, Brooklyn, in 1855. He had previously collected *Temple Melodies* in 1847. This collection marked an important development in the conduct of praise in the Puritan Churches of America which was further developed through this hymnal.

249 LORD OF MERCY AND OF MIGHT

R. HEBER (see 33)

Published *The Christian Observer*, 1811; the second verse has been omitted.

250 GOD OF PITY, GOD OF GRACE
ELIZA FANNY (*née* GOFFE) MORRIS (1821–74)

Published *The Voice and the Reply*, 1858. Originally ver. 7 was ver. 2. The volume was in two parts: 'The Voice', of eighteen pieces, and 'The Reply', of sixty-eight pieces. This is entitled 'The Prayer in the Temple'.

Born London. Lived much in the country and was a great lover of nature. She married in 1849 Joseph Morris, sub-editor *The Malvern News*. She edited a Bible Class Hymn-book and published in addition to above, *Life Lyrics*.

251 COME IN, OH COME!
HANDLEY CARR GLYN MOULE (1841–1920)

Educated at home and Trinity College, Cambridge. He won first-class classical and theological honours 1864–5. He was a Carus prizeman and Browne's medalist and won the Seatonian prize. Ordained 1867. Dean of Trinity College, Cambridge, 1874–7; Principal of Ridley Hall, Cambridge. Fellow of his College, 1865.

252 TWO TEMPLES DOTH JEHOVAH PRIZE
T. DAVIS (see 14)

From *Devotional Verse for a Month*, 1855.

253 COME, DEAREST LORD, DESCEND AND DWELL
ISAAC WATTS (see 2)

In enlarged edition of *Hymns and Spiritual Songs*, 1709. In 1753 Whitefield included it in his Collection, where he changed 'dearest' to 'gracious'.

254 NO HUMAN EYES THY FACE MAY SEE
THOMAS WENTWORTH HIGGINSON (1823–1911)

While at Harvard Divinity School he contributed four hymns to Longfellow and Johnson's *Book of Hymns*, 1846. A Unitarian minister and contributor to the *Atlantic Monthly*. During the Rebellion he was Colonel of the first Negro Regiment in South Carolina.

255 LEND ME, O LORD, THY SOFTENING CLOUD
GEORGE MATHESON (1842–1906)

From *Sacred Songs*, his one volume of verse, 1890.

Matheson always suffered from defective vision, and was practically blind at the age of eighteen, but in spite of this he greatly distinguished himself at Glasgow Academy and Glasgow University, especially in philosophy. Ordained in 1866, after two years as assistant in Glasgow he became minister of the parish of Innellan,

Argyllshire. He became well known as a writer of theological and devotional books. In 1886 he became minister of St. Bernard's Parish Church, Edinburgh, where he remained until 1899. His hymns have freshness and insight, and a delicately woven poetical texture.

See also 320, 343, 358, 544.

256 O BLESSÈD LIFE! THE HEART AT REST

W. T. MATSON (see 37)

Under the title 'Christ the life of men'.

257 APPROACH, MY SOUL, THE MERCY SEAT

JOHN NEWTON (see 146)

From the *Olney Hymns*.

258 I WOULD COMMUNE WITH THEE, MY GOD

GEORGE BURDEN BUBIER (1823–69)

Educated at Homerton. Congregational minister at Ossett, Essex, and then at Buxton. He became professor at Springhill, Birmingham, now Mansfield College, Oxford. He was joint editor with George Macdonald and his brother of *Hymns and Sacred Songs for Sunday Schools and Social Worship*, 1855, in which he had eleven hymns.

See also 282, 584, 730.

259 SPEAK TO US, LORD, THYSELF REVEAL

C. WESLEY (see 4)

260 MADE LOWLY WISE, WE PRAY NO MORE

F. L. HOSMER (see 45)

First printed in the *Boston Christian Register* with the title, 'The Larger Faith'. Later in his book *The Thought of God*.

261 JESUS, THESE EYES HAVE NEVER SEEN

RAY PALMER (see under 139)

'Christ loved though unseen.' Written as the result of an impulse while preparing a sermon. When published in 1858 in the *Sabbath Hymn Book* it was given 1 Peter i. 8 as a text. On his death-bed he was heard repeating ver. 5.

262 O FOR A CLOSER WALK WITH GOD

W. COWPER (see 60)

Written in 1769 during the serious illness of his friend Mrs. Unwin. First published in 1772 in Conyer's *Collection of Psalms and Hymns*, and afterwards included in the *Olney Hymns* with the title, 'Walking with God', Genesis v. 24.

263 O WALK WITH GOD, AND THOU SHALT FIND
ARTHUR CLEVELAND COXE (1818–96)

Appeared in *Hallow E'en and other Poems*, 1844.

Son of a well-known Presbyterian minister, he entered the Protestant Episcopal Church. Ordained in 1842, after various pastorates he became Bishop of Western New York in 1865.

See also 697.

264 THE LORD IS RICH AND MERCIFUL
T. T. LYNCH (see 70)

Like his other hymns it appeared first in the once famous *Rivulet*, where it was headed, 'Have faith in God'.

265 NEARER, MY GOD, TO THEE   S. F. ADAMS (see 71)

Based on Jacob's dream at Bethel, Genesis xxviii. 10–22. Written at Loughton and first contributed to the Unitarian *Hymns and Anthems*, compiled by her minister, the Rev. W. J. Fox, in 1841. It is said, though not without challenge, that the band of the *Titanic* played the hymn as the ship was sinking after collision with an iceberg on April 15, 1912. Many well-known people have testified to the helpfulness of the hymn.

266 WALKING WITH THEE, MY GOD
G. RAWSON (see 179)

From *Hymns, Verses and Chants*, 1876.

267 WHERE IS THY GOD, MY SOUL?
T. T. LYNCH (see 70)

From the first edition of the *Rivulet*, 1855.

268 STILL WITH THEE, O MY GOD
J. D. BURNS (see 244)

Included in *The Evening Hymn*, 1857.

269 MY GOD, IS ANY HOUR SO SWEET?
C. ELLIOTT (see 137)

Published in her *Hours of Sorrow*, 1836, entitled the 'Hour of Prayer'. In ver. 5 'there' has been substituted for 'here'.

270 COME, O THOU TRAVELLER UNKNOWN
C. WESLEY (see 4)

Entitled 'Wrestling Jacob' in *Hymns and Sacred Poems*, 1742. Wesley frequently preached on this subject. John Wesley, in the obituary of his brother, quotes Isaac Watts as saying, 'that single poem "Wrestling Jacob" was worth all the verses he himself had written'—a generous but exaggerated tribute. Preaching at Bolton a fortnight after his brother's death, John Wesley gave out this hymn and broke down in tears on reading the words, 'My company before is gone', while the congregation wept with him. The *Handbook to the Church Hymnary* says that 'this is undoubtedly the greatest of Wesley's hymns'.

271 'LIFT UP YOUR HEARTS!'
HENRY MONTAGU BUTLER (1833–1918)

In the *Harrow School Hymn Book*, 1881. Became headmaster of Harrow, of which his father had also been head, in 1859. In 1886 he was made Master of Trinity College, Cambridge.

272 STILL, STILL WITH THEE
MRS. HARRIET (*née* BEECHER) STOWE (1812–96)

Daughter of Lyman Beecher and sister of Henry Ward Beecher. Married Professor Calvin Stowe. She achieved fame through the writing of *Uncle Tom's Cabin* in 1852. She contributed three hymns, including this, to her brother's *Plymouth Hymnal*, 1855.

See also 309.

273 HOW SHALL I FOLLOW HIM I SERVE?
J. CONDER (see 9)

274 SO LET OUR LIPS AND LIVES EXPRESS
ISAAC WATTS (see 2)

275 MY GOD I LOVE THEE, NOT BECAUSE
(?) FRANCIS XAVIER (1506–52)

Translated by Edward Caswall (see 139) from a Latin hymn in a book published in Cologne in 1669, based upon a Spanish sonnet attributed to Xavier, though there seems little reliable evidence for this belief. The translation appeared in Caswall's *Lyra Catholica* in 1849.

Xavier was one of the founders of the Society of Jesus in 1534. He laboured as a missionary in the Far East with great devotion. He was canonized by the Roman Catholic Church in 1621.

276 OUR FATHER, HEAR OUR LONGING PRAYER
GEORGE MACDONALD (1824–1905)

Novelist, poet and critic, most of his hymns were contributed to *Hymns and Sacred Songs for Sunday School and Social Worship*, of which he was one of the editors, in 1855.

He was trained at Highbury Theological College, but after a short time as Congregational minister at Arundel he turned to literature. He was tutor in English Literature at King's College, London. He became a member of the Church of England and was a close friend of F. D. Maurice. His novels, *David Elginbrod* and *Robert Falconer*, made him well known. He also issued several volumes of poetry.

See also 617.

277 O FOR A HEART TO PRAISE MY GOD
C. WESLEY (see 4)

In *Hymns and Sacred Poems*, 1742, based on Psalm li. 10. The original has eight verses, and in ver. 1 (line 4), reads 'spilt' for 'shed', and 'dear' for 'great' in ver. 2, and 'dearest' for 'gracious' in ver. 5.

278 LORD, AS TO THY DEAR CROSS WE FLEE
J. H. GURNEY (see 51)

In the *Collection of Hymns*, 1838, which he prepared for his parish at Lutterworth. One verse is omitted.

279 WE PRAISE AND BLESS THEE, GRACIOUS LORD
KARL JOHANN PHILIPP SPITTA (1801–59)

Educated at Göttingen. Ordained in 1828 he ultimately became Superintendent in Hanover. He had written songs and poems as a student, but in 1824 he started to write hymns. He wrote to a friend: 'In the manner in which I formerly sang I sing no more. To the Lord I consecrate my life and my love and likewise my song. His love is the great theme of all my songs; to praise and to exalt it worthily is the theme of the Christian singer. He gave me song and melody. I give it back to Him.' He published two volumes of hymns.

See also 365, 641, 681.

JANE LAURIE BORTHWICK (1813–97) published, with her sister Sarah, Mrs. Findlater (see 218), four volumes of *Hymns from the Land of Luther*, between 1854 and 1862. The title of this furnished the initials H. L. L., over which she published many of her own hymns in *The Family Treasury*. She belonged to the Free Church of Scotland and was a devoted supporter of Christian work at home and abroad.

See also 341, 365, 419, 630, 647.

280 WALK IN THE LIGHT   BERNARD BARTON (see 195)

From his *Devotional Verses*, 1826, with the text, 1 John i. 7. In some other collections it is differently arranged, e.g. with our ver. 4 first. There is an additional verse:

> Walk in the light, and thine shall be
> A path, though thorny, bright;
> For God, by grace, shall dwell in thee
> And God Himself is Light.

281 THOUGH LOWLY HERE OUR LOT MAY BE

WILLIAM GASKELL (1805–84)

Appeared in Miss Courtald's *Psalms, Hymns and Anthems*, 1860. He was Unitarian minister of Cross St. Chapel, Manchester, Professor of English in Manchester New College, and an influential figure in the life of the city. He published eighty hymns, chiefly in Beard's *Collection*, 1837. His wife was the writer of *Cranford* and other novels famous in their day and the biographer of Charlotte Brontë.

282 MY GOD, I LOVE THEE FOR THYSELF

G. B. BUBIER (see 258)

283 HELP ME, MY GOD, TO SPEAK

HORATIUS BONAR (see 40)

284 TEACH ME, MY GOD AND KING

GEORGE HERBERT (see 26)

A selection from a poem in *The Temple*, 1633, with the title 'The Elixir'. The word is defined by the *Oxford Dictionary* as 'alchemist's preparation designed to change metals into gold'. The elixir here is the 'tincture, "for Thy sake"'. It may be doubted whether Wesley's changes, adopted here, are really improvements. Our ver. 2 is entirely Wesley's. Ver. 3 originally read:

> All may of Thee partake;
> Nothing can be so mean
> Which with this tincture, 'for Thy sake',
> Will not grow bright and clean.

Instead of Wesley's ver. 4 Herbert wrote these two:

> A servant with this clause
> Makes drudgery divine.
> Who sweeps a room, as for Thy laws,
> Makes that and th' action fine.

> This is the famous stone
> That turneth all to gold;
> For that which God doth touch and own
> Cannot for less be told.

285 THOU SAY'ST, 'TAKE UP THY CROSS'

FRANCIS TURNER PALGRAVE (1824–97)

First published in *Macmillan's Magazine*, 1865.
After a distinguished career at Oxford he became private secretary to Gladstone for a short time. Working in the Education

Department he rose to be Assistant Secretary. In 1885 he became
Professor of Poetry at Oxford. He compiled the famous anthology,
The Golden Treasury, 1861.

See also 455, 609, 621.

286 BLEST ARE THE PURE IN HEART
JOHN KEBLE (see 53)

Verses 1 and 3 are by Keble, who wrote 'cradle' instead of
'dwelling' in ver. 3. Verses 2 and 4 are from the *Mitre Hymn-book*,
1836. It is not certain if they are by W. J. Hall or his fellow editor,
E. Osler. The present text was authorized by Keble.

WILLIAM JOHN HALL (1793–1861), joint editor of the *Mitre
Hymn-book*, was priest of the Chapel Royal, St. James's, and later
vicar of Tottenham.

287 NEVER FURTHER THAN THY CROSS
MRS. E. R. CHARLES (see 99)

288 HARK, MY SOUL! IT IS THE LORD
W. COWPER (see 60)

First published in Maxfield's *New Appendix*, 1768. It was written
at Huntingdon three or four years earlier. In the *Olney Hymns* it had
John xxi. 16 as text. In ver. 2 'bleeding' was originally 'wounded'.

289 FILL THOU MY LIFE   HORATIUS BONAR (see 40)

From his *Hymns of Faith and Hope*, third series, 1866, headed
'Life's Praise'.

290 WE LOVE THEE, LORD, YET NOT ALONE
MRS. JULIA ANNE (*née* MARSHALL) ELLIOTT (1803–41)

Married in 1833 the Rev. H. Venn Elliott, brother of Charlotte
Elliott. Eleven hymns by her appeared, at first anonymously, in
Psalms and Hymns for Public, Private and Social Worship, published
by her husband.

291 FATHER, I KNOW THAT ALL MY LIFE
ANNA LETITIA WARING (1823–1910)

Written at Clifton, 1846. Printed in her *Hymns and Meditations*,
1850, with the text 'My times are in Thy hands', Psalm xxxi. 15.

Brought up in the Society of Friends, when in Cardiff she
worshipped at our Bethany Church. In 1842 she joined the Church
of England. She learned Hebrew so as to read Old Testament
poetry in the original. She was rich in friendships. She visited the
prisons in Bristol and was a friend of the Discharged Prisoners'
Aid Society.

See also 305, 336, 424.

292 NOT WHAT I AM, O LORD   H. BONAR (see 40)

From his *Hymns of Faith and Hope*, second series, 1861.

293 TEACH ME, MY LORD
ELLEN ELIZABETH BURMAN (1837–61)

Printed in the 1872 edition of Snepps' *Songs of Grace and Glory* as from 'a Dublin leaflet'. In the musical edition of 1880 he gives the writer's name as above.

294 GRACIOUS SPIRIT, HOLY GHOST
CHRISTOPHER WORDSWORTH (see 105)

A paraphrase of 1 Corinthians xiii., published in *The Holy Year*, 1862. The eight verses of the original covered more fully the contents of the Scripture chapter.

295 IT PASSETH KNOWLEDGE
MARY SHEKLETON (1827–83)

Printed in broadsheet form. She was an invalid in Dublin for many years, during which she wrote several hymns. She founded the Invalids' Prayer Union.

296 BELOVED, LET US LOVE   HORATIUS BONAR (see 40)

First appeared in the Supplement to our Baptist *Psalms and Hymns*, 1880, and in his *Communion Hymns*, 1881.

297 O LORD OF HEAVEN AND EARTH AND SEA
C. WORDSWORTH (see 105)

From his *Holy Year*, third edition, 1863. He agreed to certain alterations when the hymn was inserted in *Hymns Ancient and Modern*. The last line of the first three verses originally read 'Giver of all'. Ver. 4 (line 3) was changed from 'And e'en that gift Thou didst outrun'.

298 THEE WILL I LOVE
JOHANN ANGELUS (SILESIUS) (1624–77)

In his *Heilige Seelenlust* (sacred joy of the soul), 1657. Translated by John Wesley. Ver. 1 (last line) originally read, 'with chaste desire'. Richard Cobden is said to have repeated the last verse on his death-bed.

Angelus, with Silesius to indicate his birthplace, was the name adopted on joining the Roman Church, by Johann Scheffler. He studied medicine at four universities and graduated M.D. He came under the influence of Jacob Boehme, which provoked controversies with the clergy of the Lutheran Church to which he then belonged.

He became a Roman Catholic in 1653 and in 1671 entered the Jesuit monastery of St. Mathias at Breslau. Most of his hymns were written while he was a Lutheran.

See also 300.

299 THOU HIDDEN LOVE OF GOD

G. TERSTEEGEN (see 27)

John Wesley's translation was made while he was in Georgia, but published after his return to England.

300 O LOVE WHO FORMEDST ME TO WEAR

JOHANN ANGELUS (see 298)

The translation was published in *Lyra Germanica*, second edition, 1858.

C. WINKWORTH (see 11).

301 O LOVE DIVINE, HOW SWEET THOU ART

C. WESLEY (see 4)

From *Hymns and Sacred Poems*. Ver. 1, line 4, originally 'and die'.

302 LORD GOD, BY WHOM ALL CHANGE IS WROUGHT

T. H. GILL (see 94)

Written in 1869 and first published in *Songs of the Spirit*, New York, 1871.

303 BEHOLD, WHAT WONDROUS GRACE

ISAAC WATTS (see 2)

304 COME, WE THAT LOVE THE LORD

ISAAC WATTS (see 2)

In *Hymns and Sacred Songs*, 1707. Ver. 3 (line 3) read, 'But fav'rites of the heavenly King'.

305 MY HEART IS RESTING, O MY GOD

A. L. WARING (see 291)

Based on Lamentations iii. 24, 'The Lord is my portion, saith my soul; therefore will I hope in Him'.

306 HOW VAST THE TREASURE WE POSSESS

ISAAC WATTS (see 2)

307 HOW FIRM A FOUNDATION

ROBERT KEEN (eighteenth century)

First appeared in Rippon's *Selection of Hymns*, 1787.

Keen was precentor at Carter Lane Chapel, 1776–93. He was manager of the Particular Baptist Fund, and was appointed by

Whitefield as trustee of his Tabernacles on Moorfields and in Tottenham Court Road.

308 LONG DID I TOIL   HENRY FRANCIS LYTE (1793–1847)

In *Poems Chiefly Religious*, 1833, Lyte says that this hymn is 'imitated from Quarles', the seventeenth-century poet.

At Trinity College, Dublin, Lyte won the prize for the English poem three times. Already ordained, he experienced a change of heart when attending the death-bed of a fellow clergyman. Both together found a deeper faith and peace in Christ. From that day his work and his preaching had a new vitality. After curacies in many places he went in 1823 to the fishing village of Lower Brixham, Devon. His delicate and sensitive nature was unsuited to the kind of work he had to do and his health became undermined. He died in Nice in 1847. The clergyman fetched by a servant to minister to him at the last was H. E. Manning, then Archdeacon of Chichester and later the Roman Catholic Cardinal. Lyte died pointing upwards and saying, 'Peace! Joy!'

309 THAT MYSTIC WORD OF THINE
                                     H. B. STOWE (see 272)
In the *Plymouth Hymnal*, 1855.

310 OBJECT OF MY FIRST DESIRE
                                     A. M. TOPLADY (see 225)
Three stanzas of his hymn, 'Happiness thou lovely name', first printed in the *Gospel Magazine*, 1774.

311 JESUS, LOVER OF MY SOUL   C. WESLEY (see 4)

In *Hymns and Sacred Poems*, 1740; the third stanza is omitted. The often criticized phrase 'lover of souls' is found applied to God in Wisdom of Solomon xi. 26.

The omitted stanza ran:

> Wilt Thou not regard my call?
>   Wilt Thou not accept my prayer?
> Lo! I sink! I faint! I fall—
>   Lo! on Thee I cast my care:
> Reach me out Thy gracious hand!
>   While I of Thy strength receive,
> Hoping against hope I stand,
>   Dying, and behold I live.

Henry Ward Beecher said, 'I would rather have written that hymn of Wesley's . . . than to have the fame of all the kings that ever sat on the earth. . . . That hymn will go on singing until the last trump'. C. H. Spurgeon told how 'an ungodly stranger stepping

into one of our services at Exeter Hall was brought to the cross by
the words of Wesley's hymn, "Jesus, Lover of my soul". "Does
Jesus love me?" he said. "Then why should I live at enmity with
Him?"'

312 SAVIOUR, WHO EXALTED HIGH
RICHARD MANT (see 19)

From '*The Holy Days of the Church*, or Scripture Narratives of
our blessed Lord's Life and Ministry, with biographical notices
of the apostles, evangelists, and other saints, with reflections,
collects, and metrical sketches', Vol. I, 1828; Vol. II, 1831.

313 MY FAITH LOOKS UP TO THEE
RAY PALMER (see 139)

First published in Mason's *Spiritual Songs for Social Worship*,
1831, entitled 'Self Consecration'. It was his first hymn, written
when he was only twenty-one, shortly after leaving Yale. 'I gave
form to what I felt by writing with little effort the stanzas. I
recollect I wrote them with very tender emotion and ended the
last lines with tears'. The tune 'Olivet' was written for it by
Dr. Lowell Mason, who said, 'Mr. Palmer, you may live many
years and do many good things, but I think you will be best
known to posterity as the author of "My faith looks up to Thee"'.

314 I GIVE MY HEART TO THEE
Latin hymn translated by RAY PALMER (see 139)

The Latin began, '*Cor meum tibi dedi, Jesu dulcissime*'. Dr. Schaff
in his *Christ in Song*, 1869, says that the Latin text was 'freely
and happily reproduced by the Rev. Ray Palmer for this collection,
August 20, 1868'.

315 I LAY MY SINS ON JESUS HORATIUS BONAR (see 40)

First published in his *Songs for the Wilderness*, 1844, but written
some ten years earlier when he was assistant in St. John's Church,
Leith, 'in a desire to provide something which children could
sing and appreciate in divine worship'. It was perhaps the first
hymn he ever wrote.

316 I LIFT MY HEART TO THEE
CHARLES EDWARD MUDIE (1818–90)

Bookseller and founder of Mudie's Library. A Congregationalist
and a director of the London Missionary Society, he carried on
home mission work in Vauxhall Bridge Road and at Hampstead.
In 1872 he published *Stray Leaves*, a volume of verses most of
which had been written during a long illness.

317 LOVE DIVINE, ALL LOVES EXCELLING
C. WESLEY (see 4)

In the second verse Wesley wrote 'second rest' and 'power of sinning'. In other collections, including the *Methodist Hymnal*, the second verse is often omitted.

Luke Wiseman in his *Charles Wesley, Evangelist and Poet*, makes the interesting suggestion that Wesley was inspired to write this by Dryden's Song of Venus in his play *King Arthur*, beginning 'Fairest Isle, all isles excelling'. The hymn was originally sung to Purcell's tune for this song, which was given the name Westminster in *Sacred Harmony*.

318 O HOLY SAVIOUR, FRIEND UNSEEN
CHARLOTTE ELLIOTT (see 137)

319 O MASTER, LET ME WALK WITH THEE
WASHINGTON GLADDEN (1836–1918)

Published in March, 1879, in *Sunday Afternoon*, of which Dr. Gladden was editor. Ver. 1 (line 3) read 'Teach me'. He was a well-known Congregationalist pastor, author and editor in the United States, and a pioneer of the 'social Gospel'.

320 JESUS, FOUNTAIN OF MY DAYS
GEORGE MATHESON (see 255)

321 WHO, AS THOU, MAKES BLEST
JOHANN ANASTASIUS FREYLINGHAUSEN (1670–1739)

Attracted by the preaching of Francke and Breithaupt, the Pietist leaders, he moved to Erfurt and then to Halle. He married Francke's daughter and became his assistant in St. Ulrich's and as director of the Paedagogum and the Orphanage. In 1727 he succeeded him. He has been called the Charles Wesley of the Pietist movement. He published two hymn-books and also composed tunes.

FREDERICK WILLIAM GOTCH (1807–90) was President of Bristol Baptist College and one of the Old Testament Revisers.

322 O JESUS CHRIST, GROW THOU IN ME
JOHANN CASPAR LAVATER (1741–1801)

Pastor in Zurich, when the French in 1799 deported ten of its leading citizens Lavater protested vigorously in the pulpit and in print. He was seized by French dragoons but allowed to return to Zurich. He was shot by a French soldier and never fully recovered. He was a much loved pastor and preacher. He wrote about 700 hymns.

The translation appeared in the *British Messenger*, November 1, 1860. Dr. Schaff said that the translator was MRS. ELIZABETH LEE (*née* ALLEN) SMITH (1817–98), wife of Dr. Boynton Smith of Union Seminary, New York.

323 TO ME TO LIVE IS CHRIST   W. C. SMITH (see 38)

From *Hymns of Christ and the Christian Life,* from which comes also his better known 'Immortal, invisible'.

324 OH, THE BITTER SHAME AND SORROW
                                          THEODORE MONOD (1836–1921)

Written in English during meetings in Broadlands, Hants, in July, 1874.

Monod was born in Paris of a well-known French Protestant family. Trained in America at Western Theological Seminary, he became pastor of the French Reformed Church in Paris.

325 BEGONE, UNBELIEF   JOHN NEWTON (see 146)

From the *Olney Hymns,* headed 'I will trust and not be afraid'.

W. T. Stead said that this hymn had helped him more than any other. 'To this day whenever I am in doleful dumps and the stars in their courses appear to be fighting against me that one doggerel verse comes back clear as a blackbird's note through the morning mist, "His love in time past forbids me to think".'

326 MY GOD AND FATHER, WHILE I STRAY
                                          C. ELLIOTT (see 137)

From her *Invalids' Hymnbook,* 1835.

It is unfortunate if the hymn is allowed to encourage people to associate the will of God *only* with suffering and loss.

327 MY GOD, I THANK THEE
                                          ADELAIDE ANNE PROCTER (1825–64)

From *Legends and Lyrics,* 1858.

Daughter of 'Barry Cornwall', once well known as poet and dramatist, a friend of Charles Lamb and Dickens. Her first poems appeared in *Household Words,* though Dickens as editor did not at first know that they were by the daughter of his friend. In 1851 she became a Roman Catholic. She wrote the words of 'The Lost Chord'. Dickens bore witness to her unselfish devotion to the service of those in need, under the strain of which she broke down in health and died at an early age.

See also 345, 635.

328 COMMIT THOU ALL THY GRIEFS
                                          PAUL GERHARDT (see 87)

Wesley's fine version is a very free rendering of the German original. It has been said that, like Luther's *Ein Feste Burg,* this hymn is surrounded by a cloud of witnesses.

329 THY WAY, NOT MINE, O LORD

HORATIUS BONAR (see 40)

From his *Hymns of Faith and Life*, 1857.

330 QUIET, LORD, MY FROWARD HEART

JOHN NEWTON (see 146)

331 LORD, IT BELONGS NOT TO MY CARE

RICHARD BAXTER (see 31)

From Baxter's *Poetical Fragments*, 1681, published soon after his wife's death. It is a selection from a long poem called 'the Covenant and Confidence of Faith', with a note 'This covenant my dear wife in her former sickness subscribed with a cheerful will'. It had been signed by Margaret Baxter, then Charlton, after her recovery from serious illness in 1660. This was before her marriage or engagement to Baxter. Baxter dates the preface of his book: 'London—at the door of Eternity, August 7th, 1681'.

This was a favourite hymn of the great scientist, James Clerk Maxwell.

332 MY FATHER, IT IS GOOD FOR ME

GEORGE RAWSON (see 179)

333 O THOU FROM WHOM ALL GOODNESS FLOWS

THOMAS HAWEIS (1734–1820)

Studied medicine for a time but decided to enter the ministry. He became a prominent Evangelical. After various charges, including assistantship to Martin Madan at the Lock Hospital, London, he became chaplain to Lady Huntingdon's chapel in Bath and manager of her chapels. He published a collection of hymns, *Carmina Christo or Hymns to the Saviour*, which was used as a companion to the *Select Collection of Hymns* edited by the Countess of Huntingdon for her chapels. He is the composer of the tune Richmond, set in *Baptist Church Hymnal* (*Revised*) to 72 (Praise to the holiest) and 513 (City of God).

Henry Martyn quotes ver. 5 in his diary with reference to the sneers of Muhammadan teachers and also found comfort in this hymn in the following year in Persia.

334 MAN'S WEAKNESS, WAITING UPON GOD

F. W. FABER (see 42)

335 THY WAY IS IN THE DEEP, O LORD

JAMES MARTINEAU (1805–1900)

After ministries in Dublin and Liverpool, he became in 1840 Professor of Philosophy and Political Economy at Manchester

New College. He went with the college to London in 1857 and in 1869 became Principal. He wrote a number of philosophical and theological works and edited three hymn-books.

336 GO NOT FAR FROM ME, O MY STRENGTH

A. L. WARING (see 291)

337 THROUGH THE LOVE OF GOD OUR SAVIOUR

MRS. MARY (*née* BOWLY) PETERS (1813–56)

The wife of an Anglican clergyman, she wrote *The World's Story from the Creation to the Accession of Queen Victoria* in seven volumes. In 1847 she issued *Hymns Intended to Help the Communion of Saints*, containing fifty-eight hymns. Some had already been published in *Psalms, Hymns, and Spiritual Songs* of the Plymouth Brethren.

338 O, LET HIM WHOSE SORROW

HEINRICH SIEGMUND OSWALD (1751–1837)

With the text Psalm l. 15. In Miss Cox's *Sacred Hymns from the German*, 1841.

Oswald was a German business man and civil servant who devoted himself to writing after his retirement. He wrote a hundred hymns. This hymn was sung at the funeral on Thursday, May 11, 1882, at Chatsworth, of Lord Frederick Cavendish, Chief Secretary for Ireland, who had been murdered in Phoenix Park, Dublin, on the previous Saturday.

FRANCES ELIZABETH COX (see 12).

339 STILL WILL WE TRUST

WILLIAM HENRY BURLEIGH (1812–71)

Descended through his mother from Governor Bradford of the *Mayflower*. After working as printer and journalist he published *The Christian Witness* and *The Temperance Banner*. In 1843 he became editor of *The Christian Freeman*, an anti-slavery journal. He then acted as secretary of the New York State Temperance Society and later became Harbour Master of New York. He was a Unitarian. He issued a volume of poems in 1841.

See also 356, 421.

340 DOST THOU BOW BENEATH THE BURDEN

G. T. COSTER (see 49)

An imitation of Neale's 'Art thou weary'. Published in 1880 in the Supplement to *Psalms and Hymns*.

95

341 THOU KNOWEST, LORD, THE WEARINESS AND SORROW
J. L. BORTHWICK (see 279)

342 IN THE HOUR OF TRIAL
J. MONTGOMERY (see 13)

Based on Luke xxii. 32, 'I have prayed for thee'. Published in his *Original Hymns*, 1835.

343 LORD, THOU HAST ALL MY FRAILTY MADE
G. MATHESON (see 255)

Shows the spiritual insight and poetic gift characteristic of this remarkable man.

344 SOMETIMES A LIGHT SURPRISES
W. COWPER (see 60)

In *Olney Hymns* with the title 'Joy and Peace in Believing'. Ver. 4 refers to Habakkuk iii. 17. Perhaps ver. 2 refers to Matthew vi. 34.

Palgrave in his *Treasury of Sacred Song* calls this a 'brilliant lyric'; its trustful faith is no less impressive than its poetic grace.

345 I DO NOT ASK, O LORD
A. A. PROCTER (see 327)

Gains added meaning from the writer's strenuous and self sacrificial life. See note on 327.

346 LEAVE GOD TO ORDER ALL THY WAYS
GEORGE NEUMARCK (1621–81)

At the age of twenty, on his way to Koenigsberg University, he was robbed of all his possessions except his prayer book and a little money sewn into his clothes. This made attendance at the university impossible and he could not find employment until in Kiel a fellow Thuringian, a pastor, found him a post as tutor, where he was able to earn enough to matriculate at Koenigsberg. This sudden relief was the occasion of his composing hymn and tune. A poet and musician, he became librarian at the Court of Weimar. The *Companion to the Church Hymnary* comments, 'The hymns of his prosperous years were markedly inferior to those written during his years of hardship'.

CATHERINE WINKWORTH (see 11).

347 HE THAT IS DOWN NEEDS FEAR NO FALL
JOHN BUNYAN (1628–88)

Bunyan's genius did not move in the direction of poetry. Most of his verses are pedestrian enough. But two lyrics in the *Pilgrim's Progress* have achieved independent status and are in many modern hymn-books—this and the Pilgrim hymn (407). This is the song of the shepherd boy in Part II: 'Now as they were going along and talking they espied a boy feeding his father's sheep. The boy was in very mean clothes, but of a fresh and well favoured countenance, and as he sat by himself he sung. "Hark", said Mr. Greatheart, "to what the Shepherd's boy saith." So they hearkened and he said, "He that is down . . . " Then said their Guide, "Do you hear him? I will dare to say this boy lives a merrier life, and wears more of that herb called Hearts-ease in his bosom than he that is clad in silk and velvet."'

The immortal John Bunyan scarcely needs a brief biographical note here. Passing through the acute spiritual turmoil which is recorded in *Grace Abounding* he reached a secure faith. For persisting in preaching he had to spend altogether some twelve years in imprisonment. Happily he was allowed to write and among the fruits of his stay in Bedford jail was *Pilgrim's Progress*, the first part of which appeared in 1678. A second part was added in 1684. It had a phenomenal sale in his own lifetime and has never stopped selling. Popularly nicknamed Bishop Bunyan he had a great influence in Nonconformist circles. He had a great gift for preaching and large crowds gathered wherever he went. He was minister of an Independent-Baptist Union Church in Bedford. Himself a Baptist he refused to allow difference of opinion about 'water-baptism' to separate him from his fellow Christians.

348 THROUGH ALL THE CHANGING SCENES OF LIFE
TATE AND BRADY (see 81)

This version of Psalm xxxiv is perhaps one of the most successful of those in the *New Version of the Psalms of David*, 1696.

349 WE BLESS THEE FOR THY PEACE, O GOD
CHRISTIAN MELODIES (U.S.A.), 1858

350 I SEE THE WRONG THAT ROUND ME LIES
J. G. WHITTIER (see 59)

A selection from a poem of twenty-two verses called 'The Eternal Goodness' which contains the often quoted lines:

> And so beside the silent sea
> I wait the muffled oar;
> No harm from Him can come to me
> On ocean or on shore.
> I know not where His islands lift
> Their fronded palms in air.
> I only know I cannot drift
> Beyond His love and care.

351 I WAITED FOR THE LORD MY GOD

Rous and Barton (see 62)

A metrical version of Psalm xl. 1–5.

352 NOT SO IN HASTE, MY HEART!

Bayard Taylor (1825–78)

American traveller, journalist, diplomat, translator.

353 MY TIMES ARE IN THY HAND

William Freeman Lloyd (1791–1853)

From *Hymns for the Poor of the Flock*, 1838.
Became secretary of the Sunday School Union in 1810. He started the *Sunday School Teachers' Magazine* and produced other Sunday school literature. He was also associated with the R.T.S. He issued a volume of verse, *Thoughts in Rhyme*, 1853.

354 SAY NOT, MY SOUL, FROM WHENCE

T. T. Lynch (see 70)

355 STRONG SON OF GOD   Alfred Tennyson (1809–92)

Selected verses from the prologue to *In Memoriam*, 1850.
The son of an Anglican clergyman, Tennyson succeeded Wordsworth as Poet Laureate in 1850. He was buried in Westminster Abbey. He was outstanding in an age of great poets. With an alert mind keenly aware of the doubts and questionings of his generation, he never lost his firm grasp of spiritual realities. His faith in God added the note of prophetic preaching to a rarely rivalled gift of poetic skill. Tennyson was not, by intention, a hymn-writer. When asked the reason he replied, 'A good hymn is the most difficult thing in the world to write. In a good hymn you have to be both commonplace and poetical.'

356 FATHER, BENEATH THY SHELTERING WING

W. H. Burleigh (see 339)

357 DEAR LORD AND FATHER OF MANKIND

J. G. Whittier (see 59)

From a long poem 'The Brewing of Soma'. Soma is an intoxicating Indian drink. He describes the pagan custom of seeking communion with the deity through such intoxication. Some, he thinks, still seek sensuous excitement in worship.

> In sensual transports wild as vain
> We brew in many a Christian fane
> The heathen soma still.

In these concluding verses he extols instead the quietness of true Christian intercourse with God.

358 O LOVE THAT WILT NOT LET ME GO

G. MATHESON (see 255)

First appeared in *Life and Work*, January 1882. Written in the Clydeside manse of Innellan. 'It was composed with extreme rapidity. It seemed to me that its construction occupied only a few minutes and I felt myself rather in the position of one who was being dictated to than of an original artist. I was suffering from extreme mental stress and the hymn was the fruit of pain.' It has been said, though not with assurance, that it was written when the lady to whom he was engaged decided that his blindness made their marriage impossible.

359 DAY BY DAY THE MANNA FELL   J. CONDER (see 9)

360 PEACE, PERFECT PEACE   E. H. BICKERSTETH (see 46)

Written in August, 1875, after hearing a sermon by Canon Gibbon, vicar of Harrogate, on Isaiah xxvi. 3, 'Thou wilt keep him in perfect peace, whose mind is stayed on Thee'. Bickersteth was there on holiday. That afternoon he visited an aged relative on his death bed. Sitting beside him he wrote the hymn in a few minutes and read it to his dying friend.

It is told in his *Life* that Bishop Hannington used to sing this hymn aloud on his last journey. It has brought consolation and strength to many. Congregations sometimes fail to realize that the second line of each verse supplies the answer to the question asked in the first line.

361 O LORD, HOW HAPPY SHOULD WE BE

J. ANSTICE (see 95)

Anstice, who died at the age of twenty-eight, a man of brilliant promise, dictated his hymns to his wife. Fifty-two were printed after his death in 1836 for private circulation. This was included in Miss Yonge's *Child's Christian Year* with the text, 1 Peter v. 7.

362 NOT, LORD, THINE ANCIENT WORKS ALONE

T. H. GILL (see 94)

363 HOLD THOU MY HAND

MRS. FRANCES JANE (*née* CROSBY) VAN ALSTYNE (1820–1915)

Better known to many by her maiden name Fanny Crosby. Through mistaken eye treatment became totally blind when six weeks old. When fifteen years of age she entered the New York City Institution for the blind, and in 1847 became a teacher therein. In 1858 she married Alexander van Alstyne, a blind musician. She was a member of the Methodist Episcopal Church. Some of her verses were published when she was eight years of age, and she continued writing with unfaltering facility until her death in her ninety-fifth year. Until middle life she wrote chiefly poems and songs. Her first volume of verse was *A Blind Girl, and other poems*, 1844. Her songs were usually highly sentimental, and were very popular.

Her first hymn was published in the *Golden Censer*, 1864. Altogether she wrote about 8,000 songs and hymns. At one time she was under contract to a New York firm to produce three hymns a week. With few exceptions her hymns are not of a high quality, but they are often redeemed by their simplicity and earnestness. She lived in the great hymn-singing period of Moody and Sankey, and it was chiefly through the latter's *Sacred Songs and Solos* that her hymns became familiar in Great Britain. About sixty are in common use. 'Safe in the Arms of Jesus' is perhaps the most popular. She wrote under a number of pseudonyms. Poignancy is added to the imagery of this hymn by the fact of the writer's blindness.

See also 383.

364 THY LIFE WAS GIVEN FOR ME

F. R. HAVERGAL (see 133)

Her first hymn, written when she was twenty-one years of age. She was studying in Germany at the time. Coming into the house of the German divine where she was staying, on January 10, 1858, she noticed under a picture of Christ the words, 'I did this for thee: what hast thou done for me?' The lines of the hymn flashed into her mind and she wrote them down in pencil on a scrap of paper. Reading them over she thought them so poor that she tossed them on the fire, but they fell out untouched. Later she showed them to her father who encouraged her to preserve them and wrote the tune 'Baca' especially for them.

The first line of the original copy, printed as a leaflet in 1859, was, 'I gave My life for thee: what hast thou done for me?' She reluctantly consented to its alteration for the S.P.C.K. *Church Hymns* (1871), which changed the original appeal of Christ to a disciple into an address by a disciple to Christ.

365 HOW BLESSÈD, FROM THE BONDS OF SIN

CARL J. P. SPITTA (see 279)

First published in his *Psalter und Harfe* in 1833. Miss Borthwick's version is a free translation of four of its seven verses. She included it in her *Hymns from the land of Luther* (1845).

For Miss Borthwick, see 279.

366 BE STILL MY HEART
WILLIAM EDWARD WINKS (1842–1926)

Educated for the Baptist ministry at Chilwell College, Nottingham. From 1865 he held pastorates at Allerton and Wisbech, and was minister of Bethany Chapel, Cardiff, from 1876–1914. Most of his hymns were written for special services. No. 366 is taken from a collection of seventy-two of his hymns published in 1897.

See also 527.

367 FOUNTAIN OF GOOD, TO OWN THY LOVE
P. DODDRIDGE (see 55)

This hymn, undated in the author's MS., begins 'Jesus, my Lord, how rich Thy grace'. It was published in his posthumous *Hymns*, 1755. Its present form is largely the work of Edward Osler.

368 DISMISS ME NOT THY SERVICE, LORD
T. T. LYNCH (see 70)

Published in the 1st edition of his Christian poems, *The Rivulet*, 1855. This was a supplement to Dr. Watt's hymns, written for use in the author's own congregation.

369 O GOD OF TRUTH, WHOSE LIVING WORD
THOMAS HUGHES (1822–96)

The author of *Tom Brown's Schooldays* was educated at Rugby, under Dr. Arnold, and at Oriel College, Oxford. He was called to the Bar in 1848, took silk in 1869, and appointed a county court judge in 1882. He represented Lambeth (1865–8), and Frome (1868–74), as a Liberal Member of Parliament. He joined Kingsley and Maurice in the Christian Socialism Movement, and with them founded the Working Men's College, in Great Ormond Street, being its Principal from 1872–83.

This is his only known hymn, and was given by him to Mrs. Norton for her *Lays of the Sanctuary*, 1859. It expresses the distinctive thought and feeling which guided his life.

370 O, STILL IN ACCENTS CLEAR AND STRONG
S. LONGFELLOW (see 184)

Included in the Unitarian *Hymns of the Spirit*, 1864.

371 WE GIVE THEE BUT THINE OWN
W. W. HOW (see 192)

Written about 1858, and first published in the 1864 edition of Morrell and How's *Psalms and Hymns*. It strikes a characteristic, practical, and humanitarian note and is more extensively used than any other of his hymns, except 'For all the Saints'.

372 RISE UP, O MEN OF GOD
WILLIAM PIERSON MERRILL (1867–   )

Studied for the Presbyterian ministry at the Union Theological Seminary, New York. He was ordained in 1890, and after pastorates in Philadelphia and Chicago, ministered to a New York church from 1911 to 1938. Several of his numerous theological books are widely read. He was a gifted preacher, and in 1922 gave the Lyman Beecher lectures on *The freedom of the preacher*.

No. 372 was written on a Lake Michigan steamer for the use of the Brotherhood Movement. It was first published in the Presbyterian *Continent*, 1911.

373 O THOU WHO CAMEST FROM ABOVE
C. WESLEY (see 4)

Published in his *Short hymns on select passages of the Holy Scriptures*, 1762, and based on Leviticus vi. 13, 'The fire shall ever be burning upon the altar; it shall never go out'. In 1781 he told a friend that 'his experience might always be found in the first two verses of this hymn'.

374 AND DIDST THOU, LORD, OUR SORROWS TAKE?
T. H. GILL (see 94)

A Passiontide hymn, written in 1849 and published in his *Golden Chain*, 1869.

375 LORD, SPEAK TO ME, THAT I MAY SPEAK
F. R. HAVERGAL (see 133)

This popular hymn was written in 1872 and published as one of Parlane's musical leaflets in the same year. In her original MS. it is headed 'A worker's prayer: "None of us liveth unto himself" ' (Romans xiv. 7).

Bishop Bickersteth thought it her choicest hymn.

376 GO, LABOUR ON, SPEND, AND BE SPENT
H. BONAR (see 40)

Written in 1836, and printed at Kelso, 1843. It is included also in his *Songs for the Wilderness*, 1843, and is the first of his hymns not written expressly for the young. It was intended to encourage the workers in his mission district in Leith.

377 MY GRACIOUS LORD, I OWN THY RIGHT

P. DODDRIDGE (see 55)

Headed 'The Service of God a delight', and published in the posthumous edition of his *Hymns*, 1755.

378 WHO CALLS THY GLORIOUS SERVICE HARD?

J. G. WHITTIER (see 59)

This line begins the third verse of his poem 'Seedtime and Harvest'. It was written in 1850 and included in his *Complete Poetical Works*, 1876.

379 I SAID IT IN THE MEADOW PATH

LUCY LARCOM (1824–93)

Born in Massachusetts. Worked in the mills of Lawrence until she was nearly twenty-one. Then she taught in elementary schools until 1849, and, after further training, in higher grade schools. She began to write poetry while still in the mills, and later produced several books of poems, collaborating with J. G. Whittier in some of them. She was joint-editor with him of *Child Life in Poetry*, 1871. This hymn is one of her *Collected Poems*, 1885.

380 WHERE CROSS THE CROWDED WAYS OF LIFE

FRANK MASON NORTH, D.D. (1850–1935)

Entered the Methodist Episcopal ministry in 1872. From 1892–1912 he edited *The Christian City*, and was secretary of the New York City Extension and Missionary Society. His gifts as an administrator led to his appointment in 1912 as secretary to the Methodist Board of Foreign Missions, a position he held till his death. In 1916–20 he was President of the Federal Council of the Churches of Christ in America.

A few of his hymns are widely used. They were mostly written for special occasions in his own church. No. 380 was written for the compilers of a new *Methodist Hymnal*, 1905, and was inspired by a translation of Matthew xxii. 9: 'Go ye therefore unto the parting of the highways'. It was included with others of his hymns in a commemorative volume issued by his friends soon after his death.

381 TAKE MY LIFE, AND LET IT BE

F. R. HAVERGAL (see 133)

Written in 1874 and printed as a consecration hymn at the beginning of her *Loyal Responses*, 1878. Originally it consisted of eleven couplets. She invariably sang them to her father's tune 'Patmos', and always associated the two in any publication over

I

which she had influence. It was written when she was staying at Areley House. She was used to lead to Christ the two daughters of the house. In her own words: 'It was nearly midnight. I was too happy to sleep, and spent most of the night in praise and renewal of my own consecration. These little couplets formed themselves and chimed in my heart one after another till they finished with "ever, only, all for Thee".' It is translated into many languages.

382 WHO IS ON THE LORD'S SIDE?
F. R. Havergal (see 133)

Written in 1877. Published in *Loyal Responses*, 1878. Based on 1 Chronicles xii. 18.

383 RESCUE THE PERISHING   F. van Alstyne (see 363)
From the American *Songs of Devotion*, 1870.

384 SHINE THOU UPON US, LORD   J. Ellerton (see 21)

This hymn for teachers was first published in 1881, and revised by the author to its present form for the 1889 Supplement to *Hymns Ancient and Modern*.

385 LORD, GIVE US LIGHT TO DO THY WORK
H. Bonar (see 40)

Published in *Hymns of Faith and Hope*, third series, 1866.

386 O IT IS HARD TO WORK FOR GOD
F. W. Faber (see 42)

Appeared in his *Jesus and Mary*, 1849, in nineteen verses, and headed, 'The right must win'. It was repeated in his *Hymns*, 1862.

387 SOW IN THE MORN THY SEED
J. Montgomery (see 13)

Written in 1832 and printed for the Whitsuntide gathering of the Sheffield Sunday Schools. For nearly forty years he wrote annually a hymn for this festival. It was published in *The Poet's Portfolio*, 1835, and in his *Original Hymns*, 1853.

388 OFT WHEN OF GOD WE ASK   T. T. Lynch (see 70)
From the first edition of *The Rivulet*, 1855.

389 NOW, THE SOWING AND THE WEEPING
F. R. Havergal (see 133)

Written in 1870, at Leamington. First published in *The Sunday at Home*, 1870.

390 LORD OF THE REAPERS
FREDERIC GOLDSMITH FRENCH (1867–1947)

Trained for the Baptist ministry at the Midland College and Nottingham University. After three years at Chatteris he became minister at Lee, Kent, in 1894, and remained there until 1946. He was a man of rich spiritual experience and outstanding mental ability, a born student and teacher. He read widely and thought deeply. The fine quality of his mind and spirit can be seen in his books on Thomas à Kempis and on Mysticism, and also in his hymns. He wrote several of these for the Sunday School anniversaries at Lee. No. 390 was written in 1901 and first published in the *Sunday School Hymnary*, 1905.

391 MASTER, SPEAK! THY SERVANT HEARETH
F. R. HAVERGAL (see 133)

Written in 1867 at Weston-super-Mare and published in *Ministry of Song*, 1869.

392 GOD IS MY STRONG SALVATION
J. MONTGOMERY (see 13)

A version of Psalm xxvii. It appeared in his *Songs of Zion*, 1822.

393 BELIEVE NOT THOSE WHO SAY
ANNE BRONTË (1820–49)

The youngest of the three daughters of the Rev. Patrick Brontë. She was born at Thornton, near Bradford, a month before the Brontës moved to Haworth. She died of consumption at Scarborough. Her sister Charlotte wrote of her, 'Long-suffering, self-denying, reflective and intelligent', and referred to 'a constitutional reserve which veiled her mind and feelings'. 'Gentle' is the word by which many of her friends described her.

Under the pseudonym of Acton Bell she wrote *Agnes Grey* and *The Tenant of Wildfell Hall*. Some of her poems and hymns were published by Charlotte in 1851. Her poetry is 'gentle, melancholy, religious, pensive'. No. 393 appeared in 1850 in ten verses, entitled 'The narrow way'. It reveals the faith which upheld her in the testing, and sometimes tragic, years of her brief life.

394 SOLDIERS OF CHRIST, ARISE   C. WESLEY (see 4)

Printed in his *Hymns and Sacred Poems*, 1749, in sixteen verses of eight lines. Various centos have been formed from the original, sometimes with alteration of the text. Dr. Percy Dearmer refers to 'the mastered simplicity, the faultless technique, its sagacity in the use of imperfect rhymes', while W. T. Stead found it 'inspiriting as the blast of a bugle'.

395 AWAKE OUR SOULS ISAAC WATTS (see 2)

Based on Isaiah xl. 28–31. Printed in his *Hymns and Sacred Songs*, 1707. It was included by John Wesley in *Psalms and Hymns*, published at Charlestown, South Carolina, in 1736–7.

396 FATHER, THOUGH STORM ON STORM APPEAR
C. WESLEY (see 4)

Taken from his hymn, 'Hail, holy martyrs, glorious names', which was first published in twelve verses in *Hymns and Sacred Poems*, 1740, and headed 'Written after walking over Smithfield'.

397 'FORWARD!' BE OUR WATCHWORD
HENRY ALFORD (1810–71)

Dean Alford came of Somerset stock, a succession of his ancestors having been vicars of Curry Rivel. He was born in London, educated at Ilminster Grammar School and Trinity College, Cambridge, where he was contemporary with Hallam and Tennyson. Ordained in 1833 he was appointed Dean of Canterbury in 1857, a position he held until his death. He was a Fellow of Trinity, Hulsean Lecturer, 1841–2, and for some years editor of the *Contemporary Review*. He was a voluminous writer on many subjects, but his best known work is his commentary on the Greek New Testament, the fruit of twenty years' labour. This became the standard critical commentary of the later nineteenth century. He was a member of the New Testament Revision Company.

He composed and translated many hymns. These vary greatly in merit. Often both thought and expression are dull and pedestrian. The most popular is 'Come, ye thankful people, come'. His hymns were collected in *Psalms and Hymns*, 1844, and in *Year of Praise*, 1867. No. 397 was written as a Processional Hymn for the 1871 Festival of the choirs of the Canterbury diocese, and published with the music, also by the Dean, in the same year.

See also 450, 462, 670.

398 ONWARD! CHRISTIAN SOLDIERS
SABINE BARING-GOULD (1834–1924)

Born at Exeter. Lived much in Germany and France. Educated at Clare College, Cambridge. Ordained in 1864, and served at Horbury, Dalton, and East Mersea. In 1881 he succeeded to his father's estate at Lew Trenchard, Devon, and exercised his privilege as squire and patron by presenting himself to the living there as rector. He was a most versatile man, with abounding energy and an extraordinary range of interests. His writings include *Lives of the Saints*, fifteen volumes, *Curious Myths of the*

Middle Ages, *The Origin and Development of Religious Belief*, books of travel, works on Germany and her Church, and many novels. He was deeply interested in folk-songs, and collected and edited two valuable volumes of these—*Songs of the West* and *A Garland of Country Song*. Many of his hymns, both original and translations, appeared in the *Church Times* and in the 1868 and 1875 editions of *Hymns Ancient and Modern*.

No. 398 was written in 1865 for a Sunday School procession when he was in charge of a mission near Wakefield, Yorkshire. The reference in the chorus to a processional cross distressed many folk in the last century.

See also 427, 779.

399 CHRISTIAN, SEEK NOT YET REPOSE

C. ELLIOTT (see 137)

From her *Morning and Evening Hymns*, printed in 1939 for sale on behalf of a benevolent institution in Brighton.

400 AWAKE, MY SOUL

P. DODDRIDGE (see 55)

A Confirmation hymn in the Doddridge MSS. It was first published by J. Orton in his edition of Doddridge's *Hymns*, 1755, in five verses.

401 ARE WE THE SOLDIERS OF THE CROSS

ISAAC WATTS (see 2)

Printed with his *Sermons*, published in 1721-4, to accompany a sermon on 1 Corinthians xvi. 13: 'quit you like men, be strong'. The original hymn had six verses, and the first line was 'Am I a soldier of the Cross'.

402 THE SON OF GOD GOES FORTH TO WAR

R. HEBER (see 33)

Written for St. Stephen's Day when he was rector of Hodnet, and published in his posthumous *Hymns*, 1827.

Miss Florence Nightingale, in a letter dated February 18, 1874, writing to Miss Livingstone on the tragic death of her illustrious brother, said: ' He has opened those countries for God to enter in. He struck the first blow to abolish a hideous slave-trade. He, like Stephen, was the first martyr.

> He climbed the steep ascent of heaven
> Through peril, toil, and pain.
> O God! to us may grace be given
> To follow in his train.'

403 CHRISTIAN, DOST THOU SEE THEM
J. M. NEALE (see 78)

A translation of a Greek hymn, printed in his *Hymns of the Eastern Church*, 1862. He attributed it to St. Andrew of Crete (660–732), but scholars have been unable to trace any Greek hymn from which it could have been translated.

404 MARCH ON, MARCH ON, O YE SOLDIERS TRUE
MRS. ELLA SOPHIA ARMITAGE (1841–1931)

One of the first students at Newnham College. In 1874 she married the Rev. E. Armitage, Professor of Theology in the Congregational United College, Bradford. Her main interests were history, archaeology, and education. She served on the school boards of Rotherham and Bradford, and on the West Riding Education Committee. She was appointed an assistant commissioner to the Royal Commission on secondary education. For a time she was a lecturer on English history in the Women's Department of Manchester University. A degree was conferred on her by this university for her work in archaeology.

Her books include *The Childhood of the English Nation*, *The Connection of England and Scotland*, *The Education of a Christian Home*, and some on English antiquities. She also wrote a Service of Song, entitled, *The Garden of the Lord*, which contains sixteen of her original hymns. No. 404 was written for a missionary meeting at Waterhead, Oldham, about 1866. In her own words: 'I believe I was intended by nature for an archaeologist, but life has made me a hymn-writer, and I shall be content to be known as such when my archaeology is forgotten'. Her hymns are widely used here and in America.

See also 716, 756.

405 STAND UP, STAND UP FOR JESUS
GEORGE DUFFIELD (1818–88)

Trained for the Presbyterian ministry at Yale and Union Theological Seminary, New York. He held pastorates at Brooklyn, New Jersey, Philadelphia, and Michigan.

He found the inspiration for this hymn in the dying words of the Rev. D. A. Tyng, rector of the Church of the Epiphany, Philadelphia. This valiant fighter for the freedom of the slaves sent a message from his death-bed to the members of the Y.M.C.A.: 'Tell them to stand up for Jesus'. The following Sunday Dr. Duffield preached a memorial sermon on Ephesians vi. 14, 'Stand therefore, having your loins girt about with truth', and read this hymn which he had just composed. In 1858 he gave it in MS. to his Sunday School superintendent, who printed it on a handbill for the children. In the same year it was printed in *The Psalmist* in six verses. It is one of the most widely circulated of American hymns.

406 O GREAT LORD CHRIST, MY SAVIOUR

A. H. VINE (see 176)

'The Divine Call', from his *Doom of Saul*, 1895.

407 WHO WOULD TRUE VALOUR SEE

JOHN BUNYAN (see 347)

From *The Pilgrim's Progress*, Part II. Mr. Valiant-for-Truth met Christian and Mr. Greatheart towards the end of their journey, and told them of the obstacles set in his way by those who opposed his pilgrimage. He goes on: 'I believed, and therefore came out, got into the Way, fought all that set themselves against me, and by believing am come to this place'. Then follows this poem. Though Mr. Valiant's name makes this song appropriate to this setting, it is not sung by him, and in truth it sums up the noble story of the whole book. 'Monks Gate', the tune to which it is normally sung, is an arrangement, by Dr. R. Vaughan Williams, of a Sussex folk-tune.

408 GOD IS WITH US WALTER JOHN MATHAMS (1853–1931)

Born in London. His early years were spent at sea, where he had an adventurous career, including a rush, with others, to the Alaska gold fields. In 1874 he entered Regents Park College to train for the Baptist ministry and became minister of the Baptist church in Preston, Lancs. Failing health sent him to Australia in 1879, but he returned four years later and exercised most fruitful ministries at Falkirk and Birmingham. In 1900 he entered the Church of Scotland and spent three years in Egypt as Chaplain to the Forces, where his remarkable influence with men had wide scope. After service in churches in Scotland he retired in 1919. While still a student he published a small volume of his hymns and poems entitled *At Jesus' Feet*. He was a preacher of exceptional ability and force, and wrote several religious books of a popular character. His many hymns are scattered among various periodicals and some are in Baptist and other hymnals. They reveal the strength and the tenderness of this adventurous man, and his deep spiritual life. No. 408 was first sung at the Evangelical Free Church Congress in Nottingham, 1896, and printed in the *Christian Endeavour Hymnal*, 1896. This hymn was a favourite of John Clifford.

See also 420, 767.

409 MY FAITH, IT IS AN OAKEN STAFF

T. T. LYNCH (see 70)

From *The Rivulet*, 1855.

410 MY GOD, MY FATHER, MAKE ME STRONG
FREDERICK MANN (1846–1928)

A Free Church minister who later took Anglican orders and became Vicar of Ewell, and afterwards chaplain of Claybury Asylum.

411 COURAGE, BROTHER! DO NOT STUMBLE
NORMAN MACLEOD (1812–72)

Educated at the Universities of Glasgow and Edinburgh. After a period in Germany he returned to Glasgow to complete his course. After serving as parish minister at Loudoun and Dalkeith, he came to the Barony, Glasgow, where he exercised an outstanding and far-reaching ministry. He was a man of rare breadth and catholicity of spirit, an eloquent and moving preacher, a generous, warm-hearted, and courageous Christian. His deep love for the poor revealed itself in many practical ways. The first Penny Savings Bank in Glasgow was founded by him. He became one of the most influential ministers in the Church of Scotland. In 1841 he was appointed one of the Queen's chaplains, given the degree of D.D. by Glasgow University in 1858, and in 1869 elected Moderator of the General Assembly. He was one of the founders of the Evangelical Alliance, and a member of the General Assembly's Hymnal Committee in 1854–5. From 1860 until his death he edited *Good Words*. Many of the stories, verses, and sermons he wrote for this periodical were published in book form. No. 411 is the best known of his hymns. It appeared in January 1857, in the *Edinburgh Christian Magazine*.

412 MUCH IN SORROW, OFT IN WOE
HENRY KIRKE WHITE (1785–1806) and
FRANCES SARA FULLER-MAITLAND (1809–77)

H. K. White is remarkable for the early development of his genius as a poet and for the untimely ending of his life. His father was a butcher in Nottingham. His mother successfully conducted a girls' boarding school. He began work at fourteen years of age in a hosiery factory, but disliked it, and was placed in an attorney's office in Nottingham with the intention of entering the legal profession. All his spare time was given to languages and to literary pursuits. His earliest preserved poem was written when thirteen years old. Two years later he won a silver medal for a translation from Horace. His *Clifton Grove and other poems* was published when he was seventeen. About this time he felt called to enter the ministry. His employer released him from his articles and he entered St. John's College, Cambridge. Here he speedily distinguished himself, but over study undermined his health and he died at the age of twenty-one years. His death brought many tributes to his genius. Byron composed some beautiful lines on the sad event, and Southey published his *Remains*, with a short memoir of his life.

No. 412 is printed with nine other of his hymns in Collyer's *Hymns Collected and Original*, 1812. The first ten lines had been written by White on the back of a mathematical examination paper, and Collyer added six lines of his own.

Several people have essayed to complete the hymn, and No. 412 is Miss Fuller-Maitland's version, written when she was about eighteen years old.

Miss F. S. FULLER-MAITLAND was born at Shinfield Park, near Reading. In 1834 she married Mr. John Colquhoun. Her version of White's hymn was included, with two other of her hymns, in her mother's *Hymns for Private Devotion*, 1827 and 1863.

413 WHEN WE CANNOT SEE OUR WAY

T. KELLY (see 113)

From *Hymns not before published*, 1815.

414 CHILDREN OF THE HEAVENLY KING

J. CENNICK (see 168)

In his *Sacred Hymns for the children of God*, 1742, in twelve verses. George Whitefield printed six of these verses in his *Collection*, 1753.

415 LEAD, KINDLY LIGHT   J. H. NEWMAN (see 72)

Written on June 16, 1833, twelve years before he entered the Roman Church. He wrote it on an orange-boat returning to Marseilles from Palermo at a time when he was deeply concerned at the weak and divided state of the Established Church in England. It is an outburst of tense, personal emotion. He did not regard it as a hymn, or think it suitable for singing, and ascribed its popularity as a hymn to Dr. Dykes' tune. The meaning of some of its phrases is obscure. 'Kindly light' has been taken to mean conscience, a general term for divine guidance, or Christ the light of the world. 'Angel faces' has been interpreted as our guardian angels, but more usually as those we have lost by death. The lines were first printed in *The British Magazine*, 1834, and again in *Lyra Apostolica*, 1836. They have been widely translated.

416 JESUS, SAVIOUR, PILOT ME

EDWARD HOPPER (1818–88)

A Presbyterian minister in Greenville, New York, and later of the Church on Sea and Land, New York, a place of worship much used by sailors. He graduated at the Union Theological

Seminary, New York, in 1842. His hymns were issued anonymously.
No. 416 appeared in *The Sailors' Magazine*, New York, 1871,
and in the *Baptist Praise Book* of the same year.

417 LEAD US, HEAVENLY FATHER, LEAD US

JAMES EDMESTON (1791–1867)

Became an eminent London architect. Sir G. Gilbert Scott was
one of his pupils. He was a Congregationalist by descent, but
joined the Established Church early in life. He wrote eleven
volumes of verse and about 2,000 hymns. His *Cottage Minstrel*
was written in successful response to an advertisement offering £20
for fifty simple hymns suitable for cottage meetings. Few of his
hymns have proved of lasting value. His best known are this one
and 'Saviour, breathe an evening blessing'.

No. 417 appeared in his *Sacred Lyrics*, 1821, in three verses of
seven lines. It was entitled 'Hymn written for the children of the
London Orphan Asylum', an institution in which he was deeply
interested and which he often visited. It was included in the
Baptist *Psalms and Hymns*, 1858, and from there has passed into
most hymnals. It has been translated into several languages.

See also 625, 768.

418 GUIDE ME, O THOU GREAT JEHOVAH

WILLIAM WILLIAMS (1717–91)

The 'Sweet Singer of Wales' was born near Llandovery. He
began to train for the medical profession, but a sermon which he
heard Howel Harris preach at Talgarth in 1738 proved a turning-
point in his life, and he decided to enter the ministry. In 1740
he was ordained a deacon of the Established Church, but he was
refused priest's orders because of his evangelical views. So he
withdrew from the Established Church and threw himself into
evangelistic work. For nearly fifty years he travelled an average
of 3,000 miles a year on preaching journeys in Wales. The
preaching of Daniel Rowlands and Howel Harris awakened the
dormant spirit of song, and a new hymnody was created to give
it voice. Incomparably the greatest of the new singers was William
Williams. Elvet Lewis writes of him: 'What Paul Gerhardt has
been to Germany, what Isaac Watts has been to England, that
and more William Williams of Pantycelyn has been to the little
Principality of Wales. His hymns have both stirred and soothed
a whole nation for more than a hundred years; they have helped
to fashion a nation's character and to deepen a nation's piety.'

No. 418 was published in Welsh in 1744, and he issued a shorter
English version in 1771. It was included in his first book of hymns,
Alleluia, 1745.

See also 528.

419 JESUS, STILL LEAD ON
Count Nicholas Ludwig von Zinzendorf (1700–60)

The son of one of the principal ministers of State in Saxony. His family was noble, wealthy, and religious. He was educated at Halle and Wittenberg, studying law with a view to the diplomatic service. In 1722 settled down on his estate in Saxony, where he established the 'Herrnhut', a place of refuge for the Moravians driven from their homes. For them he drew up a common order of worship and established the organization which became known as the Moravian Brethren. He was consecrated their Bishop in 1737, and in the same year was banished from Saxony. He spent two years in America, and visited England. When his banishment was repealed in 1748 he returned to Herrnhut, and there spent most of his remaining years. He died a poor man, for all his wealth had been devoted to the work of God.

He wrote more than 200 hymns, publishing 128 of them in 1735. His best hymns are marked by simplicity, deep devotion, and fervent faith. No. 419 is a blending of two of his hymns, translated by Miss Borthwick, and first printed in the *Free Church Magazine*, 1846. It is repeated in her *Hymns from the land of Luther*, 1854.

See also 279.

420 CHRIST, OF THE UPWARD WAY
W. J. Mathams (see 408)

The last line was suggested by Colonel Newcome's final word *adsum* in Thackeray's novel.

421 LEAD US, O FATHER   W. H. Burleigh (see 339)

This 'prayer for guidance' appeared in the *Lyra Sacra Americana*, 1868. It had been printed before this, but the date is unknown.

422 LEADER OF FAITHFUL SOULS   C. Wesley (see 4)

Four verses of his hymn entitled 'The Traveller' in his *Hymns for those that seek, and those that have redemption*, 1747.

423 REJOICE, BELIEVER, IN THE LORD
J. Newton (see 146)

In the *Olney Hymns*, 1779. The first line is sometimes given as 'Let us rejoice in Christ the Lord'.

424 IN HEAVENLY LOVE ABIDING
A. L. Waring (see 291)

From *Hymns and Meditations*, 1850, a small book of nineteen of her hymns. Based on Psalm xxiii. 4. I will fear no evil, for Thou art with me.

425 COME THOU FOUNT OF EVERY BLESSING

R. ROBINSON (see 164)

The author records that a hymn 'Come Thou Fount, etc.' was published by Mr. Wheatley, of Norwich, 1758. This edition has not been traced, and the earliest known text is printed in 'a collection of Hymns used by the Church of Christ in Angel Alley, Bishopsgate', 1759. This is in four verses. The present form is in Madan's *Psalms and Hymns*, 1760. 'The hymn is as truly biographical as any of John Newton's, for Robinson's youth had been wild and reckless.'

426 O HAPPY BAND OF PILGRIMS

JOSEPH THE HYMNOGRAPHER. Died 883
Translated by J. M. NEALE (see 78)

St. Joseph was a native of Sicily, born about the year 800. In 830 he entered the monastic life at Thessalonica and then at Constantinople. He left here for Rome during a period of persecution, but was captured by pirates and enslaved for many years in Crete. Regaining liberty, he returned to Constantinople and established a monastery to which many were attracted by his eloquent preaching. He was banished for his defence of image worship, but recalled by the Empress Theodora and, through the favour of the patriarch Ignatius, was made Keeper of the sacred vessels in the Great Church of Constantinople. He died here, and is commemorated in the calendars of the Greek Church on the 3rd April.

He was the most voluminous of the Greek hymnwriters, and is said to have composed 1,000 canons, a canon being a series of short odes loosely linked as an acrostic.

No. 426 is Dr. Neale's translation of part of St. Joseph's canon on Saints Chrysanthus and Daria. In his preface to the 3rd edition of his *Hymns of the Eastern Church*, Dr. Neale writes that 'it contains so little that is from the Greek that it has no right to be included in this collection', and proposed that in any future edition it be put in an appendix.

See also 438.

427 THROUGH THE NIGHT OF DOUBT AND SORROW

BERNHARDT SEVERIN INGEMANN (1789–1862)
Translated by S. BARING-GOULD (see 398)

This famous Danish professor and author was the son of a Lutheran pastor. He was educated at the University of Copenhagen. From 1822 until his death he was Professor of Danish language and literature at the Academy of Sorφ, a quiet cathedral city. He wrote many historical novels, and his children's stories became as well known and loved as Hans Andersen's. A large number of his songs and hymns became widely popular and familiar to every Danish home. His collected works were published in 1851 in thirty-four volumes. He published collections of his hymns in 1822 and 1825. Only seven of his hymns have been translated into English, and No. 427 is the only one in common use. The author wrote it in 1825. Baring-Gould translated and published it in *The People's Hymnary*, 1867, and prepared this greatly improved version for *Hymns Ancient and Modern*, 1875.

428 AFTER THE DARKNESS
EDWIN PAXTON HOOD (1820–85)

Born in London, of humble parentage. He had no formal schooling but successfully educated himself. In 1852 he was invited to be the pastor of the Congregational Church of Nibley, Gloucestershire. He filled later pastorates in various parts of England. His last charge was the Falcon Square Church, Aldersgate, London. He was an impressive preacher and in great demand as a popular lecturer. His philanthropic interests were many, notably his concern for the inmates of the Hospital for Incurables. He wrote many books, including *The age and its architects*, *An exposition of Swedenborg*, and biographies of Thomas Carlyle and Oliver Cromwell. He edited the *Eclectic Review* for eight years.

He wrote many hymns. Some of them found a place in *Our Hymnbook*, 1862, which he drew up for the use of his congregation in Brighton. He published his *Children's Choir* in 1870. It is as the author of hymns for children that he is chiefly remembered. Their freshness and simplicity made an immediate appeal. Some of his best were written for Sunday School Anniversaries at Nibley. No. 428 is from the 1879 edition of *Our Hymnbook*.

See also 732, 744.

429 FOR EVER WITH THE LORD!
J. MONTGOMERY (see 13)

First published in 1835 in *The Amethyst*, an annual, and in his *Poet's Portfolio*, in twenty-two verses of four lines. Numerous centos from this are in common use.

430 ONE SWEETLY SOLEMN THOUGHT
PHOEBE CARY (1824–71)

When quite young moved with her sister, also a hymnwriter, to New York. She wrote many poems and hymns. Her published works include *Poems and Parodies*, 1854, and *Poems of faith, hope and love*, 1868. Dr. C. F. Deems compiled a collection of her hymns in 1869—*Hymns for all Christians*. No. 430 was written one Sunday morning in 1852 on her return from church. She did not intend it for public use, yet it won universal acceptance. Its inclusion in Sankey's hymnbook made it well known in Great Britain.

431 WEARY OF EARTH   SAMUEL JOHN STONE (1839–1900)

Educated at Charterhouse and Pembroke College, Oxford. Ordained in 1862. In 1870 he joined his father as curate at St. Paul's, Haggerston, succeeding him as vicar four years later. He transferred to All Hallows-on-the-Wall, London, in 1890. He wrote many religious poems and hymns. *Lyra Fidelium*, based on the Apostle's Creed, was published in 1866, *The Knight of Intercession and other poems* in 1872, *Sonnets of the Christian Year* in 1875, and *Hymns, original and translated*, in 1886. Most of the fifty hymns he wrote are in use. They vary greatly in metre and subject, although of no great quality as poetry are vigorous and nearly always didactic. A few, like this one, are plaintive and pathetic, but most resound with faith and hope. No. 431 is from his *Lyra Fidelium*, written in 1866, in eight verses, based on the tenth article of the Creed, the forgiveness of sins. He revised it to its present form for the appendix to *Hymns Ancient and Modern*, 1868. After his death F. G. Ellerton collected and edited his *Poems and Hymns* with a memoir of his life.

See also 454, 653.

432 HARK, HARK, MY SOUL!   F. W. FABER (see 42)

Published in his *Oratory Hymns*, 1854, in seven verses. It became widely known when included in the 1868 appendix to *Hymns Ancient and Modern*. Canon Ellerton writes: 'We enquire in vain into the meaning of "the Pilgrims of the night". Congregations are carried away by the rhythm and the musical ring of the lines.'

433 THE SANDS OF TIME ARE SINKING
MRS. ANNE ROSS COUSIN (1824–1906)

Born in Hull, the only child of Dr. D. R. Cundell, who served as an assistant surgeon at the Battle of Waterloo. She married the Rev. W. Cousin, minister of the Free Church in Melrose. She was a remarkable linguist and an excellent musician. She wrote many poems and hymns. A woman of deep evangelical piety, and of gentle and gracious character, all her hymns are songs of gratitude and love. They are scattered in many periodicals and hymnals. No. 433 is an interesting hymn. It consists of a skilful mosaic of passages from Samuel Rutherford's 'Letters and dying sayings'. It was published in *The Christian Treasury*, 1857, in nineteen verses, and gives its title to the collected edition of her poems, *Immanuel's Land and other pieces*, 1876. This consists of 107 hymns and poems, mostly meditations suited for private worship.

No. 433 is a form of her original hymn arranged by Mrs. Cousin for the 1900 *Baptist Church Hymnal*. It was the last hymn given out by the Rev. C. H. Spurgeon, at a brief service in his rooms at Mentone, 1892, shortly before he died.

434 IT SINGETH LOW IN EVERY HEART

JOHN WHITE CHADWICK (1840–1904)

In 1864 he graduated at the Cambridge Divinity School, Mass., and was ordained minister of the Second Unitarian Church, Brooklyn. He contributed many articles, poems, and hymns to the *Christian Examiner*, *Harper's Magazine*, and other periodicals. He wrote the lives of Theodore Parker and of William Ellery Channing, and four books of his poems and hymns were published. No. 434 was written in 1876 for the twenty-fifth anniversary of the Dedication of his church in Brooklyn.

See also 459.

435 JERUSALEM, MY HAPPY HOME

F.B.P. (late sixteenth or early seventeenth century)

In the British Museum there is a MS. copy, probably of the late sixteenth century, of a hymn in twenty-six verses with the title, 'A Song made by F. B. P. To the tune Diana'. It is a fairly close rendering of a passage in a book of meditations by St. Augustine which was frequently translated and much read in the sixteenth century. There is no certainty as to the identity of F. B. P. In its present shorter form the hymn is printed in the Eckington collection of *Psalms and Hymns for Public and Private Devotion*, 1795. The preface to the collection is written by its editor, Joseph Bromehead, and No. 435 is signed 'B'. It seems a legitimate inference that the hymn is Bromehead's version of F. B. P.'s poem.

436 CAPTAIN AND SAVIOUR OF THE HOST

G. RAWSON (see 179)

In the 1853 *Leeds Hymn Book*, which he helped to compile.

437 HUSH, BLESSÈD ARE THE DEAD

E. H. BICKERSTETH (see 46)

Written in 1873 and published in *The Shadowed House and the Light Beyond*, 1874.

438 SAFE HOME, SAFE HOME IN PORT

J. M. NEALE (see 78)

Based on JOSEPH THE HYMNOGRAPHER (see 426).

In Dr. Neale's *Hymns of the Eastern Church*, 1862. This is one of the three hymns in this collection which Dr. Neale said contained so little of the Greek original that in a future edition they should be placed in an appendix.

439 FOR THOSE WE LOVE WITHIN THE VEIL
WILLIAM CHARTER PIGGOTT (1872–1943)

Educated at Huddersfield College, and prepared for the Wesleyan ministry at Headingley College. In 1902 he joined the Congregationalists. After pastoral charges at Greville Place, London, and Bunyan Meeting, Bedford, he succeeded the Rev. C. Silvester Horne at Whitefield's Tabernacle, Tottenham Court Road, in 1912. His last church was at Streatham, 1917–43. He was chairman of the L.M.S. Committee in 1930 and of the Congregational Union in 1931–2. He was a gifted preacher, with an interesting and cultured mind, a wise counsellor, with understanding of human problems and needs. A small volume of his verse and hymns was published in 1944, and one could wish he had written more. Five of his hymns are preserved in *Songs of Praise*. No. 439 was written for a memorial service at his Streatham church.

440 GOD OF THE LIVING   J. ELLERTON (see 21)

Written when he was a curate at St. Nicolas, Brighton, for *Hymns for Schools and Bible Classes*, 1858. He rewrote it in its present form in 1867, and it was published in the Brown-Borthwick collection of hymns for church and home in 1871. It was sung at his own funeral.

441 NOW THE LABOURER'S TASK IS O'ER
J. ELLERTON (see 21)

Written for the S.P.C.K. *Church Hymns*, 1871. Mr. Ellerton acknowledges his debt for many thoughts and expressions to a poem of the Rev. G. Moultrie's. This was a favourite hymn of Queen Victoria.

442 WHEN THE DAY OF TOIL IS DONE
J. ELLERTON (see 21)

Written and published in 1870, and included in the S.P.C.K. *Church Hymns*, 1871. Sung, like No. 440, at his funeral.

443 O LORD OF LIFE, WHERE'ER THEY BE
F. L. HOSMER (see 45)

Written in 1888 for Easter Sunday in his church at Cleveland, Ohio. Published in 1894 in *Church Unity* and in *The Thought of God*.

444 WHEN ON MY DAY OF LIFE THE NIGHT IS FALLING
J. G. WHITTIER (see 59)

This moving hymn for old age, with its gentle serenity, was written in 1882, when Whittier was seventy-five. It was published in *The Bay of Seven Islands*, 1883.

445 GIVE ME THE WINGS OF FAITH TO RISE
ISAAC WATTS (see 2)

Published in his *Hymns and Spiritual Songs*, 1709.

446 THERE IS A LAND OF PURE DELIGHT
ISAAC WATTS (see 2)

Published in his *Hymns and Spiritual Songs*, 1707–9. One of his earliest hymns, composed probably in 1706. According to tradition it was while, on one summer day, he was gazing across Southampton Water that the pleasant meadows near Netley on the further side suggested 'the sweet fields beyond the swelling flood'.

447 BRIEF LIFE IS HERE OUR PORTION
448 JERUSALEM THE GOLDEN
449 FOR THEE, O DEAR, DEAR COUNTRY
BERNARD OF MORLAIX (twelfth century)
Centos by J. M. NEALE (see 78)

Little is known of this Bernard, who is overshadowed by his more illustrious contemporary and namesake, St. Bernard of Clairvaux. His parents are believed to be English. He is sometimes called Bernard of Morlaix, after the place in France where he was mistakenly thought to have been born, and sometimes Bernard of Cluny, after the Abbey which he entered as a monk somewhere between 1122–56, and where he probably spent the rest of his life. At this period the Abbey was at the height of its wealth and fame. Bernard was deeply moved by the corruption in the Church and by the lawlessness and misery in the world, and he composed a satire of some 3,000 lines on the vices and follies of his age, naming it '*de contemptu mundi*'. The first 400 lines are a description of the peace and glory of heaven, in contrast to the misery and pollution of earth, 'of such rare beauty as not easily to be matched by any medieval composition on the same subject' (Neale).

Dr. Neale translated these lines, and from them his genius produced these three hymns, some of the most widely known and loved of the hymns of the Church. They were published in his *Medieval Hymns*, 1851.

450 TEN THOUSAND TIMES TEN THOUSAND

H. ALFORD (see 397)

A Processional for Saints' Days, included in his *Year of Praise*, 1867.

451 FOR ALL THE SAINTS   W. W. HOW (see 192)

First published in Lord Nelson's *Hymns for Saints' Days and Other Hymns*, 1864, in eleven verses. The author altered his original 'For all Thy saints' to 'For all the saints'.

452 WE SPEAK OF THE REALMS OF THE BLEST

MRS. ELIZABETH (*née* KING) MILLS (1805–29)

Born at Stoke Newington. Married Mr. Thomas Mills, M.P. Written shortly before she herself was called to 'the realms of the blest'. In some versions 'speak' is altered to 'sing' or 'talk'.

453 GLORIOUS THINGS OF THEE ARE SPOKEN

J. NEWTON (see 146)

In *Olney Hymns*, 1779, in five verses.

454 THE CHURCH'S ONE FOUNDATION

S. J. STONE (see 431)

Written in 1866, based on the ninth article of the Apostles' Creed. It was written at the period when Bishop Gray, of Capetown, was engaged in controversy with Bishop Colenso over the latter's critical use of the Bible. There is a reference to the conflict in ver. 3. The seven verses of the original were printed in his *Lyra Fidelium*, 1866, and the five verses now in common use were printed in 1868 in the Appendix to *Hymns Ancient and Modern*.

455 O THOU NOT MADE WITH HANDS

F. T. PALGRAVE (see 285)

'The Kingdom of God within.' Published in his *Hymns*, 1867.

456 WE COME UNTO OUR FATHERS' GOD

T. H. GILL (see 94)

Built on Psalm xc, and intended to set forth the continuity and unity of God's people in all ages. Mr. Gill writes: 'It was inspired by a lively delight in my Puritan and Presbyterian forefathers in East Worcestershire. Descended from a Moravian martyr and an ejected minister, I rejoice not a little in the godly Protestant stock from which I spring. A staff handed down from him, and inscribed with the date 1692, was in my hand when I began the hymn.'

Also, 'The birthday of this hymn, November 22, 1868, was almost the most delightful day of my life. Its production employed the whole day, and was a prolonged rapture. It was produced while the *Golden Chain* was being printed, just in time to be the latest link.'

It is printed in his *Golden Chain*, 1869, in seven verses.

457 BLEST BE THE TIE THAT BINDS

JOHN FAWCETT (1731–1817)

Converted by George Whitefield's preaching on John iii. 14. In 1763 the Baptist Church in Bradford, of which he was a member, sent him forth to preach, and he entered on his ministry to the small congregation at Wainsgate. In 1777 he moved to Hebden Bridge, remaining there until his death. He was a gifted teacher and trained many students. Bristol Baptist College invited him to be the Principal, but he declined the call, yet his desire to promote the efficient training of ministers led him to found the Northern Education Society, known now as Rawdon College. He published two volumes of hymns, most of them summaries of his sermons sung at the close of the service.

No. 457 is published in his *Hymns*, 1782. One of his biographers recounts an unverified story of its origin which may well be true. In 1772 he received a call to succeed Dr. Gill at Carter Lane, London. He accepted, but after the farewell sermon had been preached and the wagons loaded with his furniture, he was so moved by the grief of his people that he decided to remain, sacrificing the attractions of a London pulpit to the affection of a poor but devoted flock, who had never been able to give him more that £25 a year.

See also 566.

458 LORD, FROM WHOM ALL BLESSINGS FLOW

C. WESLEY (see 4)

A poem of his, beginning 'Father, Son, and Spirit, hear', of thirty-nine verses and in six parts, was published in *Hymns and Poems*, 1740. Several centos have been taken from this, including these three verses, printed in the Baptist *Psalms and Hymns*, 1858.

459 ETERNAL RULER OF THE CEASELESS ROUND

J. W. CHADWICK (see 434)

This hymn on 'Unity' was written for the graduating class of the Divinity School, Cambridge, Mass., on June 19, 1864, shortly before his ordination. It is in his *Book of Poems*, 1876, and in Horder's *Congregational Hymns*, 1884. These lines of peace and goodwill are especially significant in that they were written during the bitter strife of the Civil War. Only a few weeks before its writing General Grant had met General Lee in desperate battle in the Wilderness.

460 MEN TRUE OF HEART AND STRONG IN FAITH
J. WAUGH BODEN

We have failed to discover any information about this hymn or its author.

461 HEAD OF THE CHURCH AND LORD OF ALL
JOSEPH TRITTON (1819–87)

Born in Battersea, educated at Charterhouse, and forty years a banker in Lombard Street. For twenty years he was Treasurer of the Baptist Missionary Society, and of many other religious and philanthropic institutions. He was an occasional writer of hymns. Two of his were written for, and sung at, the opening of the Metropolitan Tabernacle in 1861. Mr. Spurgeon included them in *Our Own Hymn Book*, 1866. No. 461 was written in 1880 for the first New Year's Day Prayer Meeting, initiated by the B.M.S. in that year. It is included in the Supplement to the Baptist *Psalms and Hymns*, 1880.

See also 522.

462 LO! THE STORMS OF LIFE ARE BREAKING
H. ALFORD (see 397)

In his *Psalms and Hymns*, 1844.

463 LORD OF OUR LIFE, AND GOD OF OUR SALVATION
PHILIP PUSEY (1799–1855) (adapted from the German)

Grandson of the first Viscount Folkestone, and elder brother of Dr. E. Bouverie Pusey, the Tractarian leader. Educated at Eton and Christ Church, Oxford. He then settled down on his estate and devoted himself to agriculture and the public service. He was one of the founders of the Royal Agricultural Society, and of the London Library. He was interested in the arts, a collector of prints and etchings, a copious contributor to the reviews, and for many years a Member of Parliament. Hymnology was one of his interests. No. 463 was written in 1834. 'It refers', he writes to his brother, 'to the state of the Church (of England) in 1834, assailed from without, enfeebled and distracted within, but on the eve of a great awakening.' It bears a close resemblance to the German ode on which it is based. This was written by Matthäus Apelles von Löwenstern in 1644, entitled 'For spiritual and temporal peace'. Löwenstern, of Silesia, was a musician, hymn-writer, and Minister of State during the Thirty Years War. His ode reflects the tragic, terrible years of that period.

Pusey's hymn was contributed to A. R. Reinagle's *Psalms and Hymn Tunes*, Oxford, 1840.

464 COME, LET US JOIN OUR FRIENDS ABOVE
C. WESLEY (see 4)

First published in his *Funeral Hymns*, 1759, in five verses of eight lines.

465 HAPPY THE SOULS TO JESUS JOINED
C. WESLEY (see 4)

From his *Hymns on the Lord's Supper*, 1745.

466 ONE HOLY CHURCH OF GOD APPEARS
S. LONGFELLOW (see 184)

From the Unitarian *Hymns of the Spirit*, 1864, of which he was joint editor.

467 HEAD OF THY CHURCH TRIUMPHANT
C. WESLEY (see 4)

First published in his *Hymns for Times of Trouble*, 1745. The special trouble then was the threatened attack on England by Charles Edward Stuart, the Young Pretender, whose forces had occupied Edinburgh. A national Day of Fasting was proclaimed. Bishop Heber admired this hymn 'as one of the most beautiful in our language for rich and elevated tone of devotional feeling'.

468 FOR THE MIGHT OF THINE ARM WE BLESS THEE
CHARLES SILVESTER HORNE (1865–1914)

The son of a Congregational minister. He was educated at Newport Grammar School, Shropshire, and at Glasgow University. In 1886 Mansfield College, Oxford, was opened and he was one of the first small group of students to enter there. His outstanding preaching gifts led to his settlement at the influential Allen Street Church, Kensington, in 1889. After fourteen fruitful years he went to the great institutional church at Whitefield's Tabernacle, Tottenham Court Road, where he worked strenuously and effectively until his death in 1914. He was elected Member of Parliament for Ipswich in 1900, Chairman of the Congregational Union in 1909, and President of the National Brotherhood Council in 1913. In 1914 he delivered the Yale Lectures on Preaching, and it was when he was returning from Niagara to Toronto that he suddenly collapsed on the deck of the steamer and died. Dr. James Moffatt wrote of him: 'His enthusiastic public spirit and zeal for all good causes, his burning interest in the social problem, his strong yet winsome personality, led to his being the admired and loved leader in his own denomination, and, far beyond, a power for righteousness'.

No. 468 was written for use at Whitefield's Tabernacle. It was suggested by Mrs. Hemans's 'Hymn of the Vaudois mountain Christians', which begins, 'For the strength of the hills we bless Thee'. The first collection in which it appears is *The Fellowship Hymnbook*, 1909.

469 I'M NOT ASHAMED TO OWN MY LORD

ISAAC WATTS (see 2)

In his *Hymns and Sacred Songs*, 1709.

On March 7, 1897, when Professor Henry Drummond was on his death-bed, his friend Dr. Hugh Barbour played several hymn-tunes to him without gaining any response. 'Then he tried the old Scots melody of "Martyrdom", to which Drummond beat time with his hand, and joined in the words, "I'm not ashamed to own my Lord". When the hymn was done, he said, "There's nothing to beat that, Hugh".'

470 MY GOD, ACCEPT MY HEART THIS DAY

M. BRIDGES (see 142)

In his *Hymns of the Heart for the use of Catholics*, 1848, and entitled 'Confirmation'.

471 FIGHT THE GOOD FIGHT WITH ALL THY MIGHT

J. S. B. MONSELL (see 6)

Written in 1834, and given in Ferguson's *Hymns for British Seamen*, 1838. Dr. Monsell included it in his *Hymns of Love and Praise*, 1863. It is based on 1 Timothy vi. 12: 'Fight the good fight of faith'.

472 HAST THOU SAID, EXALTED JESUS

JOHN EUSTACE GILES (1805–75)

He joined his father's church in Chatham, where his elder brother William gave Charles Dickens all the schooling he received. After training at Bristol Baptist College, he began his ministry at Haverford West. In 1830 he moved to Salter's Hall, London, and after six years went to South Parade, Leeds. He later held pastorates in Bristol, Sheffield, Dublin, and at Clapham Common, where he died. He was an effective preacher and platform speaker. From childhood he composed hymns and other verse. In 1834, at the request of the Baptist Missionary Society, he composed a hymn in celebration of negro emancipation. Five of his hymns appear in B.M.S. collections. No. 472 is his best known. It was written 'during a serious illness, in 1830, in anticipation of having to baptize several persons at Salter's Hall'. It was printed in six verses in 1830, with five verses in the 1858 Baptist *Psalms and Hymns*, and with the full text in the *Baptist Hymnal*, 1879.

473 O JESUS, I HAVE PROMISED   J. E. Bode (see 175)

Written when his daughter and two sons were confirmed as
'O Jesus, we have promised'. It was printed as a leaflet by the
S.P.C.K. in 1868, and included in the Appendix to the S.P.C.K.
Psalms and Hymns, 1869.

474 AROUND THY GRAVE, LORD JESUS
James George Deck (1802–84)

Educated for the Army and became an officer in the Indian
service. When he retired from the Army he joined the Plymouth
Brethren, and undertook the charge of their cause in Wellington,
Somerset, in 1843. In 1852 he settled in New Zealand. He wrote
and published several collections of his hymns. Their main theme
is the Second Advent, but several are of wider interest and of more
than average merit. They are direct, simple, and earnest. No. 474
is a shortened form of his hymn in Dr. Walker's *Psalms and Hymns*,
1855. It is printed in the Baptist *Psalms and Hymns*, 1858.

475 JESUS! AND SHALL IT EVER BE
Joseph Grigg (see 211)
Altered by Benjamin Francis (1734–99)

He published this, with three others of his hymns, in seven
rather crude verses in 1765.

Benjamin Francis was born in Wales, and trained for the Baptist
ministry at Bristol College. His first church was at Sodbury. In
1757 he moved to Horsley, where he ministered until his death
forty-two years later. He wrote much verse, including elegies on
the deaths of George Whitefield and of Caleb Evans, and two
satirical poems on the baptismal controversy. The greater number
of his hymns are in Welsh, and many are still in use. Five of his
English hymns are in Rippon's Baptist *Selection*, 1787. No. 475 is
one of these five, and is there stated to be a hymn of Joseph Grigg
altered by B. Francis. The alterations are considerable.

476 GLORY TO GOD, WHOSE SPIRIT DRAWS
Baptist W. Noel (see 65)

In the Appendix, containing thirty-nine original hymns to be
used at the baptism of believers, to his *Selection of Psalms and
Hymns*, 1832.

477 LORD OF THE BRAVE
John Huntley Skrine (1848–1923)

Educated at Uppingham and Corpus Christi College, Oxford.
He was ordained in 1874, and a Fellow of Merton College, Oxford,
from 1871–9. In 1873 he became an assistant master at Uppingham,

and was appointed Warden of Trinity College, Glenalmond, in 1888. In 1903 he accepted the living of Itchen Stoke, in Hampshire. He wrote many hymns. No. 477 was written in 1893. He included it in his *Thirty Hymns for Public School Singing*, 1899.

478 O HAPPY DAY, THAT FIXED MY CHOICE
P. DODDRIDGE (see 55)

In J. Orton's posthumous edition of his *Hymns*, 1755, in five verses. It is printed with four verses in J. W. Humphrey's edition of Doddridge's hymns, 1839.

479 JESUS, I MY CROSS HAVE TAKEN
H. F. LYTE (see 308)

In *Sacred Poetry*, 1824, with the text, 'Lo, we have left all and followed thee'.

The author of 'Abide with me' and 'Praise, my soul, the King of heaven', had a troubled life in more ways than one, and this is perhaps reflected in this hymn. Disputes with his parishioners greatly distressed him and are said to have contributed to his early death.

480 DEAR MASTER, IN THY WAY
JOHN THOMAS (1859–1944)

Contributed to the original edition of *B.C.H.*

Educated at Pontypool and Bangor University College. Baptist minister at Huddersfield; Myrtle Street, Liverpool; and Sutton.

481 STAND, SOLDIER OF THE CROSS
E. H. BICKERSTETH (see 46)

Written for *Hymnal Companion*, 1870.

The stress on individual religion, 'the single soul with his God', is characteristic of this writer.

482 BURIED WITH CHRIST!
WILLIAM WILSON SIDEY (1856–1909)

Baptist minister at Cupar and Tottenham. Written for the latter church.

483 TRUE-HEARTED, WHOLE-HEARTED
F. R. HAVERGAL (see 133)

Written for a Y.W.C.A. New Year meeting near the end of Miss Havergal's life. This simple hymn, characterized by deep 'whole-hearted' devotion to Christ, strikes the keynote of the faithful Christian life of its writer.

484 MASTER, WE THY FOOTSTEPS FOLLOW
FREDERICK ARTHUR JACKSON (1867–1942)

New in this book. Other hymns by Mr. Jackson are in *Sunday School Hymnary*, *Child Songs*, and elsewhere. His hymns are marked by originality of thought, smoothness of rhythm, and some real poetic gift.

A Baptist minister, educated at Spurgeon's College, he held several pastorates, notably at Campden, Glos., and finally at Brington, Northamptonshire. He wrote much in religious journals and published a volume of poems, *Just Beyond*.

See also 705, 707.

485 MY GOD, AND IS THY TABLE SPREAD?
P. DODDRIDGE (see 55)

First published in 1755 in a posthumous edition of his *Hymns*, with the text, Malachi i. 12. It has been translated into several languages and is said to be widely used in the Church of England.
In the original there were two other verses:

> Hail, sacred feast which Jesus makes,
> Rich banquet of His flesh and blood!
> Thrice happy he who here partakes
> That sacred stream, that heavenly food.
>
> Let crowds approach with hearts prepared;
> With hearts inflamed let all attend,
> Nor, when we leave our Father's board,
> The pleasure or the profit end.

486 LET ME BE WITH THEE   C. ELLIOTT (see 137)

Characterized by deep devotional feeling. Miss Elliott's hymns seem to have a special message for those in sickness and sorrow, to whom her own experience taught her to speak.

487 LORD, IN THIS BLEST AND HALLOWED HOUR
J. CONDER (see 9)

In his *Congregational Hymnbook*, 1836, with the motto, 'He was known of them in the breaking of bread'. In the original there is an opening stanza beginning, 'Far from my thoughts, vain world, depart'.

488 JESUS, THOU EVERLASTING KING
ISAAC WATTS (see 2)

Not perhaps one of his most impressive hymns, either in thought or expression.

489 JESUS, TO THY TABLE LED
ROBERT HALL BAYNES (1831–95)

In the *Canterbury Hymnal*, which he edited, with the text, Ephesians iii. 19. The second verse, here omitted, ran:

> While in penitence we kneel
> Thy sweet presence let us feel,
> All Thy wondrous love reveal.

Son of the Rev. Joseph Baynes, Baptist minister at Wellington, he became an Anglican and was Canon of Worcester and vicar of Holy Trinity, Folkestone. He edited several books of religious poetry.

490 BY CHRIST REDEEMED
G. RAWSON (see 179)

Himself a Congregationalist he helped in the preparation of the Baptist *Psalms and Hymns*, 1857, for which he wrote this hymn. It is one of the most widely used of all he wrote.

Originally the first line of ver. 3 read, 'His fearful drops of agony', which he later changed to 'The streams of His dread agony'.

491 FOR EVER HERE MY REST SHALL BE
C. WESLEY (see 4)

Attached to the text, 'Christ our righteousness', 1 Corinthians i. 30. The original first verse was:

> Jesu, Thou art my righteousness,
> For all my sins were thine;
> Thy death hath bought of God my peace,
> Thy life hath made Him mine.

492 O JESUS CHRIST, THE HOLY ONE
JANE EUPHEMIA (*née* BROWNE) SAXBY (1811–98)

In a long illness she wrote much poetry. This hymn was written to deplore her enforced absence from the Lord's Supper, as is clearly reflected in verses 2 and 3.

493 ACCORDING TO THY GRACIOUS WORD
J. MONTGOMERY (see 13)

From its first appearance one of the most popular of Communion hymns. It was printed in his *Christian Psalmist*, 1825, with the text, 'Do this in remembrance of Me', Luke xxii. 19.

494 BREAD OF THE WORLD
R. HEBER (see 33)

Published the year after Heber's death in 1827 in *Hymns Written and Adapted for the Weekly Church Services of the Year*.

495 JESUS WE THUS OBEY   C. WESLEY (see 4)
   From *Hymns for the Lord's Supper*, 1745.

496 DEAR LORD, BEFORE WE PART   G. RAWSON (see 179)
   Julian, in the *Dictionary of Hymnology*, says, 'This hymn is usually ascribed to G. Rawson, but on Mr. Rawson's authority this is an error. It was given anonymously in Baptist *Psalms and Hymns*, 1858.'

497 NO GOSPEL LIKE THIS FEAST   E. CHARLES (see 99)

498 HERE, O MY LORD   H. BONAR (see 40)
   The original had ten stanzas and was written in 1855 for use at a Communion service in the Church of Dr. Bonar's elder brother, a minister in Greenock. It was considerably altered before publication.

499 O CHRIST OUR GOD
                GEORGE HUGH BOURNE (1840–1925)
   Warden of St. Edmund's College, Salisbury, for which he wrote seven post-Communion hymns, including this.

500 TILL HE COME   E. H. BICKERSTETH (see 46)
   The bishop said he wrote this, in 1861, to emphasize an aspect of the Communion service too often forgotten—'Ye do shew forth the Lord's death until He come'.

501 BREAD OF HEAVEN   J. CONDER (see 9)
   The most generally popular of Conder's many hymns. First appeared in his *Star in the East*, 1824, with the text, 'I am the living bread which came down from heaven', John vi. 51.
   The fourth line of ver. 2 originally read, 'From Thy veins I drink and live'.

502 I HUNGER AND I THIRST   J. MONSELL (see 6)
   In the *Parish Hymnal*, 1873.

503 OH, LEAD MY BLINDNESS
                WILLIAM EWART GLADSTONE (1809–98)
   From a poem of ten stanzas printed in *Good Words* after his death.
   In his early days Gladstone had serious thoughts of entering the ministry, as is revealed in his letter to his father in 1830 (*Life.*

Morley. II. 793). John Morley wrote that Gladstone 'cared as much for the church as he cared for the state . . . and he was sure that the strength of a state corresponds to the religious strength and soundness of the community of which the state is the civil organ' (*Life*, p. 3). For him 'political life was only a part of his religious life' (p. 200). He records in his diary for 1854 how the Bible had helped him in times of strain and crisis. Lord Salisbury called him 'a great Christian'.

504 FATHER OF MERCIES   BENJAMIN BEDDOME (1717–93)

Baptist minister for more than fifty years at Bourton-on-the-Water, from his ordination at the age of twenty-six until his death, declining many invitations to larger churches. In accordance with a fairly general custom at the time, he wrote a hymn to follow the sermon every Sunday morning. A volume containing 822 of them was published in 1817 with a preface by Robert Hall.

505 FROM DISTANT PLACES
WILLIAM LINDSAY ALEXANDER (1808–84)

Written in 1847 for the annual meeting of the Congregational Union of Scotland. It originally read 'From distant corners'.

Dr. Alexander was principal of the Congregational Theological Hall, Edinburgh, and a Reviser of the Old Testament. He edited the *Augustine Hymnbook*, 1849.

506 SPIRIT OF CHRIST   J. KEBLE (see 53)

507 WE THANK THEE, LORD, FOR USING US
H. BONAR (see 40)

In *Hymns of Faith and Hope*, 1867, headed, 'Forget not all His benefits'. It began, 'I thank Thee, Lord, for using me'.

508 WE THANK THEE, GRACIOUS LORD
H. BONAR (see 40)

With the previous hymn, this reflects the spirit of the writer's long and faithful ministry.

509 COME, KINGDOM OF OUR GOD
JOHN JOHNS (1801–47)

Contributed to Beard's *Collection*, 1837.

Unitarian minister in Liverpool. Working among the poor, he fell a victim during a fever epidemic. A poet and hymn-writer, he published three volumes of verse.

510 REVIVE THY WORK, O LORD

ALBERT MIDLANE (1825–1909)

In the *Evangelist's Hymnbook*, 1860.

An ironmonger in Newport, Isle of Wight, he was known as 'the poet-preacher' of the Strict Brethren, among whom he exercised a regular ministry. He wrote more than 500 hymns, mostly for Sunday schools, and published six volumes.

See also 782.

511 FAR DOWN THE AGES NOW   H. BONAR (see 40)

In *Hymns of Faith and Hope*, 1857.

512 JOY TO THE WORLD   ISAAC WATTS (see 2)

The second part of his paraphrase of Psalm xcviii, 'The Messiah's Coming and Kingdom'. First published in his *Psalms of David Imitated*, 1719.

513 CITY OF GOD   S. JOHNSON (see 57)

With the caption 'The Church, the City of God', in *Hymns of the Spirit*, which he edited with Samuel Longfellow in 1864.

Written at Nice in 1860 on a visit paid with his friend, Samuel Longfellow, the brother of the poet and himself the author of four hymns in *B.C.H.* (see 184). The Kingdom of God within men can be seen at work in the great company of ages who have witnessed for 'freedom, love, many lands and truth'.

514 LIGHT OF THE LONELY PILGRIM'S HEART

EDWARD DENNY (1796–1889)

Sir Edward Denny was born at Tralee Castle, County Kerry, and succeeded his father as 4th baronet in 1831. He owned nearly the whole of the town of Tralee, and his rental income was about £13,000 a year. He was a considerate and popular landlord. The rents of his property were fixed at so just a figure that he was almost the only landlord whose rents were not reduced by the Land Commissioners. Although he was so wealthy he lived usually in a small cottage in Islington, giving liberally to the poor and to religious causes.

A member of the Plymouth Brethren, he gave much time to the study of the prophetical scriptures. This has influenced many of his hymns and made them unsuitable for general use, but 514, and a few others, are more widely used. This hymn first appeared in Deck's *Psalms and Hymns*, 1842.

515 THY KINGDOM COME! ON BENDED KNEE

F. L. HOSMER (see 45)

This noble hymn is one of the very few nineteenth-century hymns which voice the longing for the coming of the Kingdom on earth. He wrote it in 1891, when he was a minister in Cleveland, Ohio, for the commencement of the Meadville Theological School. It was published in the second series of *The Thought of God*, 1894.

516 OUR GOD! OUR GOD! THOU SHINEST HERE

T. H. GILL (see 94)

Written and published in 1846. The author rewrote it for his *Golden Chain*, 1869, heading it 'The glory of the latter days', and adding this quotation from Milton: 'The power of Thy grace has not passed away with primitive times as fond and faithless men imagine, but Thy Kingdom is now at hand, and Thou standest at the door'.

517 JESUS SHALL REIGN WHERE'ER THE SUN

ISAAC WATTS (see 2)

This glorious hymn was first published in his *Psalms of David*, 1719, as the second part of his paraphrase of Psalm lxxii. It is the earliest notable English hymn for overseas missions, and was evidently in advance of current thought since it was scarcely used in the eighteenth century.

It has been sung on many notable occasions. On Whit-Sunday, 1862, it was sung by thousands of South Sea Islanders at a service preparatory to the adoption of a Christian form of government for their Islands. 'It would be impossible to describe the deep feeling manifested. Who so much as they could realize the full meaning of the poet's words? They had been rescued from heathenism and cannibalism, and they were that day met for the first time under a Christian constitution, under a Christian king, and with Christ Himself reigning in the hearts of most of those present. Old and young rejoiced together in the joys of that day, and faces were radiant with Christian joy, love, and hope.'

518 O SPIRIT OF THE LIVING GOD

J. MONTGOMERY (see 13)

Written in 1823 for a public meeting of the Auxiliary Missionary Society of the West Riding of Yorkshire, held in Salem Chapel, Leeds. It was published in his *Christian Psalmist*, 1825, and is used extensively in all English-speaking countries.

519 THE LORD IS KING! LIFT UP THY VOICE
J. CONDER (see 9)

Published in his *Star in the East*, 1824.

520 O CHRIST, OUR TRUE AND ONLY LIGHT
JOHANN HEERMANN (1585–1647)

The son of a Silesian furrier. During a severe illness in his childhood—he was the fifth and only surviving child—his mother vowed to educate him to the ministry if he recovered. He became pastor of Köben in 1611. In 1623 a throat affection began which finally made preaching impossible. Much of his manhood was spent amid the terrors of the Thirty Years War. Köben was sacked four times, devastated by fire in 1616, and by plague in 1631. He lost all his possessions several times, and was often in danger of death, but endured all with patience and courage.

He compiled two hymn-books, and 520 was included in his *Songs of Tears*, 1630, in the section, 'In the time of the persecution and distress of pious Christians'. It is the most widely used of all his hymns. His hymns are marked by depth and tenderness of feeling, firm faith in God, and deep love to Christ. He ranks with the best hymn-writers of his century, and reveals the transition from the objective standpoint of the hymns of the Reformation period to the more subjective and experimental school that followed.

Miss Winkworth published this translation in her *Lyra Germanica*, 1858 (see 11).

521 HAIL TO THE LORD'S ANOINTED
J. MONTGOMERY (see 13)

This 'rich and splendid Messianic hymn' is described by the author as 'an imitation of' Psalm lxxii. It was included in a Christmas ode sung at one of the Moravian settlements in England, probably Fulneck, in Yorkshire, at a Christmas service in 1821. He published it in his *Songs of Zion*, 1822, and it is found in most modern hymnals and has been translated into several languages.

522 LORD GOD OF OUR SALVATION
J. TRITTON (see 461)

Included in the 1880 Supplement to the Baptist *Psalms and Hymns*. It was used at one of the early New Year's Day Prayer Meetings of the B.M.S.—possibly at the first of these meetings in 1880.

523 FROM GREENLAND'S ICY MOUNTAINS
R. HEBER (see 33)

Written when Bishop Heber was rector of Hodnet. Mrs. Heber gives this account of its origin in her 'Memoirs': 'In 1819 a royal letter authorized collections in every church and chapel of England in furtherance of the Eastern operations of the S.P.G. Mr. Heber went to Wrexham to hear the Dean of St. Asaph, his father-in-law, preach on the day appointed, and at his request he wrote this hymn on the Saturday evening. It was first sung in this beautiful church,' and published in the *Christian Observer*, in 1823.

524 LORD OF THE LIVING HARVEST

J. S. B. MONSELL (see 6)

Originally appeared in the second edition of his *Hymns of Love and Praise*, 1866. It is appointed for Ember Days and ordinations.

525 O BROTHERS, LIFT YOUR VOICES

E. H. BICKERSTETH (see 46)

Written by the Bishop of Exeter when he was a curate at Banningham, Norfolk, for the Jubilee of the C.M.S. in 1848. It was printed in the Jubilee Tract in the same year.

526 LET US SING THE KING MESSIAH

JOHN RYLAND (see 103)

This paraphrase of Psalm xlv is dated by Dr. Ryland's son as July 31, 1790. It appeared in 1798 in a collection of hymns used at the monthly meetings of the united congregations of Bristol to pray for the success of the Gospel at home and abroad. It was abbreviated to its present form in the Baptist *New Selection*, 1828.

527 LORD, THY SERVANTS FORTH ARE GOING

W. E. WINKS (see 366)

Written in 1892, for 'the departure of missionaries', when he was minister of Bethany Baptist Chapel, Cardiff. He published it among the hymns written for special services in the second edition of his *Christian Hymns and Songs for Church and Sunday School*, 1907.

528 O'ER THE GLOOMY HILLS OF DARKNESS

WILLIAM WILLIAMS (see 418)

Included in his *Gloria in Excelsis*, a collection of his hymns published at Carmarthen in 1722. Dr. J. Rippon omitted two verses and made other slight alterations when he printed it in *Selection of Hymns for Public Worship*, 1787. This is the form we have here.

The Black Mountains are seen from Pantycelyn, the poet's home, and may be responsible for 'the gloomy hills of darkness' in this hymn. It is a prophetic hymn, published seventy years before William Carey's famous sermon and the founding of the B.M.S.

529 JUDGE ETERNAL, THRONED IN SPLENDOUR
HENRY SCOTT HOLLAND (1847–1918)

This gifted and devoted servant of Christ was educated at Eton and Balliol College. In 1870 he became Senior Student and Rector of Christ Church, Oxford. He was ordained in 1872, and appointed canon of St. Paul's in 1884. In 1908 he was the Romanes lecturer, and from 1910 until his death held the Regius Professorship of Divinity at Oxford.

He wrote several books, mostly theological, but as far as is known this is his only hymn. It embodies the two chief interests of his fruitful life—social reform and missionary work. It appeared in 1902 in *The Commonwealth*, a magazine concerned with the social application of the Christian faith which he edited from 1896 until the end of his life. He was one of the founders of the Christian Social Union. He loved music and did much to improve the musical quality of the services at St. Paul's. He was part-editor of the *New Cathedral Psalter* and of the *English Hymnal*.

530 LORD, HER WATCH THY CHURCH IS KEEPING
H. DOWNTON (see 69)

Written in 1866 at Geneva, where he was resident English chaplain, and first published in D. T. Barry's *Psalms and Hymns*, 1867.

531 O NORTH, WITH ALL THY VALES OF GREEN
WILLIAM CULLEN BRYANT (1794–1878)

Born in Massachusetts. He was called to the Bar in 1815, but ten years later retired from the law and settled in New York, devoting himself to journalism and literature. He founded the *New York Review* and edited for a time the *New York Evening Post*. He was the first in time of the notable American poets, and owed to the hymns of Isaac Watts his first impulse to write poetry. His deep love of nature is reflected in more than a hundred of his poems.

He was certainly no sectarian. After his Congregationalist upbringing he became connected with the Unitarians. In New York he worshipped with the Episcopalians, and with the Presbyterians when at his country home at Long Island. Finally, in 1858, while wintering in Italy, he was baptized by a friend who was a Baptist minister.

His hymns were written at intervals in his long life. They are usually placid and contemplative. Some are in common use. 531 is included in a collection of twenty of his hymns printed in 1869.

See also 660 and 693.

532 GOD OF MERCY, GOD OF GRACE

H. F. LYTE (see 308)

This hymn is based on Psalm lxvii, and was first published in his *Spirit of the Psalms*, 1834.

533 CHRIST FOR THE WORLD WE SING

SAMUEL WOLCOTT (1813–86)

Educated at Yale College and Andover Theological Seminary. In 1840 he went as a missionary to Syria, but two years later ill-health compelled him to come home. He ministered to several Congregational churches and was secretary for some time of the Ohio Home Missionary Society.

He wrote over 200 hymns. 533 is one of the earliest, written when he was fifty-six, in 1869, and is his best known. He composed it on the way home from a service held by the Y.M.C.A.s of Ohio where the rostrum had been decorated with the motto 'Christ for the world, and the world for Christ'.

534 THOU WHOSE ALMIGHTY WORD

JOHN MARRIOTT (1780–1825)

The son of the rector of Cottesbach, near Lutterworth. After his schooldays at Rugby he had a brilliant career at Christ Church, Oxford. In 1804 he was ordained and spent the next four years as a private tutor in the family of the Duke of Buccleuch at Dalkeith. Here he became intimate with Sir Walter Scott, who dedicated to him the second canto of *Marmion*. In 1808 the Duke presented him to the living of Church Lawford, Warwickshire. He retained this until his death, though his wife's ill health compelled him to reside in Devonshire. He was an evangelical preacher and a man of great personal charm.

He wrote several hymns but was too modest to publish them or even to allow them to be quoted. A few appeared in print in his life-time without his permission. This hymn was written about 1813. Six weeks after his death it was quoted at a meeting of the London Missionary Society and deeply impressed the audience. It was printed in the *Evangelical Magazine* of June 1825.

535 FROM NORTH AND SOUTH AND EAST AND WEST

G. T. COSTER (see 49)

The original was written in 1864 and first printed in the *Evangelical Magazine*. It has been considerably altered in later collections.

536 FROM THE EASTERN MOUNTAINS
G. Thring (see 109)

A processional hymn for Epiphany, based on Matthew ii. 2: 'We have seen His star in the East and are come to worship Him'. Written in 1873, it was first published in his *Hymns and Sacred Lyrics*, 1874.

537 SOLDIERS OF THE CROSS, ARISE!
W. W. How (see 192)

First published in Morrell & How's *Psalms and Hymns*, 1854, with seven verses. It is interesting to compare it with C. Wesley's 'Soldiers of Christ, arise!' (394).

538 FATHER, LET THY KINGDOM COME
John Page Hopps (1834–1911)

Educated for the ministry at the Baptist College, Leicester. After two years ministry at Hugglescote and Ibstock, Lincolnshire, he joined George Dawson in 1856 in the pastorate of the Church of the Saviour, Birmingham. He then became a Unitarian and held pastorates in several places, including Leicester and London. He was a vigorous controversialist, and published many books and pamphlets, chiefly volumes of sermons and lectures. In 1863 he founded, and edited, a monthly periodical called *The Truthseeker*. He also compiled a number of hymn-books for congregational or school use.

He wrote several hymns. This one and his most popular children's hymn, 'Father, lead me day by day', were printed in his *Hymns, Chants, and Anthems*, 1877. The evangelical spirit in which he was trained is preserved in many of his hymns.

See also 758.

539 LIFT UP YOUR HEADS, REJOICE
T. T. Lynch (see 70)

From the second edition of *The Rivulet*, 1856, a collection of the author's hymns.

540 THY KINGDOM COME, O GOD
Lewis Hensley (1824–1905)

Educated at Trinity College, Cambridge. Graduated in 1846 as Senior Wrangler and Smith's Prizeman, Fellow and assistant tutor of Trinity College, 1846–52. Took Holy Orders in 1851. He was Vicar of Hitchin in 1856, became an honorary canon of St. Alban's in 1881. Two collections of his hymns were published, in 1864 and 1867. This Advent hymn is from the second collection, which is entitled *Hymns for the Minor Sundays*.

541 HARK! THE SONG OF JUBILEE
J. MONTGOMERY (see 13)

Composed at the request of the London Missionary Society to mark the acceptance of the Gospel by the Georgian Isles of the South Seas. The author made several alterations in the second line of ver. 2. His final authorized text is 'From the depths unto the skies'. It was first published in the *Evangelical Magazine* in 1818.

542 SEE HOW GREAT A FLAME ASPIRES
C. WESLEY (see 4)

In Jackson's *Memoirs of the Rev. C. Wesley*, 1848, there is this comment on the hymn, under the date November 1746: 'This animated and emphatic hymn was written on the joyful occasion of his ministerial success, and that of his fellow labourers, in Newcastle and its vicinity. Perhaps the imagery was suggested by the large fires connected with the collieries, which illuminate the whole of that part of the country in the darkest night.' It was published in *Hymns and Sacred Poems*, 1746.

543 OH COME, OH COME, IMMANUEL
Translated by J. M. NEALE

In the early centuries of Christian worship, sentences, usually from scripture, were introduced into the Liturgy, to be read or chanted before and after certain portions of the service. These were given the name antiphons. Among these are the Seven Greater Antiphons for use at vespers in Advent, beginning on December 17, and sung before and after the Magnificat. They are still used in the Roman Church. About the twelfth century an unknown author wove five of these prose antiphons into a hymn, beginning with 'Veni, veni, Emmanuel', and adding a refrain to each verse. Dr. Neale's translation, 'Oh come, Oh come, Immanuel', was published in the first edition of his *Medieval Hymns*, 1851.

544 GATHER US IN, THOU LOVE THAT FILLEST ALL
G. MATHESON (see 255)

Written at Row, Dumbartonshire, in 1890, and included in his *Sacred Songs*, 1890. He entitles it 'One in Christ', based on Ephesians i. 10, and it is typical of his original and catholic mind.

545 HILLS OF THE NORTH, REJOICE
CHARLES EDWARD OAKLEY (1832–65)

Educated at Oxford, where he graduated in 1855. From 1859–60 he was examiner in the School of Jurisprudence and for degrees in Civil Law, and was appointed Special Preacher in 1860 and 1862. He took Holy Orders in 1855, and after seven years as rector of Wickwar he became, in 1863, rector of St. Paul's, Covent Garden. His brief pastoral charge here was made memorable by his impressive eloquence and by his saintly life.

This hymn for Advent or the Epiphany appeared in Bishop T. V. French's *Hymns adapted to the Christian Seasons*, and hence passed into the *Hymnal Companion*, 1870. It is the only hymn preserved from his brief and brilliant life, and its merit has given it a place in many hymnals.

546 GOD IS WORKING HIS PURPOSE OUT
ARTHUR CAMPBELL AINGER (1841–1919)

Son of the Rev. T. Ainger, vicar of Hampstead. Born at Blackheath, London. Educated at Eton and Trinity College, Cambridge, gaining a First Class in the Classical Tripos, 1864. From then until 1901 he was an assistant master at Eton. One tribute to him states that 'he was one of the most distinguished of Eton masters, a man of clear head, wide accomplishments, a fine scholar with a remarkable memory . . . his justice, courtesy, and unruffled good humour won the respect and admiration of the boys'.

He was joint author of an *English-Latin Verse Dictionary*, and wrote *Eton Songs*, 1901–2, and many other poems. Some of his hymns are in common use. This one, based on Habakkuk ii. 14, was written and first printed in 1894.

547 I CANNOT TELL WHY HE, WHOM ANGELS WORSHIP
WILLIAM YOUNG FULLERTON (1857–1932)

Dr. Fullerton was brought up among the Irish Presbyterians. It was a visit of D. L. Moody to Belfast in 1874 which made him realize that he was called to be an evangelist. When he came to business in London in 1875 he worshipped at the Metropolitan Tabernacle and joined the Baptist communion. He became a close friend of C. H. Spurgeon and wrote his biography. After a course of study at Spurgeon's College he entered on evangelistic work with Mr. Manton Smith, and from 1879–94 led missions in every part of the British Isles with wonderful success. He then accepted the pastorate of the church of Melbourne Hall, Leicester, where he exercised a fruitful and memorable ministry.

For many years he was a member of the B.M.S. Committee, and became Home Secretary of the B.M.S. in 1912. He was called to the Presidency of the Baptist Union in 1917. McMaster University gave him the D.D. degree in 1927. He wrote many devotional and expository books, and several biographies, including his own. He travelled widely and was honoured in the evangelical churches of many lands.

A few of his hymns have been preserved. This one is the best known.

548 THERE'S A LIGHT UPON THE MOUNTAINS
HENRY BURTON (1840–1930)

Born at Swannington, Leicestershire. His parents emigrated to Wisconsin, and he entered Beloit College, where he graduated. After a brief ministry in the Methodist Episcopal Church he came back to England, entered the Wesleyan ministry in 1865, and worked chiefly in Lancashire and London. He married a sister of the Rev. Mark Guy Pearse.

This hymn is included in his *Wayside Songs*, 1886. He also published a collection of his poems and hymns in 1929, entitled *Songs of the Highway*. Many of his hymns are in common use, and include 'In the secret of His presence', and 'Have you had a kindness shown? Pass it on.'

See also 703.

549 SWEET IS THE WORK
ISAAC WATTS (see 2)

Based on Psalm xcii, and first published in his *Psalms of David*, 1719.

550 THOU GLORIOUS SUN OF RIGHTEOUSNESS
C. ELLIOTT (see 137)

An abbreviated form of a hymn from her *Morning and Evening Hymns for a Week*, printed in 1839 for sale on behalf of a school in Brighton for the daughters of clergymen.

551 THE DAWN OF GOD'S DEAR SABBATH
ADA CROSS (1844–1926)

Born at St. Germains, Norfolk. Married G. F. Cross in 1869, who, after ordination, moved to Australia, where he served in various parishes. Her hymns are marked by purity of rhythm, and by their naturalness and simplicity.

This hymn is included in her *Hymns on the Holy Communion*. She also wrote *Hymns on the Litany* and contributed to *Lays of the Pious Minstrels* and to *English Lyrics*.

552 O DAY OF REST AND GLADNESS
C. WORDSWORTH (see 105)

Written when Canon of Westminster. It is the opening hymn in *The Holy Year*, 1862, a volume of hymns for every season of the Church's year. Based on Psalm xcviii. 24, 'This is the day the Lord hath made'.

553 THE DAY OF RESURRECTION!

St. John of Damascus (eighth century)

The last but one of the Fathers of the Greek Church, and the greatest of her poets. A native of Damascus he took service under the Caliph. This he relinquished to enter a desolate monastery near Jerusalem. This was the centre of a school of hymn-writers, and here he wrote his theological works and his hymns. He brought renewed inspiration to Greek hymnody, strongly influencing its form and theological character, and its music. His hymns are still used in the Service Books of the Greek Church. He died at a great age, probably in 780.

No. 553 is the first of eight odes which form the great hymn known as 'The Golden Canon', used in the Easter Day Office of the Greek Church. Dr. Neale's free translation was published in his *Hymns of the Eastern Church*, 1862. It is a hymn of joyous triumph. The reference in ver. 2 is to St. Matthew xxviii. 9: 'Jesus met them, saying, "All Hail"'.

554 THIS IS THE DAY OF LIGHT   J. Ellerton (see 21)

Written in 1867, and published for use in Chester Cathedral in *Hymns for Special Occasions and Festivals*.

555 HAIL! SACRED DAY OF EARTHLY REST

G. Thring (see 109)

Written in 1863. Not originally intended for public worship, but adapted by the author and Bishop W. W. How. Based on Psalm xcviii. 24.

556 OUR DAY OF PRAISE IS DONE J. Ellerton (see 21)

Composed in 1867 for the Nantwich Choral Festival. Published in its present form 1871.

557 AGAIN AS EVENING'S SHADOW FALLS

S. Longfellow (see 184)

Taken from his *Vespers*, printed in 1859 for congregational use.

558 AT EVEN, ERE THE SUN WAS SET

H. Twells (see 190)

Written in 1868, when he was headmaster of Godolphin School, Hammersmith, while invigilating at an examination. In some hymnals the first line is altered to 'At even, *when* the sun was set' (cf. St. Mark i. 32), because such a gathering was unlawful among the Jews until the sun had set and the Sabbath ended. The *B.C.H.* preserves the original line. This hymn is found in 157 hymnals by 1898.

559 AND NOW THE WANTS ARE TOLD
WILLIAM BRIGHT (1824–1901)

Educated at University College, Oxford, and became Fellow and tutor of his College. Took Holy Orders, 1848. In 1868 became Regius Professor of Ecclesiastical History and Canon of Christ Church. His publications include works on Church history, a collection of ancient collects, and a translation of St. Leo the Great's sermons on the Incarnation. Also a book of private prayers for a week and *Hymns and Other Poems* (1866), in which this hymn is included.

560 THE LORD BE WITH US AS WE BEND
J. ELLERTON (see 21)

Written in 1870, for use at a Sunday afternoon service, when a strictly evening hymn would be unsuitable.

561 ANOTHER SABBATH ENDED
THOMAS VINCENT TYMMS (1842–1921)

Trained for the Baptist ministry at Regent's Park College. Pastorates at Berwick-on-Tweed and Accrington. In 1869 began his notable twenty-two years' ministry at the Downs Chapel, Clapton. He was a born leader of men and the church became the centre of virile educational and missionary work. Among those inspired to service by him were Holman Bentley, Oram, and Teichmann. He was Principal of Rawdon College, 1891–1904, and President of the Baptist Union, 1896. Dr. Tymms was a man of devout spirit and cultured mind. His apologetic writings include *The Mystery of God*, a book on the Atonement, and works on Baptism.

This hymn is among those he contributed to the supplement to the Baptist *Psalms and Hymns*, 1880. Some of his hymns are included in the Baptist *Psalms and Hymns for School and Home*, 1882.

562 THE DAY THOU GAVEST, LORD, IS ENDED
J. ELLERTON (see 21)

Written in 1870 for 'A liturgy for missionary meetings', and revised for *Church Hymns*, 1871. Chosen by Queen Victoria to be sung at her Diamond Jubilee Service in Westminster Abbey.

563 SAVIOUR, AGAIN TO THY DEAR NAME WE RAISE
J. ELLERTON (see 21)

Written in 1866 for the Nantwich Choral Association. Revised for *Hymns Ancient and Modern*, 1868. The last verse was sung at his funeral at Torquay.

This 'most delicate, beautiful, and tender' hymn ranks with Keble's 'Sun of my soul', Ken's 'Glory to Thee, my God, this night', and Lyle's 'Abide with me' as one of the great evening hymns of the Christian Church.

564 O SAVIOUR, BLESS US ERE WE GO
F. W. FABER (see 42)

First published in his *Jesus and Mary*, 1849, for use as an evening hymn at Brompton Oratory, of which he was then Superior. The original is slightly altered and its last verse omitted as unsuitable for Protestant use.

565 BE THY WORD WITH POWER FRAUGHT
T. T. LYNCH (see 70)

Published in the first edition of *The Rivulet*, 1855, a collection of his hymns. Intended to be sung before the sermon.

566 LORD, DISMISS US WITH THY BLESSING   ANON

First appeared in a supplement to the *Shawbury Hymn Book*, 1773.

567 HOW LOVELY ARE THY DWELLINGS, LORD
JOHN MILTON (see 15)

His *Nine Psalms done into Metre* was published 1648. They were Psalms lxxx–lxxxviii. This hymn is a cento from Psalm lxxxiv.

568 WE LOVE THE PLACE, O GOD
WILLIAM BULLOCK (1798–1874)

Educated at Christ's Hospital, and entered Royal Navy. While serving under his brother, Admiral Frederic Bullock, on a survey of the coast of Newfoundland, he resolved to take holy orders and to serve as a missionary to that colony. He worked there under the S.P.G. for thirty-two years, became Dean of Halifax, Nova Scotia, where he published in 1854 his *Songs of the Church*. All his hymns were 'written amidst the various scenes of missionary life, and are intended for the private and domestic use of Christians in new countries deprived of all public worship'.

He composed this hymn in 1827 for the dedication of the church at Trinity Bay, Newfoundland, of which he was the rector. It is based on Psalm xxvi. 8: 'Lord, I have loved the habitation of Thy house'. Only his first two verses are used in this version. Verses 3–5 were added by Sir H. W. Baker, principal editor of *Hymns Ancient and Modern*, 1861. He is known to hymnody principally through this revised and popular hymn.

569 OH, SEND THY LIGHT FORTH AND THY TRUTH
Rous and Barton (see 62)

This version of Psalm xliii. 3–5 is based on their Puritan version of the Psalter.

570 HOW HONOURED, HOW DEAR   J. Conder (see 9)

Psalm lxxxiv. The most popular of his versions of the Psalms. Published 1824.

571 LORD, WE COME BEFORE THEE NOW
William Hammond (1719–83)

Educated at St. John's College, Cambridge. In 1743 joined the Calvinistic Methodists, but in 1745, on moving to London, united with the Moravians. He is buried in the Moravian burial ground, Sloane Street, Chelsea.

Some of his translations of Latin hymns were printed with original hymns in his *Psalms and Hymns*, 1745. They are marked by earnestness and scriptural fidelity, and a few have attained a foremost position among English hymns. This hymn was abridged to its present form by M. Madan in 1760.

572 PRAISE, LORD, FOR THEE IN ZION WAITS
H. F. Lyte (see 308)

Psalm lxv. From *The Spirit of the Psalms*, 1834, written for use in his own church at Lower Brixham, where he was Perpetual Curate.

573 HOSANNA TO THE LIVING LORD
R. Heber (see 33)

For Advent Sunday. A revised form of a hymn he wrote in 1811, when he was vicar of Hodnet, accompanying a letter of protest against the familiarity assumed by some hymn-writers with the Divine and with divine things. It is included in the collection of his hymns published in 1827 after his death.

574 LORD GOD, THE HOLY GHOST
J. Montgomery (see 13)

A Whit-Sunday hymn. Published in 1819 in Cotterill's *Selection of Psalms and Hymns*.

575 COME, YE DISCONSOLATE, WHERE'ER YE
LANGUISH   THOMAS MOORE (1779–1852)

Born in Dublin, son of a grocer and wine-merchant. Educated
at a private school and Trinity College, Dublin. Read for the Bar
at the Middle Temple. Held a post under the government in
Bermuda for a short time. His first volume of poetry was published
in 1801, his second in 1806. His sparkling wit, social gifts, and
musical accomplishments made him a favourite in London Society.
He retired to Derbyshire and there wrote *National Airs*, *Sacred
Songs*, *Irish Melodies*, and *Lalla Rookh*. In later life, spent in
retirement near Devizes, he experienced heavy domestic trials.
His memoirs, journal, and correspondence were published by
Lord John Russell in 1855.

This hymn is included in his *Thirty-two sacred songs written to
the popular airs of various nations*, 1816. Alterations and additions
were made by Dr. T. Hastings in *Spiritual Songs for Social Worship*,
1832.

576 WHEN THE WEARY, SEEKING REST

H. BONAR (see 40)

From *Hymns of Faith and Hope*, published 1866, with the last
verse omitted. The refrain is based on Solomon's prayer in
2 Chronicles vi. 29, 30.

577 HOW PLEASED AND BLEST WAS I

ISAAC WATTS (see 2)

A paraphrase of Psalm cxxii, published 1719 in his *Psalms of
David*.

578 LORD OF THE WORLDS ABOVE ISAAC WATTS (see 2)

A rendering of Psalm lxxxiv which ranks among the best of his
paraphrases of the Psalms. Published in his *Psalms of David*, 1719.

579 PRAISE, MY SOUL, THE KING OF HEAVEN

H. F. LYTE (see 308)

Psalm ciii. One of his most successful paraphrases of the Psalms,
and more jubilant than most of his renderings. Published in his
Spirit of the Psalms, 1834. In some hymnals line 5 in each verse is
altered to 'Alleluia, Alleluia'.

580 PLEASANT ARE THY COURTS ABOVE

H. F. LYTE (see 308)

A free paraphrase of Psalm lxxxiv. Published in *Spirit of the
Psalms*, 1834.

581 OUR HEAVENLY FATHER CALLS

P. DODDRIDGE (see 55)

Among his MSS., but undated. Printed in the posthumous edition of his hymns, 1755.

582 BEHOLD THE THRONE OF GRACE

J. NEWTON (see 146)

Written when curate of Olney, Bucks. It is found in *Olney Hymns*, 1779, but abridged. Based on 1 Kings iii. 5.

583 JESUS, WE LOOK TO THEE   C. WESLEY (see 4)

An abridged form of a hymn published in his *Hymns and Sacred Poems*, 1749.

584 GREAT IS THY MERCY, LORD

G. B. BUBIER (see 258)

Written in 1854 towards the end of his ministry in Cambridge. Published in *Hymns and Sacred Songs for Sunday School and Social Worship*, 1855.

585 FATHER OF MEN, IN WHOM ARE ONE

HENRY CARY SHUTTLEWORTH (1850–1900)

Educated at the Forest School, Walthamstow, and St. Mary's Hall, Oxford. Ordained 1873. Chaplain at Christ Church, Oxford. Appointed minor canon of St. Paul's, 1876–84, and rector of St. Nicolas, Cole Abbey, London, from 1883. He held the Professorship of Pastoral and Liturgical Theology, and was a lecturer in Ecclesiastical History, English Literature, and the New Testament at King's College, London. He was 'a red-hot ritualist' and a prominent Christian Socialist of the school of Maurice and Kingsley. G. W. E. Russell writes that he was enthusiastic, buoyant, light-hearted, and devoted to his church and parish.

His publications include *Songs*, 1855, *The Place of Music in Public Worship*, second edition, 1893, and *Hymns for Private Use*, 1896, which is a small appendix to *Church Hymns* for use in St. Nicolas' Church, where he was rector. In these several of his own hymns appear.

No. 585 appeared, with music by the author, in the *Church Monthly*, 1898. It is headed 'Friendly Societies'.

586 JESUS! STAND AMONG US

WILLIAM PENNEFATHER (1816–73)

Born in Dublin, son of Richard Pennefather, Baron of the Irish Court of Exchequer. Educated at Westbury College, Bristol, and at Levans Parsonage, Kendal. Graduated Trinity College, Dublin, 1840. Ordained 1841. After serving as curate and vicar in Ireland he moved to England and held incumbencies at Walton, 1848, Barnet, 1852, and Mildway Park, 1864. He organized conferences at Barnet and Mildmay. At Mildmay he founded and super-intended large religious and charitable organizations and introduced into England the Order of Deaconesses. He was a man of saintly character and his life impressed Francis Ridley Havergal as 'illustrating in a peculiar degree the power of holiness'.

His hymns were mainly written for the Barnet and Mildmay Conferences, published as leaflets. For the 1872 Conference twenty-five were included in a pamphlet entitled *Hymns Original and Selected*. They are rich in evangelical doctrine and feeling, simply and musically written.

This hymn had been used at his conferences, but was not published until after his death. It is included in *Seventy-one Original Hymns and Thoughts in Verse*.

587 O GOD, WHO DIDST THY WILL UNFOLD

J. CONDER (see 9)

Entitled 'Holy Scriptures'. Published in *The Congregational Hymnbook*, 1836, of which he was the editor.

588 FROM EVERY STORMY WIND THAT BLOWS

HUGH STOWELL (1799–1865)

Graduated at St. Edmund's Hall, Oxford, 1822. Ordained 1823. Curate at Shepscombe, Glos., and at Holy Trinity, Huddersfield. Rector of Christ Church, Salford, from 1831 till his death. Appointed Rural Dean of Chester, and hon. canon of Chester Cathedral, 1845. A *Memoir* of him published 1868.

He was a powerful and effective preacher. Bishop Blomfield licensed him to the Salford charge with great hesitation as the young Manxman had the reputation of being 'an extemporaneous fire-brand'. In a few weeks there was no standing room in his church. He wrote on religious subjects, in prose and verse, sermons and pamphlets, and became a public force in Manchester and one of the leaders of the Evangelical school in the Anglican Communion. His love for children was intense and his enormous Sunday schools his especial pride.

He published a *Selection of Psalms and Hymns* in 1831 containing nine of his own, and added about thirty more in the 1864 edition. All were written for the anniversary services of his Sunday schools at Salford. His children's hymns are his most successful.

He headed this hymn 'The Mercy Seat'. It appeared in 1828, but he rewrote it in its present form for his 1831 *Selection*.

See also 764.

589 PRAYER IS THE SOUL'S SINCERE DESIRE

J. Montgomery (see 13)

Written in 1818, at the request of the Rev. E. Bickersteth, for his *Treatise on Prayer*. First printed in 1818, together with three other of his hymns on prayer, for the use of Nonconformist Sunday schools in Sheffield. This great hymn teaches the principle and practice of prayer with truth and power, and he received more testimonies to the benefit derived from it than about any other he wrote.

590 LORD, I HEAR THE SHOWERS OF BLESSING

Elizabeth Codner (1824–1919)

Born at Dartmouth. Married the Rev. David Codner, an Anglican clergyman. She was associated for many years with the Rev. W. and Mrs. Pennefather at the Mildmay Mission. She edited a monthly magazine called *Women's Work*, and published several small books.

An account of religious revival in Ireland prompted her to write this hymn, in 1860, for a group of children, in the hope that they might share the blessings experienced in Ireland. 'I had no thought of sending it beyond the limits of my own circle, but passing it on to one and another it became a word of power, and I then published it as a pamphlet.' It was written at Weston-super-Mare, and printed in *The Revival*.

591 WHAT A FRIEND WE HAVE IN JESUS

Joseph Medlicott Scriven (1819–86)

An Irish graduate of Trinity College, Dublin, who settled in Ontario, 1845, and lived the remainder of his life there. He won high esteem for his kindness and self sacrifice. He lived to help people, and was pointed out as 'the man who saws wood for poor widows and sick people who are unable to pay'. The people helped by him, and the people of the district, erected a monument to his memory near Rice Lake.

Ira D. Sankey, in *My Life and Sacred Songs*, 1906, writes that 'a neighbour, sitting up with Joseph Scriven in an illness, happened upon this hymn in MS. Reading it with great delight, he found Mr. S. had written it to comfort his mother in a time of special sorrow, not intending anyone else to see it.' There is no trace of any other hymn composed by him, but according to Dr. A. W. Mahon, in *Canadian Hymns and Hymn-writers*, this has become the most popular contribution to Canadian hymnody.

592 COME, MY SOUL, THY SUIT PREPARE

J. Newton (see 146)

Published in *Olney Hymns*, 1779. C. H. Spurgeon often had ver. 1 or ver. 2, or both, sung very softly before the main prayer of the service.

593 LIGHT OF LIFE, SERAPHIC FIRE C. WESLEY (see 4)

An abridged form of a hymn published in *Hymns and Sacred Poems*, 1749.

594 SWEETLY THE HOLY HYMN
CHARLES HADDON SPURGEON (1834–92)

The world-famous preacher was born at Kelvedon, Essex, in 1834, where his father was the Congregational minister. Educated at Colchester and St. Augustine's College, Maidstone, and acted as usher in schools at Newmarket and Cambridge. Minister of the Waterbeach Baptist Church, 1851. Called in 1854 to New Park Street Baptist Church, London, where Dr. Rippon and Dr. Gill had ministered. The building proved inadequate to hold the crowds who came to hear him, and the Exeter Hall and then the Surrey music-hall were used for worship until the erection of the Metropolitan Tabernacle.

He is chiefly known as a preacher mightily used of God, and as the author of many volumes of sermons, expositions, and other homiletical literature. But his activities were almost boundless, and include the founding of Spurgeon's College and of the Stockwell Orphanage.

In 1866 he compiled *Our Own Hymnbook* for the use of the congregation at the Tabernacle. Twenty of his hymns, including this one, and versions of the Psalms are in this hymnal.

595 WHERESOEVER TWO OR THREE J. CONDER (see 9)

Published in *The Congregational Hymnbook*, 1836, of which he was the editor.

596 LORD, WHEN WE BEND BEFORE THY THRONE
JOSEPH DACRE CARLYLE (1758–1804)

Sometime Professor of Arabic at Cambridge, and later vicar of Newcastle. In 1799 he accompanied the Earl of Elgin to Constantinople to explore the literary treasures of the city's library. Among his MSS. were '*Poems*, suggested chiefly by scenes in Asia Minor, Syria, etc.', published 1805. He also published *Specimens of Arabian Poetry*, 1796. His hymns appeared in the *Psalms and Hymns*, 1802, of John Fawcett, an intimate friend.

This is the first hymn in the book and was originally written as an introductory hymn to public worship for use at St. Cuthbert's Church, Carlisle, where he regularly attended when in residence as Chancellor of Carlisle.

597 THOU WHO OUR FAITHLESS HEARTS CANST READ JAMES BALDWIN BROWN (1820–84)

Born at the Inner Temple, the son of J. B. Brown, himself a hymn-writer. Graduated at University College, London, 1839.

Notes on the Hymns and Their Authors

For a short time he studied for the Bar, but soon entered Highbury College to train for the Congregational ministry. He held pastorates at Derby, 1843, and Clapham Road, London, 1846. In 1870 his congregation moved to a new chapel in Brixton. In 1878 he was elected Chairman of the Congregational Union.

His prose writings were numerous, but he is known to hymnology chiefly through this hymn, entitled 'For the increase of faith'.

598 O FOUNT OF GRACE THAT RUNNETH O'ER
JANE CREWDSON (see 238)

Probably from *A Little While, and Other Poems*, written during her long illness and published in 1864, after her death.

599 WHEN COLD OUR HEARTS AND FAR FROM THEE
J. S. B. MONSELL (see 6)

From his *Hymns and Miscellaneous Poems*, published in Dublin, 1837.

600 BEHOLD US, LORD, A LITTLE SPACE
J. ELLERTON (see 21)

Written in 1870 'for use at a midday service in a city church'. It must be one of the earliest hymns in which science and art and commerce are mentioned and recognized as having a place in God's providence.

601 HEAL US, IMMANUEL! WE ARE HERE
W. COWPER (see 60)

Published in the *Olney Hymns*, 1779, in six verses.

602 THERE IS NO SORROW, LORD, TOO LIGHT
JANE CREWDSON (see 238)

An altered version of a hymn entitled 'Divine Sympathy'. Published posthumously in *A Little While, and Other Poems*, 1864.

603 OH, HELP US, LORD, EACH HOUR OF NEED
H. H. MILMAN (see 102)

This hymn, a 'piece of pure, deep devotion', was among the thirteen hymns he contributed to Heber's *Hymns*, 1827.

604 THOU GRACIOUS POWER, WHOSE MERCY LENDS
O. W. HOLMES (see 39)

Each year he wrote a poem for the annual reunion of his old college class. This is the eighteenth of the series and was written in 1869.

605 WITH THE SWEET WORD OF PEACE

GEORGE WATSON (1816–98)

In business in London as a printer until 1866. From his office, and with his co-operation, originated *The Band of Hope Review*, in 1851, and *The British Workman*, in 1855, which were pioneers of cheap illustrated publications. He was a Congregationalist. His hymn-writing was limited. Two appeared in Paxton Hood's *Our Hymnbook*, 1868. This one was written in 1867 as a hymn of farewell to Paxton Hood when the latter was leaving his Brighton church for a long period of rest and change. He revised it for general use in 1871.

606 NOW MAY HE, WHO FROM THE DEAD

J. NEWTON (see 146)

Printed in *Olney Hymns*, 1779.

607 PART IN PEACE! CHRIST'S LIFE WAS PEACE

S. F. ADAMS (see 71)

First published in her *Vivia Perpetua*, 1841, a drama of Christian martyrdom. At the close of Act iii. the persecuted Christians, in a dimly lighted cave, hear that the edict has gone forth that they must perish. Before parting, possibly never to meet again, they all sing this hymn.

608 FORTH IN THY NAME, O LORD, I GO

C. WESLEY (see 4)

Entitled 'For believers before work'. First published in *Hymns and Sacred Poems*, 1749. John McNeill, the evangelist, used to hear his father repeat the first verse with his hand on the latch of the door as he set out to his work at the quarry shortly after five in the morning.

609 LORD GOD OF MORNING AND OF NIGHT

F. T. PALGRAVE (see 285)

Written in 1862, the year after he published his *Golden Treasury of English Lyrics*. It was given in MS. to Lord Selborne, who included it in his *Book of Praise*, 1862.

610 AWAKE, MY SOUL, AND WITH THE SUN

THOMAS KEN (1637–1711)

Scholar of Winchester. Fellow of New College, Oxford, 1657, and of Winchester, 1666. Chaplain to Princess Mary at The Hague, 1679. Returned to Winchester, 1680. Bishop of Bath and Wells, 1681. Deprived 1691. Died at Longleat, 1710 or 1711.

His parents died when he was young, and he was brought up by his brother-in-law, Isaak Walton. He was a man of firm principle. He was dismissed by Princess Mary for his protest against a case of immorality at the Court. When Charles II visited Winchester, Ken refused Nell Gwynne the use of his house. After the Battle of Sedgemoor, he interceded with the King for the prisoners, gave with great generosity to relieve the sufferers, and attended Monmouth on the scaffold. He was one of the seven bishops who refused to read the Declaration of Indulgence, and James sent him to the Tower. When William III came to the throne, he refused to take the oaths, and was deprived of his See. His charities had left him a poor man, and Lord Weymouth gave him hospitality at Longleat until his death.

There was in his character an unusual mingling of firmness and conciliation. He could stand like a rock, yet be gentle, modest, and loving. His saintliness was such that Macaulay could describe him 'as near as human infirmity permits to the ideal perfection of Christian character'.

His poetical works were published in 1721, after his death. They include *Hymns for the Festivals*, which are said to have suggested to Keble the idea of *The Christian Year*. These hymns are full of tender devotion, but are not equal in style and strength to the three great hymns for morning, evening, and midnight, which he wrote for the private devotions of the scholars of Winchester College. This hymn is a shortened version of the morning hymn. It was printed with the 1709 edition of his manual for the scholars of Winchester College, and originally ended, as 620 ends, with the Doxology.

See also 620.

611 O JESUS, LORD OF HEAVENLY GRACE

ST. AMBROSE (340–397)

Son of Ambrosius, a Christian Prefect of the Gauls. He entered the law, and in 374 became Governor of Liguria, North Italy, residing in Milan. Soon after, a new Bishop of Milan had to be elected. Feeling ran high between the followers of the Arian and of the Catholic candidates. As civil magistrate, Ambrose had to intervene. His personality so deeply impressed the multitude that they clamoured for his election as Bishop. He was consecrated in 374. He achieved an outstanding reputation as scholar, statesman, and orator, and was a brilliant defender of the faith against the Arians. His preaching proved a decisive influence in St. Augustine's life.

He introduced from the Eastern Church the antiphonal chanting of psalms and hymns and collected and used simple, melodious tunes for congregational song. His own hymns are marked by severity and depth. A large number have been attributed to him, but the Benedictine editors of Ambrose accept only twelve as genuine. This is one of them. It was translated by John Chandler and published in his *Hymns of the Primitive Church*, 1837.

See also 616.

612 NEW EVERY MORNING IS THE LOVE

J. KEBLE (see 53)

A cento from the original hymn written in 1822 and published in *The Christian Year*, 1827.

613 CHRIST, WHOSE GLORY FILLS THE SKIES

C. WESLEY (see 4)

First published in the Wesleys' *Hymns and Spiritual Songs*, 1740. Described by James Montgomery as 'one of Charles Wesley's loveliest progeny'.

614 BEGIN THE DAY WITH GOD   H. BONAR (see 40)

Written while minister of the Free Church of Scotland in Kelso, and published in his *Hymns of Faith and Hope*, 1861.

615 RISE, MY SOUL, ADORE THY MAKER

J. CENNICK (see 168)

Published in *Sacred Hymns for the Children of God* in 1741, when he was working with George Whitefield.

616 NOW THAT THE SUN IS GLEAMING BRIGHT

ANON

Jam lucis orto sidere. Wrongly ascribed to St. Ambrose. First found in eighth-century German MSS. Translated by J. H. Newman in his *Verses on Religious Subjects*, and dated 'Littlemore, 1842', three years before he was received into the Roman Church.

617 O LORD OF LIFE, THY QUICKENING VOICE

G. MACDONALD (see 276)

From *The Disciples, and Other Poems*, 1860.

618 MY SOUL, AWAKE! JANE ELIZABETH LIVOCK (1840–1925)

Written in 1880 in Norwich, for a prize competition in the *Sunday School Chronicle*. Included in the *Congregational Church Hymnal*, 1887.

619 TO THEE, MY GOD AND SAVIOUR

T. Haweis (see 333)

Published in *Hymns to the Saviour*, 1792, a companion volume to the *Select Collection of Hymns* compiled by the Countess of Huntingdon for use in the churches of her connexion.

620 ALL PRAISE TO THEE, MY GOD, THIS NIGHT

T. Ken (see 610)

Composed of selected verses from the evening hymn printed in the 1709 edition of his *Manual* for the use of the scholars of Winchester College.

621 O LIGHT OF LIFE, O SAVIOUR DEAR

F. T. Palgrave (see 285)

Written in 1865, and included in his *Hymns*, 1867.

622 SUN OF MY SOUL, THOU SAVIOUR DEAR

J. Keble (see 53)

A cento from ' 'Tis gone, that bright and orbèd blaze', dated 1820, and published in *The Christian Year*, 1827. Based on the words of St. Luke xxiv. 29: 'Abide with us, for it is toward evening'. The opening verses of the original hymn picture the fading evening light, and the traveller pressing on alone and in the darkness. Then follows 'Sun of my soul, Thou Saviour dear. It is not night if Thou be near.'

623 AS DARKER, DARKER FALL AROUND

Anon

This anonymous hymn first appeared in William Young's *Catholic Choralist*, 1842, in 13 verses, as 'Hymn of Calabrian Shepherds'.

624 THE TWILIGHT FALLS, THE NIGHT IS NEAR

Anon

An anonymous hymn in Cheever's *Commonplace Book of American Poetry*, 1831.

625 SAVIOUR, BREATHE AN EVENING BLESSING

J. Edmeston (see 417)

Published in *Sacred Lyrics*, 1820. It is thus introduced: 'At night the native Christians' evening hymn—"Jesus, forgive us"—stole through the camp' (Salte's *Travels in Abyssinia*).

626 FATHER, IN HIGH HEAVEN DWELLING
G. RAWSON (see 179)

Published in *The Leeds Hymnbook*, 1853, which he helped the Congregational ministers of Leeds to compile. It is based on part of the Lord's Prayer.

627 FATHER OF LOVE AND POWER G. RAWSON (see 179)

Published in *The Leeds Hymnbook*, 1853. In an MS. note to this hymn the author states that finding he had unconsciously given three lines from ver. 3 of Marriott's 'Thou, whose almighty Word' (*B.C.H.*, 534), he would substitute:

> 'Spirit of holiness,
> Gentle, transforming grace,
> Indwelling light.'

628 GOD THE FATHER, BE THOU NEAR
G. RAWSON (see 179)

Published in the Baptist *Psalms and Hymns*, 1858.

629 HOW CALMLY THE EVENING ONCE MORE IS DESCENDING
T. T. LYNCH (see 70)

Published in *The Rivulet*, 1855, a collection of hymns for the use of his own congregation.

630 THE DAY DEPARTS   J. A. FREYLINGHAUSEN (see 321)

Written in 1704. Translated by Miss Jane Borthwick and printed in *The Family Treasury*, 1861.

631 THE DAY IS GENTLY SINKING TO A CLOSE
C. WORDSWORTH (see 105)

It was printed separately from his *Holy Year* and was pasted into the unsold copies of the third edition of that work, 1863.

632 THE RADIANT MORN HATH PASSED AWAY
G. THRING (see 109)

Written in 1864, when he was rector of Alford-with-Hornblotton, Somerset. Under date of August 24, 1899, he asked the hymnal committee of the S.P.C.K. to substitute for the second verse:

> Our life is but an autumn sun,
>   Its glorious noon how quickly past!
> Lead us, O Christ, our life-work done,
>   Safe home at last.

633 THE SUN IS SINKING FAST ANON

From an anonymous Latin hymn '*Sol praeceps rapitur*'. The original has not been discovered, but it is probably not older than the eighteenth century. Caswall paraphrases and expands the hymn and includes it in his *Masque of Mary*, 1858.

634 THE ROSEATE HUES OF EARLY DAWN
C. F. ALEXANDER (see 131)

Appeared in S.P.C.K. *Hymns*, 1852.

635 THE SHADOWS OF THE EVENING HOURS
A. A. PROCTER (see 327)

Included in her *Legends and Lyrics*, 1862.

636 GOD THAT MADEST EARTH AND HEAVEN
R. HEBER (see 33)

His vesper consisted of the first verse, and was published in his *Hymns*, 1827. Archbishop Whately added the second verse in 1838.

637 THROUGH THE DAY THY LOVE HATH SPARED US
T. KELLY (see 113)

Published in the second edition of his *Hymns on Various Passages of Scripture*, 1806.

638 THE DAY IS PAST AND OVER ANON

This anonymous Greek hymn of the sixth or seventh century formed part of the 'Great after-supper' service of the Greek Church. It was translated by J. M. Neale in 1853, and included almost as we have it here in his *Hymns of the Eastern Church*, 1862. He writes 'this little hymn is a great favourite in the Greek Isles. It is, to the scattered hamlets of Chios and Mitylene, what Bishop Ken's evening hymn is to the villages of our own land.'

639 DAY IS DYING IN THE WEST
M. A. LATHBURY (see 198)

A vesper hymn written in 1880 for the Chautauqua Literary and Scientific circle.

640 ABIDE WITH ME: FAST FALLS THE EVENTIDE
H. F. LYTE (see 308)

Published in his *Remains*, 1850. In a prefatory memoir his daughter states that he placed in the hands of a near and dear relative 'the little hymn "Abide with me" ' on the evening of September 4, 1847. That day he had preached a farewell sermon to his congregation 'though in much weakness and ill health'. He died on November 20.

W. S. Kelynack, in his *Companion to the School Hymnbook of the Methodist Church*, 1950, writes of evidence held by Lyte's great-grandson, W. Maxwell Lyte, that the original was first written in the summer of 1847. But T. H. Bindley, in a letter to the *Spectator* of October 3, 1925, states that it was composed in 1820. In that year Lyte, as a young clergyman, visited an old friend who lay dying, and who kept repeating the phrase 'abide with me'. After leaving the bedside Lyte wrote the hymn and gave a copy of it to his host's brother, Sir Francis le Hunte, among whose papers it remained. He adds 'No doubt, when Lyte felt his own end approaching, his mind reverted to the lines he had written many years before'.

The hymn is based on St. Luke xxiv. 28 and is usually classed as an evening hymn. But it is concerned not with the close of the day but with the close of life.

641 O LORD, WHO BY THY PRESENCE HAST MADE LIGHT   C. J. P. SPITTA (see 279)

First published in his *Psalter und Harfe*, 1833.

Translated by RICHARD MASSIE (1800–77). Born in Chester. He was a wealthy Cheshire landowner who devoted himself to literature. He published a translation of Martin Luther's *Spiritual Songs* in 1854. *Lyra Domestica*, 1860, contains his translations of Spitta's German hymns. He contributed translations of other German hymn-writers to various collections of hymns.

642 ERE I SLEEP, FOR EVERY FAVOUR
J. CENNICK (see 168)

Published in his *Sacred Hymns*, 1741.

643 NOW GOD BE WITH US, FOR THE NIGHT IS CLOSING   PETRUS HERBERT (?–1571)

The date and place of his birth are not known. He lived at Fulnek, in Moravia, and belonged to the Unity of the Bohemian Brethren, from which sprang the Moravian Church. He was ordained a priest of the Unity in 1562, and rose to a position of leadership. He was chosen to represent the Unity on several important missions, including visits to Calvin and to the Emperor Maximilian II. He was one of the principal compilers of the *Brethren's German Hymnbook*, 1566, and contributed to it over ninety hymns, some translated from the Bohemian.

This is one of the hymns included, and it was written at a time of fierce persecution. Miss Winkworth's translation was printed in *The Chorale Book for England*, 1863.

644 DAYS AND MOMENTS QUICKLY FLYING

E. CASWALL (see 139)

Included in his *Masque of Mary*, 1858.

645 ACROSS THE SKY THE SHADES OF NIGHT

JAMES HAMILTON (1819–96)

Born at Glendollar, Scotland. Educated at Corpus Christi College, Cambridge. Ordained 1845. He held various incumbencies. He was the author of a few hymns of great merit, including 'Praise, O praise the Lord of harvest'.

This is a hymn for New Year's eve, and included in Thring's *Collection*, 1882. It was written to the old chorale in Mendelssohn's *St. Paul*.

See also 669.

646 COME, LET US ANEW   C. WESLEY (see 4)

Published in *Hymns and Sacred Poems*, 1749. It is much used by Methodists in Watchnight and Covenant services. Bernard L. Manning comments on 'the gift of elemental simplicity and stinging direct speech in this hymn'.

647 STILL ON THE HOMEWARD JOURNEY

J. L. BORTHWICK (see 279)

Included in Dr. Stevenson's *Hymns for Church and Home*, 1873.

648 AT THY FEET, OUR GOD AND FATHER

J. D. BURNS (see 244)

Appeared in *The Family Treasury*, 1861, and in the Presbyterian *Psalms and Hymns*, 1867.

649 GREAT GOD, WE SING THAT MIGHTY HAND

P. DODDRIDGE (see 55)

Published in a posthumous edition of his hymns in 1755. Based on Acts xxvi. 22.

650 FATHER, LET ME DEDICATE   L. TUTTIETT (see 153)

Printed in his *Germs of Thought on the Sunday Special Services*, 1864.

651 BREAK, NEW-BORN YEAR, ON GLAD EYES BREAK

T. H. GILL (see 94)

Written in 1855 and published in his *Golden Chain of Praise*, 1869.

652 THE NEW YEAR, LORD, WE WELCOME MAKE

T. H. GILL (see 94)

Written in 1888, and included in the second edition of *Golden Chain of Praise*, 1894. Some verses of the original are omitted.

653 THE OLD YEAR'S LONG CAMPAIGN IS O'ER

S. J. STONE (see 431)

Written in 1868, when curate of Windsor, and published in *The Knight of Intercession, and Other Poems*, 1872.

654 LORD, THY CHILDREN GUIDE AND KEEP

W. W. HOW (see 192)

Based on St. Matthew vii. 14, 'Narrow is the way which leadeth unto life'. First published in Morrell and How's *Psalms and Hymns*, 1854.

655 O THOU WHOSE HAND HATH BROUGHT US

FREDERICK WILLIAM GOADBY (1845–80)

Son of a Baptist minister. Educated for the Baptist ministry at Regent's Park College. Graduated M.A. of London University, 1868. Minister of the Baptist Church of Bluntisham, Hunts, and later at Watford, 1876. 'A crowd fills the court of the Temple' is one of his three hymns which have been preserved. This one was written for the opening of a new building for Beechen Grove Church, Watford.

656 CHRIST IS OUR CORNER-STONE

J. CHANDLER (see 611)

Translation of part of the anonymous Latin hymn '*Urbs beata Hierusalem*', and published in his *The Hymns of the Primitive Church*, 1837. The fifth verse begins '*Angularis fundamentum lapis Christus missus est*'. 'This rugged but fine old hymn' (Archbishop Trench) is probably of the sixth or seventh century.

657 JESUS, WHERE'ER THY PEOPLE MEET

W. COWPER (see 60)

Written in 1769, one of the sixty-eight hymns he contributed to *Olney Hymns*, 1779.

In a letter of 1769 Newton writes: 'We are going to remove our prayer meeting to the great room in the Great House. It is a noble place . . . and holds 130 people conveniently.' Cowper composed this hymn for their first meeting. In a letter of November 30, 1793, Cowper refers to the time 'when on Sabbath mornings in winter I rose before day, and by the light of a lanthorn trudged, often through snow and rain, to a prayer meeting at the Great House, as they call it, near the church at Olney. There I always found assembled forty or fifty poor folk, who preferred a glimpse of God's countenance and favour to the comforts of a warm bed.'

658 O THOU TO WHOM IN ANCIENT TIME

JOHN PIERPOINT (1785–1866)

Graduated Yale College, 1804. He had a varied life. In 1812 he was admitted to the Bar, but soon went into business. Then he studied theology at Harvard and was pastor of three Unitarian churches—Boston, Troy, and another church in Massachusetts. When over seventy he served as a chaplain in the U.S.A. army, and finally became a clerk in the Treasury Department at Washington. He was zealous against intemperance and slavery. His publications include *Airs of Palestine*, 1816, some school books, and *Poems and Hymns*, 1840 and 1854. The last includes his anti-slavery and temperance poems and songs, and also this hymn, which was written for the opening of an Independent Congregational church in Salem, 1824.

659 COME TO BLESS THY PEOPLE, LORD

BARBARA MACANDREW (1840–1929)

Daughter of Dr. John Miller, of Edinburgh, and lady bountiful at Harford, Devon. She wrote this hymn for the opening of All Saints' Church at Hoole, Cheshire, in 1871. Printed in her *Ezekiel and Other Poems*.

660 THOU WHOSE UNMEASURED TEMPLE STANDS

W. C. BRYANT (see 531)

The original version of this hymn was written in 1835 for the dedication of a chapel in New York. It was altered to its present form by 1867, when it was included in the American Presbyterian *Psalms and Hymns*.

661 LIGHT UP THIS HOUSE WITH GLORY, LORD

JOHN HARRIS (1802–56)

Educated for the Congregational ministry at Hoxton Academy. Minister of Epsom Congregational Church, 1825. Became President of Cheshunt College in 1838 and Principal of New College, London, from 1850 until his death. His numerous works include a volume of poems, *The Incarnate One*, but only one hymn as far as is known. This hymn was contributed to the *New Congregational Hymnbook* of 1859.

662 THE GLORY OF THE SPRING   T. H. GILL (see 94)

Written 'on the Whit-Sunday of 1867, a day of singular loveliness'. It combines the thoughts of Psalm civ. 30 (Thou renewest the face of the earth) and Ephesians iv. 23 (Be renewed in the spirit of your mind).

663 SUMMER SUNS ARE GLOWING
W. W. HOW (see 192)

A hymn of warmth and encouragement, fitting its theme, first published in *Church Hymns*, 1871, of which How was joint editor.

664 HERE, LORD, WE OFFER THEE
ABEL GERALD WILSON BLUNT (1827–1902)

Written for a flower service at St. Luke's, Chelsea, of which the author was rector, òn Hospital Sunday, June 15, 1879. A Broad Churchman, he was associated with Maurice, Kingsley and Dean Stanley, and a friend of Thomas Carlyle.

665 MANY THINGS IN LIFE THERE ARE
F. L. HOSMER (see 45)

First published with the motto: 'the peace of God which passeth understanding'. Included in this section presumably because of the reference to flowers in verse 1, it conveys primarily a lesson of trust where we cannot see.

666 PRAISE, OH, PRAISE OUR GOD AND KING
H. W. BAKER (see 63)

Founded on Milton's version of Psalm cxxxvi.
See also 15.

667 WE PLOUGH THE FIELDS
MATTHIAS CLAUDIUS (1740–1815)

This vigorous and straightforward hymn is a translation of the peasants' song in *Paul Erdmann's Feast* by Claudius (Hamburg, 1783), a description of a harvest thanksgiving in a German farmhouse. Claudius at first planned to enter the Lutheran ministry, but was discouraged under the free-thinking influence of Goethe and others. Later he regained his faith after a severe illness. He practised as a journalist and wrote a number of poems which are said to have 'exercised a great influence on the religious life' of Germany.

Jane Montgomery Campbell (1817–78) contributed several translations to *A Garland of Songs*, edited by the Rev. C. S. Bere. She also published *A Handbook for Singers* based upon her experience in teaching children.

668 TO THEE, O LORD, OUR HEARTS WE RAISE
W. C. DIX (see 89)

From *Hymns for the Service of the Church* (St. Raphael's, Bristol, 1864). Perhaps more popular, because of the tune and the easy flow, than the sentiments and form warrant.

669 PRAISE, OH PRAISE THE LORD OF HARVEST
JAMES HAMILTON (see 645)

670 COME, YE THANKFUL PEOPLE, COME
HENRY ALFORD (see 397)

The author made considerable changes after its original publication. This is his own final version, except for two trivial alterations: in ver. 4 (line 2), which read, 'to Thy final harvest home'; in line 6, 'In God's garner to abide'.

671 FOR THE SUNSHINE AND THE RAIN
MRS. JANE CREWDSON (see 238)

Posthumously published. The author had been an invalid for years.

672 FAIR WAVED THE GOLDEN CORN
J. H. GURNEY (see 51)

Applies to harvest festivals the idea of the Jewish feast of first fruits. See Exodus xxii. 29 and xxiii. 16; Deuteronomy xxvi.

673 THE YEAR IS SWIFTLY WANING
W. W. HOW (see 192)

Impresses by the sincere feeling characteristic of Bishop How's hymns. Written for his *Church Hymns*.

674 WINTER REIGNETH O'ER THE LAND
W. W. HOW (see 192)

675 O THOU THROUGH SUFFERING PERFECT MADE
W. W. HOW (see 192)

676 THOU TO WHOM THE SICK AND DYING
GODFREY THRING (see 109)

Associated by the author with Matthew iv. 24: 'And they brought unto Him all sick people . . . and He healed them'.

677 THINE ARM, O CHRIST, IN DAYS OF OLD
E. H. PLUMPTRE (see 10)

Written in 1864 for use in the chapel of King's College Hospital, London. Plumptre was a professor in King's College. See Matthew xiv. 34–36.

678 FROM THEE ALL SKILL AND SCIENCE FLOW
CHARLES KINGSLEY (1819–75)

A courageous idealist, who felt deeply and cared greatly for the sufferings of the artisan class in his time. Not infrequently his heart over-ruled his head. At the time of the Chartist troubles in 1848 he joined with F. D. Maurice and J. M. Ludlow to form the 'Christian Socialist' group. Ludlow, a barrister, was its father; Maurice, the theologian, its thinker and prophet; Kingsley, its voice to the people. They committed themselves to conflict 'with the unsocial Christians and the un-Christian Socialists'. Kingsley later became Professor of Modern History at Cambridge and Canon of Westminster. He was a prolific writer, but is best known by his novels, such as *Yeast*, *Hypatia*, and *Westward Ho!* He was one of the great leaders of the Church in his day and left his mark in many fields.

This hymn was written in 1871 for the laying of the foundation stone of a new block of Queen's Hospital, Birmingham. It had as its first verse:

> Accept this building, gracious Lord,
> No temple though it be;
> We raised it for our suffering kin,
> And so, good Lord, for Thee.

Kingsley was always much concerned in questions of the national health. He wrote once, 'Human beings have bodies as well as souls, and the state of the soul too often depends on that of the body'.

679 IS THY CRUSE OF COMFORT WASTING?
MRS. CHARLES (see 99)

The writer spent much time in social service in East London, where her husband had a business. The hymn reflects her experience. See 1 Kings xvii. 8–16.

680 O LOVE DIVINE AND GOLDEN

J. S. B. MONSELL (see 6)

One who knew Monsell's own home at Guildford, where he was rector of St. Nicholas, said of it: 'It was quite an ideal household, with genial brightness and gaiety playing like sunshine over all the troubles of life'.

681 O HAPPY HOME

C. J. SPITTA (see 279)

Written with the heading: 'Salvation is come to this house' (Luke xix. 9). It soon came into general use in Germany.

For Mrs. Findlater, see 218.

682 O PERFECT LOVE

MRS. DOROTHY FRANCES GURNEY (1858–1932)

Written by the author, when Miss Blomfield, for her sister's wedding in 1883. It was set as an anthem by Sir Joseph Barnby for the marriage of Princess Louise and the Duke of Fife in 1889.

Writer was grand-daughter of Bishop Blomfield of London. Became a Roman Catholic in 1919. She published two volumes of verse, including the often quoted lines:

> The kiss of the sun for pardon,
> The song of the birds for mirth:
> One is nearer God's heart in a garden
> Than anywhere else on earth.

683 HOW WELCOME WAS THE CALL

H. W. BAKER (see 63)

Said to be very popular as a marriage hymn in America.

684 ETERNAL FATHER, STRONG TO SAVE

WILLIAM WHITING (1825–78)

For twenty years master of the Winchester College Choristers' School. Published a volume of poems, but is known only by this hymn, popular with sailors the world over, both in the original and in a French version. Ver. 1 originally read:

> O Thou who bidd'st the ocean deep,
> Its own appointed limits keep,
> Thou who didst bind the restless wave,
> Eternal Father, strong to save, . . .

Ver. 2 read:

> O Saviour, whose almighty word
> The wind and waves submissive heard.

In ver. 4 (line 3):

> From rock and tempest them defend,
> To safety's harbour them attend,
> And ever let there rise to Thee . . .

These and smaller changes made by the editors of *Hymns Ancient and Modern* were accepted by the author. The hymn is inseparably wedded to Dr. Dykes' tune, fittingly named Melita in recollection of St. Paul's shipwreck.

685 O LORD, BE WITH US WHEN WE SAIL
EDWARD ARTHUR DAYMAN (1807–90)

(Not Edwin.) Fellow of Exeter College, Oxford, he later became a Prebendary of Salisbury. He contributed several translations and original hymns to the *Sarum Hymnal*, of which he was joint editor together with the Rev. J. R. Woodford and Lord Nelson, grand-nephew of the famous sailor.

686 FATHER, WHO ART ALONE
EDITH JONES (1849–1929)

Contributed to *The Home Hymn Book* in 1885. The writer wished to remain unknown and no information about her is available.

687 HOLY FATHER, IN THY MERCY
ISABELLA STEPHANA STEVENSON (1843–90)

Spent her entire life uneventfully at Cheltenham. For many years she was an invalid. She is known only by this one hymn, inspired by the stress of a special occasion; she is not recorded to have written anything else. This was written when her invalid brother sailed for South Africa, and privately printed. It was used in services on H.M.S. *Bacchante*, in which the future King George V and his brother went round the world in 1881–2. The princes sent a copy to their mother and it was sung by the royal family at home during the cruise.

688 IN CHRIST THERE IS NO EAST OR WEST
'JOHN OXENHAM' (1852–1941)

The pen-name of William Arthur Dunkerley, born and educated in Manchester. He wrote more than forty novels and twenty other volumes in verse and prose. His verse in particular achieved a great popularity and sold in large cheap editions during the first world war. Much of his writing had a strong Christian message. This hymn was sung at the close of 'The Pageant of Darkness and Light', written by Oxenham, produced at the Agricultural Hall, London, in 1908, for the London Missionary Society.

689 LORD, WHILE FOR ALL MANKIND

JOHN REYNELL WREFORD (1800–81)

A Unitarian minister, he was compelled to resign in 1831 owing to throat trouble. He became a schoolmaster. He wrote a history of Unitarianism in Birmingham, and contributed fifty-five hymns to the Rev. J. R. Beard's *Unitarian Collection*, which rejected all the great hymns of the Church on doctrinal grounds. It is interesting to note that the hymn was published in the year of Queen Victoria's Accession.

690 GOD SAVE OUR GRACIOUS KING

'The words to which the tune is sung are no part of the National Anthem. It is only the tune which is the National Anthem.' (Philip Snowden, Chancellor of the Exchequer, in the House of Commons, February 25, 1931.) The history of both words and music is very uncertain. There is some reason to think that it was originally a Jacobite song. A writer in *The Gentleman's Magazine* for 1796 says that he was present in 1740 when Henry Carey, composer and singer, sang it after dinner. It was first printed anonymously in *Harmonica Anglicana* about 1745, in two verses only. The second verse read:

> O Lord our God arise,
> Scatter his enemies
>   And make them fall!
> Confound their politics,
> Frustrate their knavish tricks.
> On him our hopes we fix.
>   O save us all!

The present second verse was written by Dean Hole for the Diamond Jubilee in 1887. SAMUEL REYNOLDS HOLE (1819–1904) was Dean of Rochester.

691 GOD BLESS OUR NATIVE LAND!

WILLIAM EDWARD HICKSON (1803–70)

An attempt to write a more religious national anthem. Several versions are to be found in different hymn-books. There is also a distinct hymn with the same first line by an American writer, C. T. Brooks.

Hickson was a boot manufacturer in London who retired at the age of thirty-seven to devote himself to social service and literature. He was member of a Royal Commission on the condition of the hand-loom weavers, and an advocate of the repeal of the Corn Laws. He was a keen musician and published three books on teaching singing. Education was another of his interests. He was editor of the *Westminster Review*.

692 PRAISE TO OUR GOD JOHN ELLERTON (see 21)

As editor and writer the author made an outstanding contribution to English hymnody.

693 LOOK FROM THY SPHERE OF ENDLESS DAY
W. C. BRYANT (see 531)

Bryant was the first American poet to become well known in Britain. He was one of the inspirers of the anti-slavery movement. This was composed for a missionary meeting.

694 LAND OF OUR BIRTH RUDYARD KIPLING (1865–1936)

Poet, story-teller, 'poet laureate of the Empire', writer of children's books of genius. An ardent patriot and preacher of the Stoic virtues, he did not always avoid the snares of 'imperialism', but in some of his most inspired verses he brought patriotism and human life into the searching presence of God. This is particularly true of this 'Children's Song' from *Puck of Pook's Hill*, which reflects his deep love for his country, and in 'Recessional' (699).

695 THESE THINGS SHALL BE
JOHN ADDINGTON SYMONDS (1840–93)

A brilliant scholar, Fellow of Magdalen, Oxford, ill health forbade him an active career in England. Settling in Switzerland, he wrote many works of history and literary criticism.

This is a selection from a longer poem called 'A Vista', beginning 'Sad heart, what will the future bring?' Written in 1880 it came into general use at the time of the first world war. 'Inarmed' in ver. 3 means 'arm in arm'. It is often wrongly printed as 'unarmed'.

696 WHOM OCEANS PART HOWELL ELVET LEWIS (1860–)

Written for a Colonial Missionary Society anniversary in London by the well-known Congregational minister, latterly at the Welsh Tabernacle, King's Cross, London. Arch Druid of Wales, 1924–7. Chairman of the Congregational Union, 1933–4. Author of several biographies and volumes of verse in Welsh and English.

697 NOW PRAY WE FOR OUR COUNTRY
A. C. COXE (see 263)

From a longer poem, by an American bishop, on the history of England, inspired by visits to her cathedrals. Originally it read, 'Now pray we for our *Mother*', and was a call to Americans to pray for their 'mother country' of England.

698 GOD BLESS OUR MOTHERLAND!

N. BARNABY (see 227)

Originally it read 'fatherland'. The author, the Director of Naval Construction, was for fifty years superintendent of the Sunday School at Lee Baptist Church.

699 GOD OF OUR FATHERS   RUDYARD KIPLING (see 694)

Second thoughts about imperialism by one of its prophets. Published in *The Times* on the occasion of Queen Victoria's Diamond Jubilee in 1897. Verses 2 and 3 refer to the great procession and the naval review.

700 WHEN WILT THOU SAVE THE PEOPLE?

EBENEZER ELLIOTT (1781–1849)

A hymn of moving dignity by a poet whose sensitive heart not only responded to the beauties of nature but also burned with sympathy for the sufferings of the oppressed workers. He wrote in Chartist days when feeling was bitter, leading to blind revolt, and when all too few of the Church leaders had realized their responsibilities for the Christian ordering of society.

Elliott was in business as an iron founder in Sheffield and was active in literature and politics. He became known as the 'Corn Law Rhymer' through his poems, first published in a local newspaper, recording with deep feeling the miserable conditions of the poor in his day. His *Corn Law Rhymes* were published in 1831 and his collected poems in 1844.

701 I VOW TO THEE, MY COUNTRY

SIR CECIL SPRING-RICE (1859–1918)

In the British Diplomatic Service at Brussels, Tokio, Berlin, and Washington. The spirit of his life is summed up in this poem which he wrote the day before his death on the eve of his intended return to England on retiring from the ambassadorship to the U.S.A. 'He gave his life for his country as surely as though he had been slain on the field of battle.'

702 MINE EYES HAVE SEEN

MRS. JULIA (*née* WARD) HOWE (1819–1910)

American poetess and social reformer, an enthusiastic advocate of international peace and women's suffrage. An influential speaker and preacher. Her publications included three volumes of verse.

This hymn was written six months after the outbreak of the American Civil War. Mrs. Howe heard the troops singing 'John Brown's Body' and it was suggested to her that she should write new words for the tune. That night she wrote these lines, which were published in *The Atlantic Monthly*, entitled 'The Battle Hymn of the Republic'. The fifth verse has been added.

Though now sung by students and others in light-hearted mood the original song enshrined the memory of the heroic, though perhaps unwise, John Brown, who attempted a rising in 1859 to secure freedom for the slaves, a cause for which he had worked apparently fruitlessly for years. His arrest and execution roused the conscience of the North and the doggerel lines became the marching song of their armies.

703 O KING OF KINGS   HENRY BURTON (see 548)

Based upon an ode written for a Jubilee Commemoration in the Albert Hall in 1887 and set to music by Stainer.

704 O VALIANT HEARTS
SIR JOHN STANHOPE ARKWRIGHT (1872–   )

Barrister and Chief Steward of the city of Hereford. At Christ Church, Oxford, won the Newdigate Prize in 1895. M.P. for Hereford, 1900–12. Published two volumes of poems. This was written during the first world war. (*Who's Who* gives his second name as Stanhope, not Stanley as in *B.C.H.*)

705 WHERE THE FLAG OF BRITAIN FLIES
F. A. JACKSON (see 484)

An Empire hymn by the one-time Baptist minister at Campden, Glos.

706 STANDING FORTH ON LIFE'S ROUGH WAY
WILLIAM BRYANT (1850–1913)

Born at Brighton. Presbyterian minister in Michigan, U.S.A. Not to be confused with W. C. Bryant.

Some versions read '*Starting* forth'.

707 FATHER, NOW WE THANK THEE
F. A. JACKSON (see 484)

A hymn for infant dedication services by the then Baptist minister at Campden, Glos.

708 GRACIOUS SAVIOUR, GENTLE SHEPHERD
JANE ELIZA LEESON (1807–82)

For many years a prominent figure in the Catholic Apostolic Church in London, she later became a Roman Catholic. She contributed nine hymns and translations to the *Catholic Apostolic Hymnal*. Some were improvised as 'prophetic utterances' at meetings of the church.

This hymn was adapted by John Keble.

See also 759.

709 LORD JESUS CHRIST, OUR LORD MOST DEAR
HEINRICH VON LAUFENBURG (*c.* 1400–58)

The Swiss author has been described as the most important and prolific hymn-writer of the fifteenth century, and as one of the fathers of German hymnody. Many of his hymns were based on popular songs and tunes. From 1445 till his death he was a monk in St. John's monastery at Strassburg.

This was originally written as a mother's cradle song. For the translator, see 11.

710 O LIGHT, WHOSE BEAMS ILLUMINE ALL
E. H. PLUMPTRE (see 10)

Written as one of five hymns for school and college by a distinguished scholar and prolific writer.

711 FOR ALL THE LOVE
LEONARD JAMES EGERTON SMITH (1879–)

Baptist minister at Kettering, Sheffield, and at Burnham-on-Sea since 1921. Chaplain to the Forces, 1917–21. The hymn was written for Vaughan Williams's noble tune '*Sine Nomine*'.

712 LORD, IN THE FULNESS OF MY MIGHT
T. H. GILL (see 94)

A call to youth to give the best of life to God's service, prefaced by the author with Cromwell's saying: 'How good it is to close with Christ betimes'.

713 O JESU, STRONG AND PURE AND TRUE
W. W. HOW (see 192)

Written in 1893 for the Jubilee of Marlborough College.

714 LORD, WE THANK THEE FOR THE PLEASURE
THOMAS WILLIAM JEX-BLAKE (1832–1915)

Written by the then Headmaster of Rugby at the request of Dr Cotton, the Head of Marlborough. It reflects the gladness of life as a boy sees it. He later became Dean of Wells. He is not known to have published any other verse.

715 LIGHT AND LIFE AND JOY ARE FOUND
C. E. MUDIE (see 316)

The author was founder of the famous lending library. An active Christian worker, he carried on a mission church in Hampstead. Published a volume of poems.

716 O LORD OF LIFE AND LOVE AND POWER
MRS. E. S. ARMITAGE (see 404)

Written for the opening of a new Sunday School at Oldham in 1875. A verse suitable to the occasion is omitted.

717 TELL ME NOT IN MOURNFUL NUMBERS
HENRY WADSWORTH LONGFELLOW (1807–82)

American poet. Professor of Modern Languages and Belles Lettres at Harvard. There is a bust in Westminster Abbey. Had a great popular vogue and many of his poems still live. But he was not in intention a hymn-writer and of the selections from his works used as hymns this alone has survived in current use.

718 GIVE LIGHT, O LORD
L. TUTTIETT (see 153)

This hymn is something of a puzzle. It is dated 1904, but is attributed to Lawrence Tuttiett, a Scottish Episcopal minister who lived 1825–97. The idea is very similar to that of 242.

719 HOW SHALL WE WORSHIP THEE, O LORD?
ANNIE MATHESON (1853–1924)

Daughter of a Congregational minister. Composed children's hymns from the age of thirteen. Her verses appeared in such magazines as *Macmillan's*, *The Spectator* and *St. Nicholas*. She published several anthologies, volumes of verse and biographies. This shows the characteristic simplicity and sincerity of her well-loved hymns.
See also 757, 770.

720 GENTLE JESUS, MEEK AND MILD
CHARLES WESLEY (see 4)

Selected from an original of twenty-eight verses in Charles Wesley's *Hymns for Children*, this is the one children's hymn of his still in general use.

721 O'ER THE HILLS AND BY THE VALLEYS
GEORGE ERNEST DARLASTON (1876–1931)

A much loved Congregational minister at Sydenham and Crouch End. Was a leader of the Free Church Fellowship in the days of its greatest influence.

722 SAVIOUR, LIKE A SHEPHERD LEAD US
H. F. LYTE (see 308)

Published anonymously in *Hymns for the Young*, edited by Miss D. A. Thrupp. It was possibly written by Lyte, but the *Methodist Hymnbook* attributes it to Miss Thrupp herself.

723 IN LIFE'S EARNEST MORNING
EBENEZER SHERMAN OAKLEY (1863–1934)

An L.M.S. missionary in India, Principal of Ramsay College, Almora. He contributed three hymns to John Hunter's *Hymns of Faith and Life*. This is there called 'A Student's Hymn'.

724 THOU PERFECT HERO KNIGHT
ALICE MURIEL PULLEN

Daughter of a Baptist missionary in Italy. Was long associated with Children's House, Bow, and one of the pioneers of the Graded Sunday School. Author of many biographies and tales for children.

725 WHAT PURPOSE BURNS WITHIN OUR HEARTS
MINOT JUDSON SAVAGE (1841–1918)

American Unitarian minister in Boston. Editor and poet. Written to be sung at the reception of new church members.

726 YIELD NOT TO TEMPTATION
HORATIO RICHMOND PALMER (1834–1907)

Professional musician, held teaching posts in New York and Chicago. In 1884 took charge of the Church Choral Union for the improvement of church music, which came to have a membership of four thousand singers. His collections of songs had a wide circulation. He said that while he was at work on technical musical theory the idea of this hymn 'flashed upon me', and he 'hurriedly penned both words and music as fast as I could write them'. In the original the first line reads, 'for weakness is sin'.

727 THY WORD IS LIKE A GARDEN
EDWIN HODDER (1837–1904)

Civil servant, author of devotional and biographical works. Lived in New Zealand from 1856–61. A Bible hymn for youth.

728 GOD MIGHT HAVE MADE THE EARTH BRING FORTH
MRS. MARY (*née* BOTHAM) HOWITT (1804–88)

The Quaker author called this 'The Ministry of Flowers'. She was the translator of some of Hans Andersen's stories, and the author of 'Will you walk into my parlour, said the spider to the fly'. This hymn was first published in a volume called *Birds and Flowers and Other Country Things*.

729 I SING THE ALMIGHTY POWER OF GOD
ISAAC WATTS (see 2)

From *Divine Songs Attempted in Easy Language for the Use of Children*, 1715, which was constantly reprinted for a century and has been described as the fountainhead of English children's hymnody. Judged by modern standards, however, Watts's genius in hymn-writing did not extend to children. This survives almost alone.

730 'TWAS GOD THAT MADE THE OCEAN
G. B. BUBIER (see 258)

'God the author and maker of all things.'

731 HOW DEARLY GOD MUST LOVE US
SAMUEL WILLIAM PARTRIDGE (1810–1903)

Written for a flower service. The author was a London publisher.

732 GOD WHO HATH MADE THE DAISIES
E. P. HOOD (see 428)

Based on Matthew xix. 13–15 by a celebrated preacher who wrote many hymns for children.

733 ALL THINGS BRIGHT AND BEAUTIFUL
MRS. C. F. ALEXANDER (see 131)

The author's most famous book, *Hymns for Little Children*, in which this was included, went into one hundred editions. This admirably simple and objective hymn is an undying favourite with children, though the survival of the erroneous statement about the rushes in ver. 5 is surprising. The original version included

> The rich man in his castle,
> The poor man at his gate,
> God made them high and lowly
> And ordered their estate.

734 I LOVE TO HEAR THE STORY
MRS. EMILY (*née* HUNTINGTON) MILLER (1833–1913)

Dean of Women Students in North Western University, U.S.A., 1891–8. Wrote many stories and published a volume of verse. This hymn is said to have been written in less than a quarter of an hour.

735 THERE CAME A LITTLE CHILD TO EARTH
EMILY ELIZABETH STEELE ELLIOTT (1836–97)

A niece of Charlotte Elliott (see 137). She was greatly interested in the mission work at Mildmay Park in London, and was editor of the *Church Missionary Juvenile Instructor*. She published two volumes of hymns, most of them first used at St. Mark's, Brighton, where her father was rector.

See also 739.

736 IN THE FIELD WITH THEIR FLOCKS ABIDING
FREDERIC WILLIAM FARRAR (1831–1903)

Headmaster of Marlborough, then Canon of Westminster and rector of St. Margaret's, the House of Commons church; later Dean of Canterbury. An eloquent preacher and popular writer, he was an outstanding national figure in his later years. This hymn was written for a concert at Harrow, where Farrar was then an assistant master.

737 ONCE IN ROYAL DAVID'S CITY
MRS. C. F. ALEXANDER (see 131)

One of a series of hymns on the Apostles Creed: 'Who was conceived of the Holy Ghost, born of the Virgin Mary'.

738 O LITTLE TOWN OF BETHLEHEM
PHILLIPS BROOKS (1835–93)

This great preacher was in the ministry of the Protestant Episcopal Church of the U.S.A. After notable ministries in Philadelphia and Boston he became Bishop of Massachusetts two years before his death. He was greatly loved and influential throughout America and beyond. This was written for his Sunday school in Boston in recollection of a Christmas spent by him in Bethlehem in 1866.

739 THOU DIDST LEAVE THY THRONE
EMILY ELLIOTT (see 735)

Written with Luke ii. 7 as text, for the school children at St. Mark's, Brighton.

740 JESUS WHEN HE LEFT THE SKY
MRS. MARY RUMSEY (about 1860)

Though the hymn has been attributed to her in many selections nothing seems to be known about her.

741 AWAY IN A MANGER   AUTHOR UNKNOWN

Exhaustive research by R. S. Hill, of which the results were published in the (American) *Music Library Association Notes* for December 1945, has definitely established that this is not by Martin Luther, but is American in origin. It was probably written in connexion with the four hundredth anniversary of Luther's birth in 1883, which started the Luther legend about it.

742 IN THE BLEAK MID-WINTER
CHRISTINA ROSSETTI (see 96)

One of four Christmas poems by the author.

743 SEE AMID THE WINTER'S SNOW
EDWARD CASWALL (see 139)

Caswall joined Newman, whose close friend and disciple he was, in the Church of Rome. He greatly enriched English hymnody, especially by his translations from the Latin. Some versions of this hymn begin 'See in yonder manger low'.

744 I LOVE TO THINK   E. P. HOOD (see 428)

745 I THINK WHEN I READ THAT SWEET STORY OF OLD   MRS. JEMIMA (*née* THOMPSON) LUKE (1813–1906)

Daughter of one of the founders of the British and Foreign Sailors' Society and the Sunday School Union. Illness thwarted an early ambition to become a missionary in India, but for a time she edited a missionary magazine for children. She married the Rev. Samuel Luke, Congregational minister in Clifton. This was sung first at the village Sunday school at Blagden, where her father was superintendent.

746 JESUS, WHO LIVED ABOVE THE SKY
MRS. ANN (*née* TAYLOR) GILBERT (1782–1866)

A prolific writer of children's hymns. *Hymns for Infant Minds*, issued in 1809 in collaboration with her sister Jane, were notable for their attempt to express the thoughts of children themselves in natural language. The two sisters were valuable pioneers in religious education and their numerous volumes were very popular in Britain and America. Many of their hymns were translated into other languages. Ann married a Congregational minister, who served churches in Hull and Nottingham. This hymn is a happy illustration of the child-like simplicity of their work, a very rare achievement in children's hymns.

See also 760.

747 WHEN HIS SALVATION BRINGING
JOHN KING (1789–1858)

The vicar of Christ Church, Hull, wrote this with a refrain for each verse:

Hosanna to Jesus we'll sing.
Hosanna to Jesus, our king.

748 THERE WAS A TIME
THOMAS RAWSON TAYLOR (1807–35)

Classical tutor at Airedale Independent College, Bradford. Published a volume containing this hymn and 783.

749 O SON OF MAN, OUR HERO STRONG AND TENDER
SIR FRANK FLETCHER (1870–)

Intended to supplement the portrait of the meek and gentle Jesus by a reminder of His strength and sympathy. Written for Charterhouse where the author was headmaster and used there for some time before publication. He was knighted in 1937.

750 TELL ME THE STORIES OF JESUS
WILLIAM HENRY PARKER (1845–1929)

Head of an insurance company. Active worker in the Chelsea Street Baptist Church, Nottingham, for whose Sunday school anniversaries he wrote hymns, fifteen of which are in the *Sunday School Hymnary*. He published a volume of poems. He wrote this on return from school one Sunday afternoon, remembering the request, 'Teacher, tell us another story'.

751 WHO IS HE IN YONDER STALL?
BENJAMIN RUSSELL HANBY (1833–67)

Educated for the ministry he was led to make music his life-work, but died in early manhood. He collaborated with G. F. Root in Chicago in editing a volume of *Chapel Gems*, collecting pieces from a musical quarterly they produced together. He wrote both words and music of this hymn.

752 THERE IS A GREEN HILL FAR AWAY
MRS. C. F. ALEXANDER (see 131)

Composed while sitting at the bedside of a sick child. Gounod was so moved by it that he wrote a setting which he sent to the authoress. The 'green hill' was confessedly suggested by a hill near Derry rather than by the Gospels or the topography of Palestine.

753 IT IS A THING MOST WONDERFUL
W. W. How (see 192)

754 WHEN THE LORD OF LOVE WAS HERE
Stopford Augustus Brooke (1832–1916)

As an Anglican clergyman he became distinguished as one of the outstanding London preachers, and through his published sermons and his *Theology in the English Poets*. In 1880 he resigned his Anglican orders, continuing to preach and lecture though attached to no denomination. In 1881 he edited *Christian Hymns*, in which many were revised to suit his liberal theology, and in which he included a number written by himself. This hymn reflects his wide human sympathies.

755 JESUS HIGH IN GLORY
Harriet Burn McKeever (1807–86)

For thirty-six years teacher in a girl's school in Philadelphia, and for nearly as long a Sunday school teacher in a Protestant Episcopal Church. Wrote many hymns and books for children. This was called an infant hymn when first published by the Methodist Episcopal Church. Ver. 1 (line 4), originally read, 'infants' praises hear'.

756 IN OUR DEAR LORD'S GARDEN
Mrs. E. S. Armitage (see 404)

'Christ's love for children.'

757 JESUS, THE CHILDREN ARE CALLING
Annie Matheson (see 719)

Written at the age of thirteen and published in *Good Words* on the recommendation of George Macdonald.

758 FATHER, LEAD ME DAY BY DAY
J. P. Hopps (see 538)

'A child's prayer for divine guidance.'

759 SAVIOUR, TEACH ME DAY BY DAY
Jane E. Leeson (see 708)

The refrain comes from 1 John iv. 19.

760 GREAT GOD AND WILT THOU CONDESCEND
Mrs. Ann Gilbert (see 746)

The work of the two sisters, Jane and Ann Taylor (Mrs. Gilbert), in many ways broke new ground in hymns for children.

761 WE ARE BUT LITTLE CHILDREN WEAK

Mrs. C. F. Alexander (see 131)

First written for 'very poor children' at a crowded city Sunday school. Between the first and second verses were verses referring to the deaths of martyrs and saints. This explains the rather unexpected last two lines of ver. 2. Some hymn-books have altered them to read:

> A life to live for Jesus' sake,
> A constant war to wage with sin.

Ver. 5 originally read:

> With smiles of peace and looks of love
> We may light up our dwellings dim,
> Bid kind good humour brighten there
> And consecrate our homes to Him.

762 SAVIOUR, WHILE MY HEART IS TENDER

John Burton (1803-77)

Congregational deacon in Plaistow, and a Sunday school teacher for twenty-seven years. He published several volumes of original hymns for children. This is taken from *One Hundred Original Hymns for the Young*.

763 LOOKING UPWARD EVERY DAY

Mary Butler (1841-1916)

Sister of Samuel Butler, author of *Erewhon*, *The Way of All Flesh*, etc. She took a keen interest in social work in Shrewsbury and many of her hymns were written for the St. Saviour's Home for girls which she founded. She is remembered as a strong, sweet-tempered, cheerful woman. This was written for the confirmation of her niece and god-daughter.

764 JESUS IS OUR SHEPHERD   Hugh Stowell (see 588)

Written for Sunday school anniversary services at Christ Church, Salford, of which Canon Stowell was rector.

765 HUSHED WAS THE EVENING HYMN

J. D. Burns (see 244)

Based on 1 Samuel iii. 1-10.

766 JUST AS I AM, THINE OWN TO BE

'Marianne Farningham' (1834-1909)

Farningham, from her birth-place, was the pen-name of Marianne Hearn, a Sunday school teacher and active worker at College Street

Baptist Church, Northampton, for many years. She exercised wide influence through her large Bible class. She was on the staff of the *Christian World* and editor of the *Sunday School Times*. She published several volumes of verse.

767 JESUS, FRIEND OF LITTLE CHILDREN
W. J. MATHAMS (see 408)

Composed for *Psalms and Hymns for Church and Home* published by the Baptist Union in 1882. He later became a minister of the Church of Scotland. This hymn is in wide use, and is said to be a great favourite in Congo.

768 GOD INTRUSTS TO ALL   JAMES EDMESTON (see 417)

Many of Edmeston's numerous hymns were written for the London Orphan Asylum.

769 GOD MAKE MY LIFE
MATILDA BARBARA BETHAM-EDWARDS (1836–1919)

Novelist and poet.

770 DEAR MASTER, WHAT CAN CHILDREN DO?
ANNIE MATHESON (see 719)

Written for a Harvest Festival, with the heading 'Children as workers for Christ'.

771 O WHAT CAN LITTLE HANDS DO?
MRS. GRACE WEBSTER (*née* HADDOCK) HINSDALE (1833–1902)

Was included in *Daily Meditations for Children* by Mrs. Hinsdale, but she said that she was not the author of the hymn. Congregationalist in New York.

772 BRIGHTLY GLEAMS OUR BANNER
THOMAS JOSEPH POTTER (1827–73)

Roman Catholic priest and professor of Pulpit Eloquence and English Literature in the Missionary College of All Hallows, Dublin. Published several volumes on preaching and some stories. This hymn first appeared in a R.C. collection and was drastically revised for *Hymns Ancient and Modern*. Ver. 3 was added later.

773 GOD WHO CREATED ME
HENRY CHARLES BEECHING (1859–1919)

Professor of Pastoral Theology, King's College, London, later Dean of Norwich. Edited editions of several poets and himself wrote poetry. Author of a number of volumes, religious and literary.

774 THE WISE MAY BRING THEIR LEARNING

From *The Book of Praise for Children*, 1875.

775 THE FIELDS ARE ALL WHITE

Based on John iv. 35. Like the previous hymn, taken from *The Book of Praise for Children*, 1875.

776 WE'VE A STORY TO TELL

'COLIN STERNE' (1862–1926)

Pen-name of Henry Ernest Nichol, musician of Hull. Published a large number of Sunday school hymns with original tunes. Wrote both words and music of this hymn.

777 LITTLE DROPS OF WATER

MRS. JULIA ABIGAIL CARNEY (1823–1908)

Written for use in the Boston Primary School, where the authoress was a teacher. A controversy as to authorship was started when a Dr. Brewer added verses of his own to Mrs. Carney's first verse. Brewer's version has now dropped out of use.

778 FAR ROUND THE WORLD

BASIL JOSEPH MATHEWS (1879–1951)

After service on the staff of the *Christian World*, he became editorial secretary of the London Missionary Society. Later worked for World's Committee of the Y.M.C.A. in Geneva, and subsequently held professorships of missions or Christian World Relations in Boston, Newton-Andover, and Vancouver. His many books for children and adults had a wide circulation in English and other languages. Few men did more in his generation to serve the Christian cause. This hymn was written in 1909 for a Sunday school anniversary at Bowes Park, London.

779 NOW THE DAY IS OVER   S. BARING GOULD (see 398)

Written for one of the Sunday school festivals so popular in Lancashire and Yorkshire. Published with Proverbs iii. 24 as a text.

780 JESUS, TENDER SHEPHERD

MRS. MARY (*née* LUNDIE) DUNCAN (1814–40)

The first prayer taught to thousands of little children by their mothers. Written for her own children a few months before her sadly early death at the age of twenty-six. Daughter of a minister in the Church of Scotland, she married another who left the Church at the Disruption and became Free Church minister at Peebles.

781 EVERY MORNING THE RED SUN
Mrs. C. F. Alexander (see 131)

Written to illustrate the clause in the Creed, 'And the life everlasting'.

782 THERE'S A FRIEND FOR LITTLE CHILDREN
Albert Midlane (see 510)

Belonged to the Strict Brethren. In business as an ironmonger in Newport, Isle of Wight, he wrote more than three hundred hymns.

783 CHILDREN'S VOICES HIGH IN HEAVEN
T. R. Taylor (see 748)

Written in 1833 and revised in 1858 by George Rawson for *Psalms and Hymns*.

784 AROUND THE THRONE OF GOD IN HEAVEN
Mrs. Anne (*née* Houlditch) Shepherd (1809-57)

Daughter of an Anglican rector. Wrote sixty-four hymns, published as *Hymns adapted to the Comprehension of Young Minds*. Two years after its first publication in 1836, Robert Moffat translated this hymn into Sechuana.

785 GOD BE WITH YOU TILL WE MEET AGAIN
Jeremiah Eames Rankin (1828-1904)

Congregational minister. President of Howard University, Washington, D.C. Edited two hymnals. Said this was not written for any special occasion but to interpret the derivation of good-bye from God be with you.

786 FAREWELL, MY FRIENDS BELOVED
Joseph Harbottle (1778-1864)

Classical teacher at Horton College, Bradford. Afterwards Baptist minister at Accrington, where Joseph Angus studied Hebrew under his guidance. His hymn is much used in the north of England at Association meetings. It was written for the traditional melody of Bunyan's 'Who would true Valour see'.

INDEX OF AUTHORS AND TRANSLATORS

(The Biographical Note will be found under the first hymn of each author.
The arabic numbers refer to hymns.)

Index of Authors and Translators

Index of Authors and Translators

Newton, John, xv, 146, 156, 257, 325, 330, 423, 453, 582, 592, 606.
Nichol, Henry Ernest, 776.
Noel, Caroline, 145.
Noel, Baptist, 65, 476.
North, Frank Mason, 380.

OAKELEY, Frederick, 86.
Oakley, Charles Edward, 545.
Oakley, E. S., 723.
Olivers, Thomas, 17.
Osler, Edward, 367.
Oswald, Heinrich, 338.
Oxenham, John, 688.

P., F. B., 435.
Palgrave, Francis, 285, 455, 609, 621.
Palmer, H. R., 726.
Palmer, Ray, 154, 185, 261, 313.
Parker, W. H., 750.
Partridge, S. W., 731.
Pennefather, W., 586.
Perronet, Edward, 140.
Peters, Mrs. Mary, 337.
Pierpoint, F. S., 56.
Pierpont, John, 658.
Piggott, W. Charter, 439.
Plumptre, E. H., 10, 677, 710.
Pollock, T. B., 243.
Pott, Francis, 25.
Potter, T. J., 773.
Procter, Adelaide, 327, 345, 635.
Prudentius, Aurelius, 78
Prynne, G. R., 245.
Pullen, Alice, 724.
Pusey, Philip, 463.

RANKIN, J. E., 785.
Rawson, George, 179, 200, 266, 332, 436, 490, 626, 627, 783.
Reed, Andrew, 181.
Richter, Mrs. Anne, 108.
Rinckart, Martin, 11.
Robert of France, 185.
Robinson, R. H., 35.
Robinson, Robert, 164, 425.
Rossetti, Christina, 96, 160, 742.
Rous, Francis, 62, 64, 73, 130, 569.
Rumsey, Mrs. Mary, 740.
Russell, A. T., 34.
Ryland, John, xxi, 103, 526.

SAVAGE, M. J., 725.
Saxby, Mrs. Jane, 492.

Schutz, J. J., 12.
Scriven, Joseph, 591.
Sears, E. H., 82.
Shekleton, Mary, 295.
Shepherd, Mrs. Anne, 784.
Shuttleworth, H. C., 585.
Sidebotham, Mary, 239.
Sidey, W. W., 482.
Skrine, J. H., 477.
Small, J. G., 158.
Smith, Mrs. Elizabeth Lee, 322.
Smith, L. J. Egerton, 711.
Smith, Walter Chalmers, 38, 83, 323.
Spitta, C. J. P., 279, 365, 641, 681.
Spring-Rice, Sir Cecil, 701.
Spurgeon, C. H., xxiii, 594.
Stanley, A. P., 106, 134.
Steele, Anne, xxiv, 193, 208.
Stephen the Sabaite, 212.
Sterne, Colin, 776.
Stevenson, Isabel, 687.
Stockton, Mrs. Martha, 221.
Stone, S. J., 431, 454, 653.
Stowe, Harriet Beecher, 272, 309.
Stowell, Hugh, 588, 764.
Symonds, John Addington, 695.

TATE, Nahum, 81, 348.
Taylor, Ann. See Gilbert.
Taylor, Bayard, 352.
Taylor, T. R., 748, 783.
Tennyson, Alfred, Lord, 355.
Tersteegen, Gerhardt, 27, 218, 299.
Theodulph of Orleans, 107.
Thomas, John, 480.
Thring, Godfrey, 109, 142, 144, 536, 555, 632, 676.
Toke, Mrs. Emma, 127.
Toplady, A. M., xiv, 225, 310.
Tritton, Joseph, 461, 522.
Tuttiet, Lawrence, 153, 167, 242, 650, 718.
Twells, Henry, 190, 199, 247, 558.
Tymms, T. Vincent, 561.

VAN ALSTYNE, Mrs. Frances, 363, 383.
Vine, A. H., 176, 406.
Von Loewen, Arnulf, 116.

WADE, J. F., 86.
Walker, Mrs. Mary, 222.
Walmsley, Robert, 28.
Waring, Anna Letitia, 291, 305, 336, 424.

185

GENERAL INDEX

INDEX TO FIRST LINE OF HYMNS

Index of Hymns

Index of Hymns

Index of Hymns

Index of Hymns